Preface to
Public Administration:
A Search for
Themes and Direction

Preface to Public Administration: A Search for Themes and Direction

Richard J. Stillman II
George Mason University

ST. MARTIN'S PRESS
New York

Senior editor: Don Reisman
Project management: The Book Studio, Inc.
Cover design: Jeannette Jacobs Design

For information, write:
St. Martin's Press, Inc.
175 Fifth Avenue
New York, NY 10010

ISBN: 0-312-05207-3 (cloth)
        0-312-03746-5 (paper)

Library of Congress Cataloging-in-Publication Data

Stillman, Richard Joseph, 1943–
        Preface to public administration / by Richard J.
    Stillman, II.
        p. cm.
        ISBN 0-312-05207-3.—ISBN 0-312-03746-5 (pbk.)
        1. Public administration.   I. Title.
    JF 1351.S84   1990
350—dc20
                                                                90-39078
                                                                CIP

*For Dwight Waldo, who first raised the question that deserves an answer,
and for my wife, Kathleen, who prodded me to "chink along" toward one*

Preface

In the lead article of the January/February 1989 issue of the *Public Administration Review*, Darrell L. Pugh raises an embarrassing question for students of public administration. Much of the considerable educational, academic, publication, and associational resources in public administration, indicates Pugh, are currently devoted to "producing professionals" and "being professional." Yet, no matter how much public administration may wish to acquire a professional identity, argues Pugh, the vast bulk of the normative, empirical, and political evidence is weighted against defining the field as such; indeed, the overwhelming evidence seems decisively opposed to the pursuit of that goal.

What is public administration in the United States today? Is it a profession? If not a profession, what is it? A discipline? a field? a focus? an enterprise? Or . . . ? How can this topic of study be defined and described? As a field in which thousands of students each year receive professional graduate and undergraduate degrees? As a discipline to which millions more devote what they view as lifelong professional careers? As a focus or an enterprise in which billions of dollars are spent to "professionalize" administrative practices? On the other hand, is there a possibility that modern public administration, like the emperor in the ancient fable, is prancing around as if it wore all the accoutrements of professional or disciplinary respectability when, in fact, it stands stark naked without a stitch on? In reality, does the emperor wear no clothes?

Of course, this problem is not new. More than two decades ago Dwight Waldo posited that public administration suffered from a profound "identity crisis," or, as another distinguished scholar, Vincent Ostrom, termed it, "an intellectual crisis." More recently, Nicholas Henry called the dilemma "a paradigmatic quandary." Whatever its label, this problem of identity has not gone away but persists and even seems to intensify as the years pass.

The aim of this book is therefore to wrestle with this central controversy: namely, what is the scope and substance of public administration theory in America today? Ultimately, this text seeks to offer a new way of thinking about this question as the United

States enters the last decade of the twentieth century. It is therefore *not* a textbook on public administration or a history of the subject (although it covers much history). Rather, this book offers a general perspective on the field, if you will—a theory of public administration, or a way of looking at the principles and methods of public administration in the United States.

Ideally, this book can provide a new way of seeing and understanding an old subject. Yet, it must be quickly added—lest people will be put off by the words "theory" or "philosophy"—this book is not written primarily for specialized academic theorists. Instead, it seeks to be an introduction to introductory texts—hence, the "preface" in its title—for students new to the field who may wish to gain a better insight into their future occupation before they embark on careers in public administration. It can also be read by old hands who have long labored in the administrative vineyards and who may be puzzled—even frustrated—by the seemingly vague purposes of their line of work. And it may appeal to general readers interested in learning more about this subject, as well as to college and graduate students within government and political science who are being introduced to this field and are grappling with understanding its theory and practice for the first time. I hope that several kinds of readers may gain from this book a deeper appreciation of a subject that perhaps seems confusing and hard to define precisely, yet is important enough to study and to pursue as a vocation because of its critical place in the context of American society, its government, and the broader world scene.

Therefore we will deal with such questions as the following: What is public administration? How did it originate as a distinctive study and a unique set of institutions in the United States? What is the relationship between its ideas and its institutions? What are its basic doctrines and its identity in America? How is it studied and practiced today? Is it a discipline, a profession, or what? What are the major contemporary intellectual controversies and academic trends in the field? What is its place in the modern global setting? What are its future directions?

I would like to thank the following reviewers whose comments were invaluable for my preparation of final manuscript: Richard T. Green, University of Wyoming; Rebecca Hendrick, University of Wisconsin, Milwaukee; Patricia W. Ingraham, State University of New York at Binghamton; David H. Rosenbloom, Syracuse University; James A. Stever, University of Cincinnati; and Ronald D. Sylvia, San Jose State University.

Contents

Preface to
Public Administration:
A Search for
Themes and Direction

CHAPTER ONE

What Is
Public Administration
Theory in America?

*The public administration [in America] is, so to speak, oral and
traditional. But little is committed to writing, and that little is
soon wafted away forever, like the leaves of the Sibyl, by the
smallest breeze.*

ALEXIS DE TOCQUEVILLE
Democracy in America

During the late summer of 1968 at the Minnowbrook Conference
Center in the solitude of New York's Adirondack mountains, thirty-
four young (most under age 30) administrative scholars assembled
for four days to reflect on the status of public administration theory.
To a large extent the meeting was a reaction to a conference in
1967 that was composed of some eminent senior scholars and was
sponsored by the American Academy of Political and Social Science. In the words of its chair, James C. Charlesworth, the 1967
meeting sought "to make a bold synoptic approach to the discipline
of public administration . . . ,"[1] but, instead, it had produced
diverse, even contradictory, statements about the possible future
directions of the field. "Shameful," was the reply of one younger
scholar who read the proceedings as "old men talking to old men
about irrelevancies; old men out of touch with the real problems of
a chaotic and dangerous world and the youth who would have to
deal with them."[2]

In 1968, the year of the assassinations of Robert Kennedy and
Martin Luther King, growing disillusionment with the Vietnam

War, race riots, campus protests, and an apparent unraveling of the Great Society, pleas for "relevancy" in public administration filled the air. Scholars in the field seemed to be out of touch with the significant issues of the day. In the midst of these intense social crises, the Minnowbrook conferees came together "to discuss what was important *to them*" and to search for a "new" public administration that would speak directly and cogently to current issues.

The resulting conference papers, however, which were eventually published as a book,[3] reached no definite conclusions either. Like the Academy's proceedings the year before, the Minnowbrook proceedings reflected a diversity of opinions, thoughts, and themes that was almost as broad as the number of conference participants. Some claimed that public administration should focus on "an enhancement of life opportunities";[4] others favored "a politics of love";[5] still another saw it as furthering "social equity";[6] and yet another posited "a consociated model" for the field.[7] The old order was challenged, provocative questions were raised, humanistic ideals were professed, and cries for relevance were heard, but there was a striking lack of consensus on a "new paradigm" or an action agenda for public administration. As one observer put it, "what is proposed by the 'new' Public Administration is not so much programmatic as procedural. . . . very little is proposed or suggested in the way of solution."[8] At best, as another observer later remarked, Minnowbrook seemed an abstract reaffirmation of old faiths: ". . . a seemingly intransigent sense of Marxist faith in the absolute value of human dignity and self-worth, and an abiding intensity of a kind of Jeffersonian hopefulness of the future. . . . Minnowbrook adventitiously seemed to turn the love command of our Judeo-Christian heritage into an operational, categorical imperative."[9]

Two decades later, in September 1988, a second Minnowbrook conference, Minnowbrook II, convened in the same location with many of the same participants but also with twenty-five still younger scholars who entered the field in the 1980s. "The purpose," in the words of H. George Frederickson, the conference organizer, was "to compare and contrast the perspectives of the two groups on the state of public administration and its future."[10] Once again, for four days many of the ablest scholars, this time young and old, met to ponder the fate of the field. Their papers with commentaries, in shortened form, were also eventually published.[11]

Minnowbrook II projected a strikingly different image, on the whole, from that of Minnowbrook I. Except for a few passing references, the idealism of the 1960s was missing; absent were vigorous affirmations of "Marxist faith," "Jeffersonian hopefulness," and

"the love command of our Judeo-Christian heritage." Rather, Minnowbrook II's essays focused on narrower, more concrete, and
more specialized subjects that were characterized by diverse and
apparently disconnected titles, such as the following: "Theoretical
and Operational Challenges of High Reliability Organizations: Air
Traffic Control and Aircraft Carriers," "Public Administration as a
Design Science," "Recovering the Public Management Variable:
Lessons from Schools, Prisons and Armies," "Investing in America?
The Public Policy and Administration of Consumption, Saving, and
Investment," "Science, Technology, and Public Administration:
The Government-University Nexus," and "The New Public Person-
nel and the New Public Service."[12]

   Did such apparently pragmatic subjects of Minnowbrook II
reflect a genuinely "new" focus, tone, and definition for public
administration thought in the 1980s? Why do these titles bear so
little resemblance to those of the 1960s? Why had current topics
shifted so dramatically away from idealistic visions? Were there *any*
common threads linking Minnowbrook I and II or, for that matter,
connecting the apparently disconnected topics presented at the
1988 conference? Why does the field seem so malleable? so impermanent? so impossible to pin down? and seemingly recast in any
direction according to personal whim? More fundamentally, after
two decades *and more* of wrestling with public administration theory, why are we no closer to defining what "it" is? Or, as one Minnowbrook participant who had attended both conferences I and II
lamented (using an apt Biblical analogy), does public administration theory personify "the trek in the continual wilderness"?*

Public Administration: The Core of Modern Government

At noon on January 20, 1989, on the West Capitol steps in Washington, D.C., a remarkable two-century-old rite was reenacted—a new
President of the United States was inaugurated. Power was once
again peacefully transferred in America. On the surface at least, the
event seemed to follow the same prescribed routines that have

---

*This confusion seems to extend to the popular mind, for the term
"public administration" is not even listed in the dictionary, although there
are listings for "public assistance," "public health," "public service," and
"public works."

occurred every four years since 1789: the same oath was administered by the Chief Justice, holding a Bible, in an open public forum,
surrounded by officials, friends, and family and with the new President standing in plain civilian dress with his right hand raised.
Even the Bible was the same one that had been used for the first .
swearing-in ceremony of George Washington.

Although the symbolic form of the 1989 inaugural followed
patterns almost to the letter with that of the first inaugural in the
early Republic, there was another side to the peaceful transfer of
power that most Americans missed seeing. Hidden from public
view, in the rear of the inaugural stands, a young military aide to
the President held a satchel containing the top-secret code words
necessary to launch a nuclear attack. This so-called "football" had
followed President Ronald Reagan everywhere for the last eight
years and was handed over to a new aide with new code words. It
will remain with President George Bush throughout his term in
office. This unpublicized action of "passing the football" (a colorful
twentieth-century phrase) might well be thought of as reflecting the
real transfer of American power. It involves governance by a huge,
powerful administrative state composed of advanced technology,
professional expertise, and extensive global influence as opposed to
the *symbolic* event of "swearing an oath" (a characteristic eighteenth-century phrase) with all its ancient republican trappings that
many millions watched on television.

Much like the inauguration, American government today—for
better or worse or for better *and* worse—may be clothed in ancient
republican forms, but in reality it is very much governed by a vast
administrative enterprise involving technology, expertise, and globalism. Public administration comprises much of the enterprise of
government, or what Carl J. Friedrich many years ago saw as "the
core of modern government."[13] Ironically, public administration
may well be the "core of modern government," but "it" seemingly
continues to elude the grasp of the best minds who attempt to the-
orize and to define what "it" is. What explains this irony?

Alexis de Tocqueville and the Earliest View of American Administrative Thought from Abroad

Alexis-Charles-Henri-Clérel de Tocqueville, a 26-year-old French
magistrate from a liberal family of lesser nobility, arrived in New-
port, Rhode Island, aboard *The President* on May 11, 1831, ostensibly to study the American penal system (at the time considered
one of the most advanced in the world). For the next nine months

he and his friend Gustave de Beaumont traveled the length and breadth of the United States and part of Canada by stage, steamer, and horseback: to New York and Boston; as far west as Green Bay, Wisconsin; as far north as Quebec; as far south as New Orleans; and back to Washington and New York. In total they traveled 7,000 miles, visiting every state that existed at the time. Throughout their journey they took meticulous notes as they interviewed thousands of Americans from all walks of life. Upon their return to France, they not only published a comprehensive official study of American prisons, but Tocqueville went on to write one of the most remarkable analyses ever of American democracy. His two-volume *Democracy in America* (1835 and 1840)[14] remains one of the most insightful, detailed, and generalized studies of the United States. As he wrote, "I wished to show what a democratic people really was in our day. . . ."[15] Europeans were fascinated with Tocqueville's observations, and both volumes of *Democracy in America* became best sellers then—and continue to remain so. "No one has ever probed more deeply the inner nature of American Society," writes one political scientist of Tocqueville's work.[16]

What is particularly intriguing for modern students of public administration is that Tocqueville offered perhaps the earliest assessment of American thinking in contrast to European thinking about public administration. He found a strange and peculiar world in the United States:

> The art of administration is undoubtedly a science, and no science can be improved if discoveries and observations of successive generations are not connected together in the order in which they occur. One man in the short space of his life remarks a fact, another conceives an idea: the former invents a means of executing, the latter reduces a truth to a formula; and mankind gathers fruits of individual experience on its way and gradually forms the sciences. But the persons who conduct administration in America can seldom afford any instruction to one another; and when they assume the direction of society, they simply possess those attainments which are widely disseminated in the community, and no knowledge particular to themselves. Democracy, pushed to its furthest limits, is therefore prejudicial to the art of government; and for this reason it is better adapted to a people already versed in the conduct of government.[17]

Tocqueville not only noted that democracy is "prejudicial to the art of government" but also emphasized the uniqueness of American administrative thinking. He noted that American public administration was not only *not* taken seriously as a subject for study but was mostly temporal in nature. In short, there was little lasting content to public administrative ideas in the United States. "The public administration [in America] is, so to speak, oral and traditional," writes Tocqueville. "But little is committed to writing, and that little is soon wafted away forever, like the leaves of the Sibyl, by the smallest breeze."[18]

In contrast, Tocqueville's description of the European approach to administration was far different (mind you, he was writing in the 1830s):

> All the governments of Europe have, in our time, singularly improved the science of administration: they do more things, and they do everything with more order, more celerity, and less expense; they seem to be constantly enriched by all the experience of which they have stripped private persons. From day to day, the princes of Europe hold their subordinate offices under stricter control and invent new methods for guiding them more closely and inspecting them with less trouble.[19]

Developing a more refined science of administration, in Tocqueville's view, seemed to be a major continental European preoccupation, even though the subject was neglected in America of that day. Yet there was a price Europeans paid for administrative advancement. European public administration, Tocqueville concludes, "has become not only more centralized, but more inquisitive and more minute: it everywhere interferes in private concerns more than it did; it regulates more undertakings, and undertakings of lesser kind; and it gains a firmer footage every day about, above, and all around private persons, to assist, to advise, and to coerce them."[20]

If Europe's vice clearly was an overrefinement of administrative science to the point that it "interferes in private concerns," Tocqueville saw America's unique approach to administration as having the reverse problems:

> The instability of administration has penetrated into the habits of the people; it even appears to suit the general taste, and no one cares for what occurs before his time: no methodological system is pursued, no archives are formed and no documents are brought together where it would be very easy to do so. Where they exist, little store is set upon them. I have among my papers several original public documents which were

given to me in public offices in America to some of my inquiries. In America society seems to live from hand to mouth like an army in the field.[21]

In brief, Americans perhaps suffered from too great an inattention and a neglect of public administration, at least from Tocqueville's perspective.

Tocqueville viewed the American neglect of administrative science from the standpoint of several centuries of French administrative advancements. He saw the United States living a unique "hand to mouth" existence when it came to the perfection of administrative sciences because the Frenchman largely viewed "the first new nation" from the vantage point of a rich European tradition of administrative development. Whereas Americans exhibited little, if any, interest in administration at the time, France, like much of Europe, had already experienced abundant administrative experimentation, innovation, and advancement by 1830. Two centuries earlier, Cardinal Richelieu, who had been the principal minister under French King Louis XIII from 1624 to 1642, set up an office of intendant to consolidate the administrative system under the Crown and to provide continuing provincial representation of royal authority. In the intendant's hands was placed "very considerable powers covering taxes, tutelage, war supplies, recruitment, public works and so on."[22] Particularly, the Sun King, Louis XIV, in the seventeenth century, under his chief minister Jean Baptiste Colbert, further increased the efficiency and effectiveness of the intendant system by centralizing the legal, fiscal, personnel, and military aspects of administration. As Brian Chapman notes, professional public administration had long, deep roots in French soil.[23]

France's greatest administrative advances came during the Napoleonic era, an era that chronologically coincided with Tocqueville's early life. As Ferrel Heady notes of this period, "administration stressed order, specialization and accountability. As Emperor, he [Napoleon] incorporated many military-like features into a tightly knit command structure which assigned duties clearly and demanded personal responsibility for performance."[24] Napoleon created the Conseil d'Etat to act as his general staff, as well as a tightly organized chain of command through which reported five basic ministries (finance, foreign affairs, interior, justice, and war). He further developed a prefecture system for local administration, a merit system for selection of civil service personnel, and a training school for top public officials, the Ecôle Polytechnique. As historian E. N. Gladden suggests, "Napoleon's objective of shaping a highly authoritarian system and of furnishing it with an efficient administration was a remarkable achievement considering the magnitude of the task and the short time he had at his disposal."[25]

A by-product of the rapid rise of this hierarchical, rationalized, ordered, and authoritarian state system, as Daniel W. Martin recently pointed out, was a surprisingly rich French literature on the subject of public administration. In retrospect, according to Martin, that literature "is quite impressive."[26] By 1812 the first public administration textbook in France had already been published, Charles-Jean Bonnin's *Principes d'administration publique*. In 1808 Bonnin had drafted the administrative code for Napoleon. When the code needed updating, he devised sixty-eight general principles of administration for ensuring that the code would remain current. These sixty-eight principles of administration eventually became a basis for his text. Later, Alexandre Françoise Auguste Vivien's two-volume basic text, *Etudes administratives* (1845), went through three editions and had, according to Martin, "the largest impact and it is still occasionally cited in French administrative histories."[27]

Other texts by Charles Dupin, Edouard Laboulaye, and Louis Antoine Macarel exhibited fairly wide agreement on the scope and direction of public administration and emphasized commonly agreed-upon "principles" of administration. Macarel actually held a professorship of "Droit Administratif" and was an especially prolific scholar who "often sought to explain the law through administrative principles."[28] In the same era there were also several significant administrative journals that flourished with wide readership, *Revue administrative*, *Revue Française*, and *Revue de legislation et de jurisprudence*. The latter journal, after April 1839, was exclusively devoted to public administration, and in its opening issue the editors announced that they were not interested in politics, commerce, or industry but primarily in public administration. That journal regularly published high-quality articles about policy studies and organizational analysis, as well as kept readers informed on current legal, institutional, and personnel developments. It sought to exhibit commonly shared intellectual and theoretical perspectives on public administration, drawn from past, present, and even international-comparative points of view. No wonder Tocqueville thought of the American administrative theory and practice as undeveloped, perhaps "primitive," seemingly living "a hand to mouth" existence.

America's Public Administration Theory: One, Two, Many

In contrast to the French experience, the conscious study of public administration has been a comparatively recent innovation in the United States. The first American essay calling for a systematic study of the subject did not appear until 1887—"The Study of Administration" by Woodrow Wilson—and the first general American textbook—*Introduction to the Study of Public Administration*, by Leonard D. White[29]—was published much later, in 1926.

Why did it take so long for Americans to develop—even consciously think about—this field in comparison to Europeans? As reflected by the Minnowbrook I and II conference experiences, several questions remain: What accounts for America's continued lack of focus in regard to this subject when in reality public administration operates as "the core of modern government"? Why do administrative ideas remain so diffuse and impermanent, even to this day? Why does the field lack consensus and direction about what "it" is, even with the best efforts by its ablest scholars at the close of the twentieth century? Or, in the words of Nicholas Henry, is this subject, one so central to America's governance and future, at best "a paradigmatic quandary"?[30]

Here perhaps is the central characteristic—and problem— with public administration theory in America: namely, its continued failure to define its scope and substance as a coherent theory, even in the late twentieth century. Its subject matter seems uncertain and problematical today, given that three contradictory theoretical images of the field were projected throughout this century and that fundamentally they seem to be irreconcilable.

One Best Way

First, until approximately World War II, public administration thought was dominated by what some might argue as unitary visions of the field—or the "one best way" school of thinking. This approach emphasized a single, specific, *and correct* view for doing *and* thinking about public administration. Frederick Taylor's "scientific management" and Luther Gulick's so-called POSDCORB methodologies were popular manifestations of this one-best-way theorizing. Often formulated as laws of science or *the* management principles, these administrative theories were conceived to apply universally to all situations and to be used by *every* administrator. Early, first-generation theorists of public administration tended to envision the field as pragmatic and action-oriented, but, above all, as a field governed by doctrines favoring single solutions derived from the application of correct methodologies. They did not perceive alternatives as *real* alternatives. Later critics pointed out that such unitary theories of public administration, in fact, held hidden normative, value judgments, which made these methodologies hardly the universal or comprehensive theories that their authors presumed them to be. Although they were flawed and are no longer accepted as wholistic theories to explain the field, such unitary visions nonetheless continue repeatedly to find powerful support within contemporary public administration thinking. Specialized methodologies perennially advocate this or that particular one way of thinking as *the* way of thinking about public sector issues. Analytical techniques like systems analysis, operations research, and budgetary systems techniques like PPB or ZZB are contemporary reflections of such unitary models. These methodologies often advocate a one best approach, based particularly on deductive lines of reasoning from first principles that are akin to the laws of scientific rationalism.

Frequently, though not always, enthusiasts for such modern unitary methodologies advocate their one particular technique as a universal system for solving public problems without conceptualizing or visualizing any alternatives. Options go unmentioned or unquestioned. Achieving one purpose or value is stressed over other priorities, and thus important alternatives are neglected or overlooked by advocates of the contemporary one-best-way school. Consensus on ends is assumed, and conflicts over purposes are often denied as real and meaningful differences in past or present unitary models of administration. At times the "good" or "correct" system or methodology becomes an end in itself, a panacea for curing all the administrative problems at hand. The method itself rules over the goals to be achieved. To paraphrase the words of Wallace Sayre, "technique triumphs over purpose."

Frequently, technologists or students from narrow disciplinary backgrounds of science or business advocate such unitary models and see the world through these limited "lenses." Contemporary advocates of the one-best-way line of reasoning often express their ideas as ideals with the enthusiasm of religious zeal. Hence, their approaches are at times regarded as simplistic, narrow, or "too academic" and therefore find limited support and only temporary application, at least by practitioners in public administration. Certainly, the "assumed pleasing harmony" over ends seems unrealistic to those on the firing line.

Dualism

The second view found in modern public administration theory might be termed "the dialectical approach" or "dualistic vision." The dialectical study of public administration, much like Marxist ideology, is conceived largely as a repeated contest between two alternative theoretical perspectives. Outcomes are determined by a continuous clash of polar opposites. Arguments by many of the field's founders, such as Woodrow Wilson and Frank Goodnow prior to 1940, advocated the new field called "public administration" precisely in order to replace or at least to find a place for values of "efficiency" and "effectiveness" as opposed to "politics" and "partisanship" which at the time characterized "wrong," even morally "evil," values. Likewise, dichotomous perspectives are vividly seen, such as the early Hawthorne studies in which experimenters sought to replace the mechanistic rationalism of scientific management with new humanistic approaches. In much the same manner, modern-day "public choice" enthusiasts, "behavioralists," or "critical theory" theorists tend to divide the world into them versus us: the public choice framework for public administration divides the world neatly between those who maximize and those who limit the pursuit of private interests for the public good; the behavioralists contrast those who favor "behavioral methods" with the formal "structuralists"; and the critical theorists contrast those who accept "positivist interpretations" with those who reject—or at least criticize—the prevailing "positivism" and accept a "post-positivist paradigm" for the field.

Like Marxist interpretation, such dialectical thinking posits a clash of two ideas and implicitly or explicitly assumes the ultimate victory of one perspective over another. One idea is seen as a good idea and should triumph in the end for the benefit of all, while the other should ultimately fail or be made to fail because of the "incorrectness" (for whatever reason) of the idea itself. There is latent manichaeistic idealism inherent such thinking. It assumes progress in one direction for the field, an academic discipline in which even the entire human race comes about by conquest of one idea over another. According to this frame of thought, public administration theory is essentially reduced to a simplified either/or, black/white dichotomy. In the war featuring two big ideas, the "grey" in between is overlooked or ignored entirely. In this respect, the implicit belief in the idea of progress and the absolutism of dual visionaries have much in common with the unitary viewpoint.

Pluralism

A third approach to public administration thought today sees that the major attribute of the field is its pluralism. No one theory or two, say the advocates of this school, can realistically explain contemporary public administration thought. The pluralist philosophy holds that diversity of opinions and points of view is not only an appropriate way to explain present reality but is a positive strength. A struggle between numerous ideas, philosophies, and perspectives reflects health, not weakness, in the field. No single or dual paradigm(s) can or should take over entirely for theorizing about public administration. Like democracy itself, public administration is seen by pluralists as a loose set of competing ideas, points of view, methodologies, and approaches. When such unitary or dualistic visions hold sway (as was the case just before World War II), so the pluralists contend, public administration was at its weakest and most ineffectual.

The "let-a-thousand-flowers-bloom" perspective is often advocated by those who like to "see the big picture" from historical, philosophical, and literary backgrounds—people such as Ordway Tead, Mary Parker Follett, Francis Coker, Dwight Waldo, Paul Appleby, James Fesler, Don Price, and John Gaus. Their prescription(s), as Dwight Waldo perhaps most aptly describes, is that, "we should open upon [public administration] all the windows we can find, that all models and idioms have their virtues—and their vices. . . ."[31] The world is a messy place and "truth," at least for the pluralists, is held by no one approach. It is discovered by sorting through bits and pieces of truths from a wide variety of perspectives. From the give-and-take of many ideas, truth emerges. "Good" public administration theory should therefore offer a wide range of methods and let the law of the situation—inventiveness of individual or collective discussion of groups—determine the selection of the appropriate choice.

In the process, public administration becomes less of a science and more of an art form. Pluralists thus tend not to speak in absolutes—i.e., the one best way or the optimal solution—but, instead, they tend to talk with shades of grey in mind—i.e., with words like "meshing," "coping," and "satisficing." In their world, as Harvey Sherman nicely summed it up, "It all depends."[32] The situation, in other words, not the method, rules. Critics of this view tend to label it as "soft," "unscientific," and "lacking method." They contend pluralists engage in "mere description" and that their theorizing is so diffuse and unstructured that it becomes a meaningless exercise, lacking rigor, even purpose.

While the three aforementioned categories of modern-day public administration thinking may overgeneralize, they do tend to characterize in broad terms the current major patterns of conceptualizing about public administration. On the surface, their fundamental differences are seemingly irreconcilable. Individually they offer distinct and separate ways of thinking about the world of public administration, which, in turn, ultimately shapes how we "do" administration. Each one advocates different methods and, ultimately, different answers for the field. The first view essentially seeks solutions in scientific, rational, and empirical methods— which tend to lead to scientific, rational, and empirical answers; the third tends to find answers without any clear-cut methodologies but simply by appreciation of humanistic, inductive, nonscientific, and even nonrational, diverse values; and the second favors administrative theory as essentially a combat of ideas, often rooted in subjective, reformist goals of a caste or class, and visualizing the triumph of *one* for the good of the field—or, better still—for the entire world population.

The American State and Public Administration Theory

Twentieth-century American public administration theory— whether visualized as one, two, or many approaches—is not so much wrong as offers incomplete ways of understanding present-day administrative theory in the United States. With rare exceptions, as this book argues, these approaches miss the vital connection with state development in the unique context of American history for fundamentally influencing the peculiar shape, style, and content of modern American public administrative theory. Just as the development of the Napoleonic reforms in France in the early 1800s stimulated the development of a rich literature of French administrative thought in that era and hence "colored" Tocqueville's views of America, so, too, American state development in the late nineteenth and early twentieth centuries was chiefly, if not exclusively, responsible for the peculiar patterns of intellectual development of the field after 1900.

Contemporary students of public administration theory often ignore this vital link between the rise of American state institutions and the rise of public administrative theory.[33] This is a regrettable oversight for the growth of the American state that began roughly a century after the formation of the American Republic and the growth of the subject of public administration *as ideals and ideas* were intimately connected and persist to this day. Not only was America "born without a state," but the American state did not take shape until roughly a century after the Constitution of the United States was ratified. Further, the American state evolved in such a way as to make a fully matured system (in the form of most European nations) a distinct impossibility in America.

The American state was—and remains—something different: it is always on the move, never stationary long enough for one to get a firm fix on it. Because state development in America took a very different path from that in Europe, the "color and tone" of administrative theory in this country also was much different. Without a fully matured, stable state, or rather with one that was always developing, American administrative thought never could cohere, take shape, and mature in the same manner of other nations, at least for very long. American theory was always trying to hit a moving target, which makes its ideas and ideals more difficult to identify, more amorphous, and harder for theorists to grasp. Thus, to this day American administrative theory looks different from that of other nations, as Tocqueville first observed and by which he was perplexed. And if outsiders are perplexed, so too are the insiders, who keep asking the perennial questions, as did the best minds of Minnowbrook I and II and elsewhere: What is public administration? its scope and content? What are its basic paradigms? its future directions?

This book asks the same questions, but endeavors to address them from a different perspective, namely, from that of the peculiar contours of American state development. Chapters Two, Three, and Four set out to examine the evolution of the American state system from its "stateless" origins to its present-day status as a "global professional technocracy." These opening chapters study how the unusual contours of American state formation "framed" an unusual twentieth-century American administrative thought. Chapter Five specifically looks at how this changing institutional framework of the American state decisively influenced the shifting doctrines of American public administration thought after 1900. Chapters Six, Seven, and Eight, in light of the unique evolution of the American state, seek to outline the contemporary and future directions of public administrative theory in America.

One final point: since much of the following argument flows from the meaning of "state" and "stateless" or "statelessness," a brief word about their definitions is in order. The "state" often denotes confusing metaphysical metaphors or legal technicalities as in "the personality of a king" or "precise national boundaries." For the purposes of this text, however, "state" is simply meant to describe concrete national institutions and the organizations and people that carry out the basic functions common to all modern nations, such as tax collection, business regulation, national defense, public education, social welfare, and other important services. These activities evolved in continental Europe in the fourteenth, fifteenth, and sixteenth centuries in their first early forms and were fully matured by the late seventeenth, eighteenth, and early nineteenth centuries. "State" in this book thus is viewed as an historical institutional concept that decisively shaped western European development during the past several centuries, focused around the idea of centralization of power, normally in an absolute monarch (later an elected parliament and chief executive), whose authority was rationalized and extended over a nation through a developed, impersonalized public administration. In short, a nation-state system involves essential functions, structures, and people that run modern government for public purposes.

"Stateless" and "statelessness" refer to the opposite condition—that is, the lack of all or most such national functions, structures, and people. Until the late nineteenth and early twentieth centuries, the United States was specifically found wanting in these basic features, which by that time characterized much of Europe— namely, centralized power, rationalized authority, and developed administration. Until 1883, with the passage of the Pendleton Act, America had no national civil service, at least in any formal sense; until 1887, with the establishment of the Interstate Commerce Commission, it had no national public system for the regulation of private enterprise; until the passage of the sixteenth amendment in 1913, it had no federal income tax; until the Federal Reserve System (1913), it had no public credit; until 1924, it had no control over foreign immigration; and until 1921, it had no national budget. Its national defense relied upon state militias of volunteer citizen-soldiers for the most part until the Root Reforms of 1902. While its legal system was based on fundamental and common law traditions, state-made law (that is, federal administrative law made by regulatory rule-making) was largely a product of this century. America's social welfare system, moreover, was generally church-supported or local "self-help" efforts until the Great Depression of the 1930s. To this day, its public education and police systems remain largely in the hands of state agencies and local jurisdictions. Indeed, what passed for local administration until this century was manned by volunteers and amateurs, not trained managers. In short, until this century America was quite literally a United *States*, not a *united state*. From the start, we failed to measure up to European "state" standards; as Henry James commented, the United States had "No State, in the European sense of the word"[34] or many years later H. G. Wells similarly observed "a sense of the state" was missing in America.[35] But here we are getting ahead of our story. First, we need to examine the roots of the peculiar sources of American "statelessness," which is the subject of the next chapter.

Notes

1. James C. Charlesworth, ed., *The Theory and Practice of Public Administration: Scope, Objectives and Methods* (Philadelphia: American Academy of Political and Social Science, October 1968), p. ix.
2. As cited in Dwight Waldo, "Foreword," in Frank Marini, ed., *Toward a New Public Administration: The Minnowbrook Perspective* (Scranton, Pennsylvania: Chandler, 1971), p. xiv.
3. Marini, ibid.
4. Todd R. LaPorte, "The Recovery of Relevance in the Study of Public Organization," in Marini, p. 32.
5. Orion F. White, Jr., "Administrative Adaptation in a Changing Society," in Marini, p. 69.
6. H. George Frederickson, "Toward a New Public Administration," in Marini, p. 311.
7. Larry Kirkhart, "Public Administration and Selected Developments in Social Science," in Marini, pp. 159–161.
8. Waldo, p. xviii.
9. Louis C. Gawthrop, "Minnowbrook: The Search for a New Reality," *Public Administration Review* (March/April 1989), p. 194. For additional insights into the Minnowbrook experience, see: Michael M. Harmon, "The New Public Administration as a Symbol and Sociological Event," unpublished paper delivered at the National American Society for Public Administration Conference (March 1982); York Willbern, "Is the New Public Administration Still with Us?," *Public Administration Review* (July/August 1973), p. 375; Brack Brown and Richard Still-

man, *A Search for Public Administration: The Ideas and Career of Dwight Waldo* (College Station: Texas A&M University Press, 1986), pp. 105–108; Robert F. Wilcox, "The New P.A.: Have Things Really Changed That Much?," *Public Management* (March 1971), pp. 4–7; H. George Frederickson, "The Lineage of New Public Administration," *Administration and Society* (August 1976), pp. 149–175; Laurence J. O'Toole, Jr., "Lineage, Continuity, Frederickson and the 'New Public Administration,'" *Administration and Society* (August 1977), pp. 233–252; and Robert B. Denhardt, "The Continuing Saga of the New Public Administration, *Administration and Society* (August 1977), pp. 252–262.

10. H. George Frederickson, unpublished letter of invitation to Minnowbrook II, December 27, 1987.
11. "Minnowbrook II: Changing Epochs of Public Administration," *Public Administration Review* (March/April 1989), entire issue.
12. Ibid.
13. Carl J. Friedrich, chapter 2, *Constitutional Government and Democracy: Theory and Practice in Europe and America,* 4th ed. (Boston: Ginn, Blaisdell, 1968), p. 38. As Friedrich writes: "No government can function without it. . . . For a constitutional system which cannot function effectively, which cannot act with dispatch and strength, cannot live" (p. 57).
14. Alexis de Tocqueville, *Democracy in America,* vols. 1 and 2 (New York: Vintage, 1945).
15. Letter to M. Stoffels (Paris, February 21, 1835), as cited in editorial notes by Phillips Bradley in ibid., vol. 2, p. 402.
16. As cited by Bradley, ibid.
17. Tocqueville, vol. 2, p. 439.
18. Ibid., vol. 1, pp. 219–220.
19. Ibid., vol. 1, p. 219.
20. Ibid., vol. 2, p. 326.
21. Ibid., vol. 2, p. 324.
22. Ibid., vol. 1, p. 219.
23. Brian Chapman, *The Professions of Government* (London: Allen & Unwin, 1959), p. 21. For a useful guide to the historical literature of this field, read Daniel W. Martin, *The Guide to the Foundations of Public Administration* (New York: Marcel Dekker, 1989).
24. Ferrel Heady, *Public Administration: A Comparative Perspective,* 3d ed. (New York: Marcel Dekker, 1984), p. 170.
25. E. N. Gladden, *A History of Public Administration* (London: Frank Cass, 1972), vol. 2, p. 297.
26. Daniel W. Martin, "*Déjà Vu:* French Antecedents of American Public Administration," *Public Administration Review* (July/August 1987), p. 297.
27. Ibid.
28. Ibid.

29. Leonard D. White, *Introduction to the Study of Public Administration* (New York: Macmillan, 1926). It should be noted that this was the first general text on the subject, although earlier administrative law texts had appeared. The two earliest of these were by Frank J. Goodnow: *Comparative Administrative Law* (1893) and *The Principles of Administrative Law* (1905).
30. Nicholas Henry, *Public Administration and Public Affairs*, 4th ed. (Englewood Cliffs, New Jersey: Prentice-Hall, 1989), p. 20.
31. Dwight Waldo, *Perspectives on Administration* (University: University of Alabama Press, 1956), p. 49.
32. Harvey Sherman, *It All Depends—A Pragmatic Approach to Organization* (University: University of Alabama Press, 1966).
33. It would be remiss to not point out several recent students of the field who have written brilliant pieces on aspects of this connection between ideas and institutional development, such as Barry D. Karl, *The Uneasy State* (Chicago: University of Chicago Press, 1983); Stephen Skowronek, *Building a New American State: The Expansion of National Administrative Capacities, 1877–1910* (Cambridge: Cambridge University Press, 1982); John A. Rohr, *To Run a Constitution: The Legitimacy of the Administrative State* (Lawrence: University of Kansas Press, 1986); Don K. Price, *America's Unwritten Constitution* (Baton Rouge: Louisiana State University Press, 1983); Ralph C. Chandler, ed., *A Centennial History of Public Administration* (New York: Free Press, 1987), as well as numerous shorter pieces, such as David H. Rosenbloom, "Public Administration Theory and the Separation of Powers," *Public Administration Review*, vol. 43, no. 3 (May/June 1983), and Laurence J. O'Toole, "Harry F. Byrd, Sr., and the New York Bureau of Municipal Research," *Public Administration Review*, vol. 47, no. 1 (January/February 1987). Largely these works have focused on the development of American administrative institutions, not on the ideas and doctrines of American public administration. This book looks at the central issue of how administrative ideas related to institutional development in the United States.
34. Henry James, *Hawthorne* (Ithaca: Cornell University Press, 1956, originally published in 1879), p. 34.
35. H. G. Wells, as quoted in Esmond Wright, "The End of Innocence," *Political Quarterly*, 43 (January 1972), p. 35.

CHAPTER TWO

The Peculiar "Stateless" Origins of American Public Administration Theory

Nothing is more striking to a European traveler in the United States than the absence of what we term the government, or the Administration.

ALEXIS DE TOCQUEVILLE
Democracy in America

The most striking feature of America's public administration thought at the founding of the United States was its absence.[1] Not until a century after the Constitution was drafted did the first "conscious" essay on public administration appear, "The Study of Administration," written by the young political scientist Woodrow Wilson in 1887. Even then, the first textbook was not published until 1926 by Leonard White, and the flowering of most serious scholarship had to await the late 1930s and postwar 1940s—well *after* the development of major America's administrative institutions. Like the famous Sherlock Holmes story in which the clue that solves the case was "the dog that didn't bark," so, too, it can be argued that America's "missing state" at its inception fundamentally shapes our way of thinking about, as well as doing, public administration today.

Why did this peculiar absence of American public administration thought occur at the birth of our nation? How does it influence contemporary public administration theory's unique outlook and design? Why is our present difficulty in understanding public administration as a set of ideas and a field of study rooted in our past "stateless" national origins? What accounts for "the missing state" within the context of America's political development?

As scholars have noted, the U.S. Constitution is mostly silent on the subject of public administration. Article I enumerates in great detail the powers of Congress, but nowhere in the Constitution or other basic founding documents does one find public administration mentioned. The word "administration" does not even appear in the text of the U.S. Constitution, nor does "organization," "budget," "management," "planning," "public service," "civil service," or, for that matter, any other terms normally associated with public administration. Article II does open with, "The Executive Power shall be vested in a President of the United States of America," but that is about all, leaving very much a blank slate involving "administration" as something to be filled in and defined by later Americans. Of course, scatterings of the Founding Fathers' views on the topic can be cited. Alexander Hamilton, in *Federalist No. 68*, did argue that "we may safely pronounce that the true test of a good government is its aptitude and tendency to produce good administration,"[2] but few other members of the 1787 Constitutional Convention spoke at any length directly about the subject.

Paradoxically, although the Constitution and the Founding Fathers avoided the subject, certainly there was no absence of concern about bureaucracy and its administration by the framers of the Constitution. The American Revolution was largely waged against royal bureaucracy, and the administrative misdeeds of George III and his colonial governors were at the heart of the specific charges against the Crown cited in the Declaration of Independence. The "injuries and usurpations" by the King of Great Britain against the Colonists, enumerated in the Declaration, were mainly *administrative offenses:* "He has obstructed the administration of justice. . . . ;" "He has erected a multitude of new offices. . . . ;" "He has kept among us in times of peace standing armies. . . . ;" He established "an arbitrary government. . . ." For the men of 1787 the administrative state may well have been absent precisely because of their fresh memories of the Revolutionary War; it was viewed as antithetical to what they saw constituted the basics of "good government." The story of America's peculiar inability to accept administration as part and parcel of the constitutional-governing framework may well be rooted in a complicated confluence of (a) republican ideas, (b) Tudor institutions, (c) crises of events of the 1780s, and (d) the "mythos," or pattern of beliefs, behind the U.S. Constitution that created "the first new nation." What were these unusual ideas, institutions, crises of events, and myths of the 1780s? How did they each emerge and together profoundly shape the intellectual contours of American administrative thought into a unique model of democratic administration?

The Legacy of "Stateless" Ideas in the American Constitution: The Dominant Faith in Republicanism

Modern communities are formed on the basis of some idea or ideals, such as the Marxist creed, the Islamic faith, or Third World ideologies. The ideas that forged America's nationhood, unlike those that stirred many twentieth-century nations, were not created out of whole cloth. They bore the stamp of historical accumulation. The most pervasive idea—the central framing idea for forging the new national American community—was republicanism. It is an idea that did not come down to the framers from one philosopher, a Locke or a Montesquieu, for example, or as a distinctly unified set of beliefs. Rather, republicanism was at the time a loose collection of ideas that had "flitted about history," to use Isaiah Berlin's delightful phrase, "like butterflies" landing here and there in history, without any necessarily rational line of development. Republicanism had first been talked about by the ancient Roman writers and was at the time highly popular with several eighteenth-century fringe theorists of politics, especially radical writers.

Mainly, as Gordon Wood reminds us,[3] republicanism came to be used, like Marxism in the nineteenth and twentieth centuries, as a countercultural ideology of protest by radicals in a monarchically dominated age of the seventeenth and eighteenth centuries, an intellectual route by which people could criticize the luxury, selfishness, and corruption of kings. As a result of its frequent use in the context of the political fray, the ideas of republicanism were often inchoate, inconsistent, and contradictory, as well as drawn from diverse sources.

Most of all, republicanism came down to us from the era of the Roman Republic, or what Peter Gay calls the Roman Enlightenment, from roughly the middle of the second century B.C. to the creation of the Empire in mid-second century A.D. It was a golden age of Roman literature—of Cicero, Plutarch, Tacitus, and Sallust, who lived in the era of the decline of the Republic. These Romans looked back with nostalgic feeling and sympathy to the brighter days of the Republic. They left a body of literature advocating the need to restore the values of good citizenship, praising morality and integrity as the basis of a good society, and warmly embracing the virtues of simple, direct, self-government by sturdy landowning farmers. Most of these Romans did not plow new intellectual ground in their political treatises but, rather, like Cicero in his *Commonwealth*, summarized a prevailing backward-looking spirit of "a lost age" of an ideal republic. The Renaissance, especially the writings of Machiavelli, revived this classical republican tradition emphasizing the worth of "civic virtue" and moral character as prerequisites to the good, well-ordered community.[4]

While Machiavelli is more often remembered for advocating amoral statecraft in the *Prince*, in reality he idealized the ancient Roman Republic—an independent, self-governing polity of property-owning farmers based upon codified law and civic virtue. Seventeenth-century English writers—such as Milton, Harrington, and Sidney—carried on this argument in favor of republicanism that valued civic humanism. English coffee house journalists like John Trenchard and Thomas Gordon popularized and spread these republican ideas throughout the educated English-speaking world in the eighteenth century. Later these notions crossed the Atlantic and became especially popular during the American Revolution.

What precisely did republicanism mean to the Founding Fathers? It is hard to say. Certainly everyone was for it, but few tried to define it. Madison was one of the few who tried in *Federalist No. 10*, but he promptly offered a different definition in *Federalist No. 39*. Literally republicanism means "public things," "public interest," or "welfare of the people." At its roots, in terms of a political system, republicanism carries more negative connotations than positive ones: the elimination of the king, heredity, hierarchy, privilege, noble titles, and tradition as a basis of rule; above all, elimination of anything that smacks of royal bureaucracy or administration and the substitution of an electoral system based on consent of the people, but requiring a particular type of involved electorate—virtuous, egalitarian, independent, and property-owning citizens who are willing to give up selfish interests for the public good of the entire community. In short, its model person is a Cincinnatus, certainly not a Caesar or a George III, and *especially not Royal Governors or Crown administrative agents!*

Yet, the difficulty the founders faced was, as Montesquieu and other theorists of the time warned, that republics had to be small, compact territories in order to survive. The only successful examples in the eighteenth century were just that—small, compact city-states of Switzerland and the Netherlands. A larger society, like mid-seventeenth-century England, had flirted with republicanism under Cromwell and had failed miserably with its application. Large states required large bureaucracies in order to function (or, in Cromwell's case, military administration), precisely what America's Constitutional framers wished to avoid.

A genius of the framers was in adapting this essentially small-state idea into the context of a large society—*without requiring an administrative state*—and then convincing others that this experiment could succeed. Throughout the new Constitution of 1787, as already discussed, one finds no mention of public administration, but plenty of republican ideas were deeply embedded, such as providing periodic elections for the executive and legislative branches (Articles I and II); guaranteeing a republican form of government for states (Article IV, section 4); and forbidding the granting of any titles of nobility (Article I, section 9). For the choice of president, virtue was also sought through a complex indirect system called "the electoral college." The framers, like Marx a century later, seemed to believe that if only enough Republicanism was incorporated into the Constitution, a state would wither away or at least become unnecessary. In short, republicanism minus a state was taken as axiomatic in creating the new Constitution, for, as Madison indicated in *Federalist No. 39*, "no other form would be reconcilable with the genius of the people of America; with the fundamental principles of revolution; or with the honorable determination which animates every votary of freedom, to rest all our political experiment on the capacity of mankind for self-government."[5]

A significant portion of the debates between the Federalists and Anti-Federalists simply overlooked administrative machinery entirely and revolved around whether or not the Constitution was "true" to republican ideals. The Anti-Federalists essentially argued that it was not and therefore the Constitution ought to be rejected. Alexander Hamilton, James Madison, and John Jay in the *Federalist Papers* had to work especially hard to convince their fellow citizens that the Constitution was indeed "a republican design" that could be stretched to extend to such a large and diverse country as America. The brilliant *Federalist No. 10* is a justification of that very point: "Extend the sphere," writes Madison, "and you take in a greater variety of parties and interests; you make it less probable that a majority of the whole will have a common motive to invade the rights of the other citizens or if such a common motive exists . . . to act in unison with each other."[6] In *Federalist No. 14* he writes, "America can claim the merit of making the discovery of the basis of unmixed and extended republics."[7]

The idea of republicanism had been in the air, so to speak, for a very long time, and the framers justly could be credited for putting into practice such an inchoate idea and adapting it to entirely new circumstances of "an extended republic." By their very fixation on republicanism, however, neither Federalists nor Anti-Federalists deemed the place of the state or the value of administration with "an extended republic" even worthy of discussion. There was no Jean Bodin, no Hugo Grotius, no Thomas Hobbes, no John Austin, nor any strong state advocate in America's constitutional debates. State proponents were missing entirely. Unlike Europeans of this era, Americans held a common assumption, based on their devoted republican beliefs, that if only enough popular participation and political representation were built into the U.S. Constitution, state machinery would be unnecessary. In their eyes, the "natural workings" of direct political conflict and widespread citizen cooperation would be enough to allow "the first new nation" to operate successfully. Thus, in essence, their enthusiasm for republicanism blinded their understanding of the need for state machinery in order to make such a large-scale society tick. Certainly the fascination with this unique idea did make a difference in how later institutions and our understanding of them would be fashioned or, rather, overlooked.

The Legacy of Institutional Practice: The Ancient Tudor "Halfway State"

If "republicanism" or, more precisely, "extended republicanism" was the central visionary ideal, a Constitution still required some actual institutional arrangements to make self-government work in practice. By 1787 the framers had a rich legacy of institutional experiences from which to pick and choose for creating workable systems of self-government. There were over six centuries of British constitutional history and a century and a half of colonial self-government that contained ample numbers of good and bad models for government. Indeed, within four years after the Declaration of Independence (mostly between 1776 and 1777) the thirteen state governments had adopted their own state constitutions that held a considerable variety of institutional forms. Thus, there was close at hand an invaluable neighborhood laboratory for observation and judgment on modeling good government.

Contemporary students of government, such as Samuel P. Huntington, tell us that the colonial political experience was unique because it was drawn from Tudor rule, from Henry VIII and Elizabeth I, who were unquestionably strong monarchs but whose institutional practices reflected the "zenith of medieval institutionalism."[8] For our purposes, the significance of this history rests in this: a "halfway state"—neither centralized nor decentralized—was transported to America, was planted, took root in the colonies, and grew up to influence the form and content of "the first new nation." How in particular did the Tudor institutions of the sixteenth century, which were essentially medieval institutions, shape later American public administration?

Above all, there was fundamental law. Law was viewed by Tudor institutional practices as a foundation for every good government. In the Magna Carta in 1215 King John at Runnymede recognized that his duty to rule must be in accordance with law and respect for the legal rights of the people. Later in 1689, the Bill of Rights established the principle that government must be conducted according to law and constitutional limitations and must be respected by the king. Already Americans in every colony had experience with living under fundamental compacts between the rulers and ruled "whose Great Charters are fundamental, perpetual, and unalterable": the Mayflower Compact (1620), the Fundamental Orders of Connecticut (1639), and the Fundamental Constitutions of Carolinas (1669), for example.

The idea of "a government not of men but laws" was therefore an ingrained habit in America, largely derived from medieval customs via the Tudors, by the time of the Revolution and certainly by 1787. Our Tudor institutional heritage saw law as divinely inspired, not man-made. It was "discovered," not humanly created; unchanging, not changeable. This was a "characteristic medieval idea of all authority as deriving from law."[9] In short, the idea of fundamental law was based on a premodern concept—namely, that law makes the king, not the reverse.

The habit of and reverence for this ancient practice of fundamental law became something of a peculiar American preoccupation, even religious devotion as part of its constitutional and public administration enterprises. Few nations today invest such intense energy and mental effort involving administration in fathoming the meaning of "the law." Few place such faith in the highest court, the U.S. Supreme Court, or in judges and lawyers generally to "correctly" discover and interpret the law or to play such large roles in administration. The Constitution itself embodies this ancient fundamental law tradition to which all statutes and administrative practices must bow and bend. Here is the very antithesis of administrative law that is man-made, changing, and often nonlegalistic in practice.

The English Tudor experience also bequeathed to the American Constitution the practice of "balanced government." The Classical writers, like Aristotle and Cicero, had advanced ideas of a mixed government that contained elements of monarchy, aristocracy, and democracy in its ideal form, but the English had practiced just such balanced arrangements in the day of the Tudor polity with the three realms of king, lords, and commoners. The practice both diffused power and caused it to be shared among the three realms. This practice was transplanted to the colonies by the establishment of a governor, his council, and a lower House of Burgesses. Separation of powers that limited the power of the Crown and his agents especially found eighteenth-century European enthusiasts supporting the more rationalized versions of this concept. The French philosophers Voltaire and Montesquieu continually praised the virtues of a rational separation of powers, not the unification of authority in administration *or* the executive.

Americans, of course, felt comfortable with how this system actually worked. William Meager of North Carolina could write in 1776 that this was "a system that approached as near to perfection as any could within the compass of human abilities."[10] Indeed, much of the justification for the American Revolution in 1776 was ironically rooted in the view that by this time the "true" English "balanced" system had become corrupt and degenerate with the monarchy of George III absorbing all powers onto itself. A unified executive, in the minds of Americans, was associated with corruption and decay. A strong, centralized administration held a near moralistic repugnance by the founders. The revolutionaries therefore viewed the English Constitution as having become a hollow shell by 1776 precisely because it was no longer (so they believed) "true" to the Tudor system they knew and practiced as colonials. The central argument of the Declaration of Independence, as already suggested, was directed at the administrative abuses of the Crown, which the revolutionaries believed upset the "normal" balance in government (normal at least according to their experience).

It was no small wonder, then, that the state constitutions written after the Revolution began replicating the "balanced" sixteenth-century Tudor Constitution almost to the letter, although most of them also severely limited the chief executive's powers and term of office so as to avoid repetition of the colonists' unhappy monarchical experiences. Most also avoided the topic of administration for the same reason. America's written Constitution of 1787 followed this institutional practice with a vengeance. It not only set up three branches of government, but strictly excluded legislators from inhabiting executive roles and, vice versa, excluded executives from holding seats in the legislature. This exclusion was an important American innovation in the development of separation of powers in that it gave the idea a peculiar American twist. Each branch not only had its own separate membership but was given enough powers of its own to make it independent from the others and thereby act as a check, or in the words of Madison, writing in *Federalist No. 51*, "to divide and arrange the several offices in this manner as that each may be a check on the other."[11] It was, however, "the checks" on branches, not the administrative coordination, control, or centralization between branches, that the founders stressed. Again, "administration" is missing from the design.

The U.S. Constitution essentially both revitalized and rearranged old, but dying English Tudor institutional customs of fundamental law and balanced government and fashioned something new in the process of forming a national political community, a uniquely American community, but also one without an administrative state. In the words of Samuel P. Huntington: "In institutional terms, the American polity has never been underdeveloped, but it has also never been wholly modern. In an age of rationalized authority, functional specialization, mass democracy, and totalitarian dictatorship, the American system remains a curious anachronism. In today's world, the American political system is unique, if only because it is so antique."[12]

The Legacy of "Conflict within a Consensus": A Creative "Stateless" Compromise Called Federalism

So far we have been discussing the role of ideas, namely republicanism, and institutional practices, namely English Tudor institutions, in forging the *novus ordo seclorum* with a "missing state," but confluence of ideas and institutions is not enough to force people to change into new patterns of human association and to forge new communities (with or without states). Often a crisis of events is needed to precipitate a fundamental redesign in communal arrangements. Forging our new national union came from the immediate pressing practical problems of operating under the Articles of Confederation (in reality "the first American Constitution"). It was a product of what Michael Kammen has rightly referred to as "conflict within a consensus."[13] But here, too, the crisis of events in the 1780s occurred in such a way to avoid the need for administration in designing the Constitution.

Recall that the Articles of Confederation gave all the states equal representation of one vote in Congress and required nine votes to do anything significant. It provided for no independent executive, only a rotating head of Congress that changed each year as well as a standing executive committee that met when Congress was not in session. There was no independent judiciary nor much of a working public service. While the Confederation was given a broad range of powers, all thirteen states were required to approve any changes in the Articles that would strengthen or enforce these powers (and tiny Rhode Island could always be counted on to vote "nay"). Clearly the Confederation was what the country had wanted in 1777 when the Articles were drafted as well as in 1781 when they were ratified. The Articles had simply codified the existing methods of the Continental Congress or, as one of its authors, Edmund Randolph, said, the authors had "done all that patriots could do, in the infancy of the science of constitution-writing."[14]

The central flaw of the Articles, which became increasingly apparent as the 1780s progressed, was that this governmental system depended on a willing consent by the sovereign states to achieve any collective action to solve pressing national problems. As Article II of the Articles states, "Each state retains its sovereignty, freedom, independence and every power. . . ." It was "a league of friendship," "a confederacy," which because of its weak structure and authority made collective action among friends often difficult and even impossible to achieve. As Andrew C. McLaughlin observed, "This mere confederacy of sovereign states was not adapted to the social, political and industrial needs of the time."[15] It could draft laws, but not enforce them; ask for money, but not compel payment; enter treaties, but not maintain them in practice; provide for raising armies, but not fill their ranks; borrow money but not ensure repayment; advise and recommend, but not govern or control in reality. In short, it contained little in the way of a core system of administration in order to make it function effectively.

In reality, then, the Confederation may have had the outward appearance of government (after all the Confederation had fought the Revolution, secured peace with Great Britain, and framed the remarkable Northwest Ordinance of 1787), but it could not effectively *administer* affairs as the 1780s progressed in many areas of increasing national consequence. It could not:

- Make effective trade policy involving chaotic, disorganized economic matters between states or foreign nations that in turn resulted in credit and business instability;
- Control wild fluctuations in paper currency leading to economic dislocation, "stagflation," inflation, and depression;
- Compel states to pay their share of regular operating costs of the Confederacy;
- Forge consistent diplomatic policies with foreign nations;
- Deal decisively with military threats on the state borders due to Indians, the British, and Barbary Pirates;
- Handle the growing social unrest due to economic instability, such as Shay's rebellion in Massachusetts;
- Provide efficiently even the most basic public services such as postal service at home or diplomatic representation abroad.

By the mid-1780s many thoughtful national leaders sensed that the ideals for which they had fought and bled during the Revolution of 1776 were slipping away, precisely because the nation could not *administer its affairs as a nation.* As Washington wrote in 1786, "We are becoming a nation without a nation," or as Noah Webster wrote the year before, "our pretended union is but a name, and our Confederation, a cobweb."[16] For those who wished "to form a more perfect union," the Articles were blamed for every ill afflicting the states.

A crisis of authority had been reached by the mid-1780s, but what to do? Stagger along with the status quo?—This was increasingly becoming inconvenient, too costly, and too difficult. Amend the Articles in order to strengthen their powers?—This had been tried five times during the 1780s, but unanimity among the thirteen states could never be mustered. Eliminate the states and consolidate them into a national union?—Impossible, given the already (by then) entrenched state powers. Create a strong, centralized administration?—Also impossible for the same reasons. Allow total fission or break up of the Articles?—Maybe a few big states like New York and Virginia were economically self-sufficient enough to go it alone, but the rest were not. Find a creative new middle solution to form a new type of national community?—Yes, but what?

The solution of the nationalists who met at Annapolis, Maryland, in September 1786 was to urge Congress "to render the federal government adequate to the exigencies of the Union."[17] The genius of the fifty-five framers of the Constitution in Philadelphia in 1787, as we all know, was to use their wise, collective skills of compromise, deliberation, and consensus-building to fashion a creative middle way that would remedy the immediate defects of the Confederation but avoid the difficulties of full-blown national administrative consolidation.

In the process, they created a genuinely "new order" based on a federal design that balanced small-state (the New Jersey Plan) and large-state (the Virginia Plan) interests, and which enumerated in Article I, Section 8, greater specific national powers over commerce, coinage, taxation, and other matters but with clear local powers reserved for states. What they achieved in the process was, again, something that avoided creating a unified administrative state, but one with endless, open possibilities for change and adaptation: neither too loose nor too tight organizational arrangements for governing; neither too liberal nor too conservative for the times; and neither too much nor too little to secure national political authority for effective collective action to deal with problems at hand. In short, federalism was very much the product of the creative American spirit of practical compromise at its best—a pragmatic, moderate, and workable compromise between the extremes of confederation and centralized union—which, above all else, kept America "stateless." The crises of events of the 1780s had provoked the necessity for change, but at the same time they allowed the luxury of time and thought to find a middle way without imposition of a "state" to solve the pressing, immediate crisis of authority. In the process it also produced a genuinely new type of constitutional government: a "stateless" federal union.

Legitimatizing Myths: The Classical Judeo-Christian View* of Humankind

Myths, in our age of tough-minded science, carry soft-headed connotations. We like to be known as realists, not influenced by fairy tales or fiction. But as Bruno Bettelheim reminds us, myths are essential as "excellent images for development"[18] and are neces-

*The term "Judeo-Christian" in this section is used to describe an outlook, a way of thinking, a philosophy, or a world view more or less characterized by monotheism, a higher (natural) law, a divine ordering of the universe, especially as embraced by many of the founders, such as Jefferson and Franklin.

sary for forming basic emotional attachments in every community. Even the rationalist Plato in his *Republic* stressed the value of "the noble lie" in creating his ideal community. He suggested that future citizens of his ideal republic begin their education with the telling of myths, rather than mere facts. Aristotle, a master of pure reason, also said: "The friend of wisdom is also a friend of myth."[19] Modern psychologists of many schools arrive at much the same notions.

The "shared mythos" that governed the framers' conception of the U.S. Constitution in forging our new national community, as historian Page Smith points out, was "classical Judeo-Christian consciousness":

> That is to say, they shared a view of human nature that derived directly from the Judeo-Christian doctrine of original sin. In this view, all of mankind were involved in Adam's original sin in eating the forbidden apple in the Garden of Eden. . . . Men and women had an ineradicable tendency to gratify their own selfish desires; that impulse could never be entirely overcome. . . . The classical view of human nature was even more pessimistic, since while accepting man's similitude, in Aristotle's image, to a pig or a wild beast it did not envision the Christian possibility of redemption through Christ's love.[20]

Given this dark view of people, it is no wonder that the founders should construct a governing system, as Madison advised in *Federalist No. 51*, in which "ambition must be made to counteract ambition."[21] The Madisonian science of government became almost a mechanical system of balancing political interests so that any one or combination could not exploit the others. Any sort of unified administration was simply out of the question, at least according to such legitimatizing mythology. For such a unifying system would assume the reverse about humankind and society: namely, the essential goodness of people that could be shaped through positive means to achieve some fixed common goal or ideal. Most of the founders shared Madison's deep-rooted pessimism about both human nature and the potential for reaching rational societal ideals for the good of humankind or some other purpose.

There was also just enough reform Protestant utopianism that the new constitutional system could be discovered by human reason and then literally "talked into existence." As Jefferson said of the process to David Humphreys, on March 18, 1789: "The example of changing a Constitution by assembling the wise men of every state, instead of assembling armies will be worth much more to the world as the former example we had given them. The Constitution which was the result of our deliberations is unquestionably the wisest ever presented to men."[22] Note what Jefferson says: it is not guns that create a Constitution or secure its consent, but peaceful, rational discussion. Note also that *no administration* is mentioned, just talk. Here Jefferson was articulating 3,000 years of classical Judeo-Christian tradition in his belief that "the Word could become Flesh": a representative assembly of wise men, using their highest intellectual skills of compromise and deliberation could fashion an enduring "fundamental law" and then ratify it through open debate and discourse in the states. "In the beginning was the Word. . . .", as John of the New Testament tells us. Here, too, the beginning was *the word*—the U.S. Constitution—and Americans, the chosen people of a covenanted nation, a "surrogate Israel," in the words of Cotton Mather. The open, deliberative process without a state machinery produced a magical, near religious text. This event became the very key to the Constitution's legitimization, as well as the central source of our sustaining belief in the system itself. It was a belief that, as Clinton Rossiter once observed, forms "the hard core of the American political tradition."[23]

A Contradictory Basis for the New "Stateless" National Community

All together these various strands of ideas, institutions, compromises, and myths created the new American "stateless" nation of 1787, which was erected upon a highly contradictory basis, full of strains and unresolved tensions. A republican model, rooted in notions of popular sovereignty and civic virtue; ancient Tudor ideas of fundamental law and balanced divisions of power; compromised federal arrangements; and classical Judeo-Christian beliefs together fashion an awkward, clumsy design. They hardly fit together consistently or formulate any rational plan for a political community. America was formed, in other words, not only without a state, but with a hodgepodge of competing beliefs, doctrines, principles, myths, and postulates, often in conflict with one another that make fitting in any stable administrative state at a later date difficult at best and most likely an impossibility. Taken together, these elements serve to continuously pulverize administrative effectiveness and to negate possibilities for any consistent administrative design. State building would prove always to be a tricky business in America because of these foundations of quicksand.

The Great Charter of 1787, although simple, direct, and seemingly uncomplicated in its language of 6,000 words, tends to paper over these problems and give the appearance of harmony of thought and capacity for governance when, in fact, it is a jumble of philosophical and institutional contradictions that perpetually influence the breakup of steady, consistent administrative thought and action. These inherent contradictions persist on several levels in order to keep administrative thought and practice in flux and thus foster the development of a unique model for American public administration. These contradictions are as follows.

Belief in Fundamental Law and Republicanism

The fundamental law background of the U.S. Constitution forged the basic compact between the government and those governed as firm, fixed, supreme, and rooted in a higher law that is divinely inspired and naturally ordered. Man discovers law and does not make it. Yet the republican roots of the Constitution were set in precisely the reverse philosophy: the good society is founded on virtuous, self-directing citizens who deliberate and make laws (after discovering the principles) by which to govern themselves. In short, for administrative theory, the source of legal authority for government is hard to pin down as it is both humanly conceived and divinely ordained.

Popular Sovereignty, but Checked in Every Way

The United States may be rooted firmly in popular consent based on notions of republicanism (recall that the Preamble begins, "We the people. . . ."), but with the addition of the federal idea coupled with checks and balances, it served up a system that negates direct popular sovereignty at every turn. The bicameral legislature, the veto power of the President, the electoral college process, the independent judiciary, even the creation of the Senate to ensure state, not mass popular, representation, are all checks aimed, in James Madison's phrase, to be "successive filtrations" to sift and cool down popular opinion.[24] The U.S. Constitution confounds the development of clear-cut administrative theory because it contains both popular and essentially "anti-popular" devices.

Majority Rule vs. Individual Rights

The higher law background, derived from the Tudor period, bequeathed to America an important concept of individual rights.

That concept was regarded as so fundamental by framers like Madison that it was thought unnecessary to write it explicitly in the Constitution. The Bill of Rights was adopted in 1791 only at the insistence of such stout Anti-Federalists as George Mason, who had refused to sign the Constitution because protections for individual rights had not been included. But the republican foundations of the Constitution also vigorously supported the idea of majority rule. Like many, Thomas Jefferson recognized this profound paradox and tried to resolve it in his first inaugural address when he said, "though the will of the majority is in all cases to prevail, that will, to be rightful must be reasonable. . . . the minority possess their equal rights, which equal laws protect, and to violate it would be oppression."[25] The American community as a whole, as well as specifically contemporary American public administration, still has not resolved this basic tension between protecting individual rights and securing majority rule.

Enumerated Federal Powers with Secured Local Autonomy

Federalism grew out of the great compromise between large and small states at the Grand Convention of 1787, and it was genuinely a brilliant innovation that advanced the cause of good government over the weak Articles, but it did not resolve fundamental differences about the appropriate balance between central and local authority. The system perpetuates and does not resolve such struggles between the local and national levels. It simply leaves open the question as to how much power should flow to the center and how much should be reserved to its individual fifty separate parts, thus leaving public administration thought and practice in a quandary over who should be in charge. In the words of Martha Derthick, this "muddled" federalism today can properly be called, "Madison's Middle Ground."[26]

Balance of Powers vs. the Favored First Branch

Separation of powers advanced the cause of good government through the creation of an independent judiciary and chief executive. Hamilton in *Federalist No. 70* and *No. 78* makes a compelling case for their creation, their independence, and the checks and balances both afford the governmental system. Yet, Articles II and III in the Constitution only vaguely sketch out the role and powers of the presidency and the courts. Our republican traditions of popular sovereignty, in contrast, seem to favor the first branch as being the most democratic and most representative one. In Congress the enumerated powers are lodged in Article I, Section 8, which includes some of the most critical tasks of governing, such as raising revenue and the impeachment processes. Many Americans would still agree with a committee of Congress in 1816 that wrote, "Of all the powers with which the people have invested the Government, that of legislation is undoubtedly the chief."[27] Are the branches really coequal or is there clearly "a first" among equals? Public administration theory and practice in America likewise remain unsure.

Change Incorporated, but Fundamental Change Made Exceedingly Difficult and Slow

The Constitution remedied a major defect in the Confederation by making collective action on behalf of the entire American nation more feasible. After its ratification, the Constitution would become "the Supreme Law of the Land." The Constitution further allowed itself to change more readily than the Articles by setting up amendment procedures in Article V. At the same time, however, it placed extraordinary roadblocks to amending the Constitution, requiring a two-thirds vote of both houses and a three-fourths vote of state legislatures or state conventions. As a consequence, basic changes in our Great Charter have come about relatively infrequently: only twenty-six amendments have been added to it since it was written (discounting the Bill of Rights, only sixteen, many of which are relatively inconsequential in scope and substance). Thus "grafting in" an administrative state is a very tough problem, and as a result, much of what is now known as our administrative state had to be enacted in piecemeal fashion, outside the formal constitutional framework. We seem undecided about the inherent value of change: always the opportunities for change remain open but, in reality, administrative ideas are seen as something separate from constitutional theory and thus must often emerge in a fragmented, informal, "extra-constitutional" manner.

Dependence on the Virtuous Citizen but Expecting Corruption of Power

The republican heritage brought with it a profound belief in civic virtue. The good republic can only be erected with virtuous citizens acting for "the public good." We still expect much higher standards, "virtue" if you please, from our public officials than from the average citizen. But the founders, rooted in classical Judeo-Christian mythos, also viewed power as a sinister and potentially highly corrupting force on those in governnment as described by Madison's *Federalist No. 51*. So they conceived numerous devices to check and balance power. The Constitution was, thus, built on confused notions of the public man as both necessarily virtuous and yet inherently prone to corruption. This legacy was rooted into American public administration thought as well, giving it today an inherent ambivalence toward the nature of mankind, even a reluctance toward dealing directly with the topic of human nature.

Equality and Inequality of Mankind

Finally, from the Tudor fundamental law traditions and Judeo-Christian idealism grew the Bill of Rights, which is a strong, enduring statement supporting political equality. It is an American original, that has perhaps been taken further and more literally in the twentieth century than the framers ever imagined possible two centuries ago. On the other hand, beliefs rooted in the Constitution and derived from classical Judeo-Christian myths also contain strong themes of inequality and natural hierarchy. The "Three-Fifths Clause" in the Constitution, for example, that counted "others" (slaves) as only three-fifths people for census, taxation, and apportionment purposes reflects such nonegalitarian points of view that are deeply embedded in the Constitution. In short, the Constitution reflects beliefs in political equality *and* inequality. In terms of public administration theory, this issue is hardly resolved today. Indeed, the value of bureaucratic hierarchy as opposed to human equality in public organizations then, as now, remains confused and undecided.

The Consequences for Present-Day American Public Administration Theory

From the standpoint of human communities throughout recorded history, the U.S. Constitution was a remarkable invention because it forged a modern political community without a state based on a blend of contradictions that began to fade and die out shortly after its founding: classical Judeo-Christian beliefs soon gave way to a new secular-democratic ethos; the small-state vs. large-state crisis that spawned federalism disappeared entirely, never to resurface in 200 years of U.S. history as a major national controversy; both republicanism and balanced government faded from view after the Civil War, particularly with the rise of big government and mass democracy. If the Constitution's ratification had been held up just a few years, say to the early 1800s, the resulting document would have probably looked very different, possibly with one featuring a strong, central state.

The founders were "national community builders," but they framed a community with a unique "stateless' design in mind, rooted in the special time and place of late eighteenth-century America. Today, the ideas, institutions, events, and mythos on which it was based are as foreign and remote to our modern understanding as the lost monarchical worlds of the eighteenth century. Taken together, these elements also added a high degree of ambiguity to public administration theory and opened the topic to enormous opportunities for continual interpretations and reinterpretations. America's Constitution was republican, Tudor, limited, balanced, a bundle of compromises, federal, and classical Judeo-Christian! Surely, it was an American original forged from the unique confluence of ideas, institutions, events, and mythos of the time, altogether giving it its essential, contradictory character: a character with many sides—none definite, none absolute, and all sides seemingly pitted against one another—forming a highly original, complex basis for human association. In music, perhaps, this juxtaposition would be called "contrapuntal"; in literature, it would be called "paradoxical" or "ironic."

The plus side of this contradictory basis for public administration thought is that it shaped a democratic administrative machinery. Democratic administration was formed "naturally," without conscious thought or optional design, pretty much any way desired. There were few barriers to creating as little or as much as wanted or to "invent" entirely new forms of administration to fulfill the many needs of a large nation. This attitude and practice, of course, fit hand and glove with the American character, itself filled with endless contradictions and a belief in democracy and open opportunities. Hence the "stateless" Constitution that, undifferentiated from its political life, is well suited for longevity and survival. As the astute Madison observed of its qualities, "no other form would be reconcilable with the genius of the people of America; with the fundamental principles of revolution; or with the honorable determination which animates every votary of freedom. . . ."[27] Through a bloody Civil War, two global wars, and countless military, social, economic, and political upheavals, the "stateless" system of administration has proved elastic enough, neither too loose nor too tight, to adapt to vastly changing conditions—from an obscure nation bordering the Atlantic of 3 million people to a global superpower of 242 million.

Democratic administration allows us to now operate with the oldest written Constitution in the world—outdistancing most by a very long stretch. Two-thirds of the world's 160 written constitutions have been adopted or revised since 1970. Only fourteen predate World War II. The average nation has adopted two constitutions since 1945! Some, like Thailand and Syria, have had nine. Yet Americans cling to theirs precisely because—given its ambiguity and contradictions—it can be reinterpreted legally and refashioned administratively with enough ease to accommodate to rapidly changing circumstances. In short, the founders, partly by accident and partly by plan, created a Constitution without a state to make it work and succeeded in creating "a living Constitution."

On a deeper level, the consequences of these inherent contradictions for public administration thought created a governing system, in the words of Forrest and Ellen McDonald, "in which power was not quite anywhere." Power is continuously negated by checks and balances, republican ideals, dispersed Tudor institutions, federal design, and classical Judeo-Christian beliefs. Power is continuously being smashed and is in a perpetual state of motion—making it unstoppable and hard to locate. Thus, no centralized, permanent, all-powerful administrative state can probably ever exist—or be "grafted" onto America. Power is always up for grabs: it is vague, imprecise, hard to pin down, free to shift anytime and everywhere. "A machine that would go of itself," in the words of James Russell Lowell.[29] The resulting kinetic energy not only permits the machine's adaptability, but the system itself becomes so seductively open in that it continuously beckons for personal involvement and, at the same time, in the words of Lynton K. Caldwell, minimizes "temptation and opportunity for ambitious men to aggrandize themselves at public expense through public office or privilege and, in so doing, to conspire against the public good."[30] In other words, it simultaneously invites participation in the exercise of public power and prevents abuse and corruption of that very same public power. With few exceptions, this system has been remarkably successful at doing both—promoting popular participation and preventing public corruption.

But there is a flip side to the democratic model for public administration theory and action: its very "statelessness" that promotes elasticity and participation and places limits on public corruption, not only makes administration hard to define in theory, but in practice also impedes developing any stable administrative systems to carry out governmental goals by permitting delay, stalemates, cross-purposes in actions, and inefficiency. These belong part and parcel to the Constitution's inherent institutional complexity and intellectual contradictions. In other words, its "stateless" design promotes ad hoc, naturally arrived at administrative arrangements, giving it a persisting ambiguity in thought *and* action. Unlike any other nation, American public administration remains impossible to define since it is fashioned on shifting sands of its "stateless" Constitution. It is always open to change and revision. Clear, swift action that would benefit the majority and offer long-term payoffs to future generations are often infrequent and hard to come by because the system is so diffuse and open, without any well-designed, stable administrative system. Well-placed minority veto groups always have numerous opportunities to throw sand in the gears and stymie collective action. At times, this has even brought us to the brink of national disaster, as in the case of the Civil War or World War II when entrenched minorities prevented adequate advanced military preparations. In the late twentieth century, such delay can become even more perilous and deadly.

Further, the contradictory nature of this system is aimed entirely inward, onto itself, namely, toward preventing corruption of *public* power. The founders of this *novus ordo seclorum* either would not, or could not, conceive of circumstances in which the rise of large private concentrations of economic-political power in corporations, conglomerates, trusts, multinationals, trade unions, professions, media, or modern-day, big-monied PACs could threaten the existing social order. The Constitution of 1787 created, in the words of Martin Diamond, a "negative government,"[31] primarily concerned with smashing public power while turning a blind eye toward the potential dangers of *private* power. In fairness, the framers lived in an era when government was *the* power and the bulk of society was made up of simple, frugal, individual small businessmen and farmers. The haunting specter of massive, competing private sources of power would not arise until the late nineteenth century, when the American community, its Constitution, and its governmental system underwent radical transformations, and a "new American state" became essential. But even then, the American state emerged as "temporary machinery" largely outside the Constitution, in piecemeal, extraconstitutional fashion. The ingrained American habit of thinking, then as now, was that ideally the nation should get along without state machinery to make government function. At the most, only limited doses of "the stuff" are needed; at the worst, as President Ronald Reagan declared in his first inaugural address, "Government is the problem," implying we should rid ourselves of it altogether. Overall, Americans feel it is best to let things work out "naturally" without the constraints or demands of an artificially imposed state. As we shall see in the next chapters, this preference for "statelessness" not only creates problems for building effective public administration institutions in the United States but imposes serious blinders on our capacity to think realistically about contemporary public administration theory or to develop a stable, consistent, intellectual framework for the field in the twentieth century.

Notes

1. This chapter appeared in revised form as "The Peculiar 'Stateless' Origins of American Public Administration and Consequences for Government Today," *Public Administration Review*, vol. 50, no. 2 (March/April 1990), pp. 156–167.
2. Alexander Hamilton, James Madison, and John Jay, *The Federalist Papers* (New York: New American Library, 1961), p. 414.
3. Gordon Wood, *The Creation of the American Republic, 1776–1787* (Chapel Hill: University of North Carolina Press, 1969).
4. For the influence of Machiavelli's thought and especially Roman Republicanism within Machiavelli's ideas, see George H. Sabine, *A History of Political Theory*, 3d ed. (New York: Holt, Rinehart & Winston, 1961), pp. 347–350. Sabine argues that "there was nothing in Machiavelli's account of the absolute monarchy corresponding to his obviously sincere enthusiasm for liberty and self-government of the Roman Republic" (p. 347).
5. Hamilton, Madison, and Jay, p. 240.
6. Ibid., p. 83.
7. Ibid., p. 101.
8. Samuel P. Huntington, *Political Order in Changing Societies* (New Haven, Connecticut: Yale University Press, 1968), p. 96. Huntington's argument draws heavily on a rich body of historical and political science literature such as S. B. Chrimes, *English Constitutional History*, 2d ed. (London: Oxford University Press, 1953); Edward S. Corwin, *The "Higher Law" Background of American Constitutional Law* (Ithaca, New York: Cornell University Press, 1955); Charles H. McIlwain, *The High Court of Parliament and Its Supremacy* (New Haven, Connecticut: Yale University Press, 1910); A. F. Pollard, *Factors in American History* (New York: Macmillan, 1925); and Henry J. Ford, *The Rise and Growth of American Politics* (New York: Macmillan, 1900).

9. Corwin, p. 27.
10. As cited in Wood, p. 200.
11. Hamilton, Madison, and Jay, p. 322.
12. Huntington, p. 98.
13. Michael Kammen, *A Machine That Would Go of Itself: The Constitution in American Culture* (New York: Knopf, 1986), p. 29.
14. As cited in Clinton Rossiter, *1787: The Grand Convention* (New York: Macmillan, 1966), p. 48.
15. Andrew C. McLaughlin, *The Confederation and the Constitution, 1783–1789* (New York: Collier, 1962, original edition published 1905), p. 124.
16. As cited in Rossiter, p. 50.
17. Ibid., p. 54.
18. Bruno Bettelheim, *The Uses of Enchantment: The Meaning and Importance of Fairy Tales* (New York: Vintage, 1977), p. 39.
19. As cited in Bettelheim, p. 35.
20. Page Smith, *The Shaping of America: A People's History of the Young Republic*, vol. 3 (New York: McGraw-Hill, 1980), pp. 19–20.
21. Hamilton, Madison, and Jay, p. 322.
22. Ibid., as cited in Smith.
23. Clinton Rossiter, "Prefatory Note," in Corwin, p. v.
24. Max Farrand, *The Records of the Federal Convention of 1787*, vol. 1 (New Haven, Connecticut: Yale University Press, 1911), p. 50. In *Federalist No. 10* Madison refers to refining and enlarging public views by "passing them through the medium of a chosen body of citizens" (Hamilton, Madison, and Jay, p. 82). For a useful discussion of this subject, read Garry Wills, *Explaining America: The Federalist* (New York: Doubleday, 1981), chapter 29.
25. Thomas Jefferson, "First Inaugural Address," as cited in Saul K. Padover, ed., *The Complete Jefferson* (New York: Duell, Sloan & Pearce, 1943), p. 386.
26. Martha Derthick, "American Federalism: Madison's 'Middle Ground' in the 1980's," *Public Administration Review* (January/February 1987), p. 66.
27. *Annals of Congress*, 14th Congress, 2d Session (December 18, 1816), p. 317.
28. Hamilton, Madison, and Jay, p. 240.
29. James Russell Lowell, "The Place of the Independent in Politics," in *Political Essays* (Boston: Houghton Mifflin, 1888), p. 312, as cited in Kammen, p. 18.
30. Lynton K. Caldwell, "*Novus Ordo Seclorum:* The Heritage of American Public Administration," *Public Administration Review*, vol. 36, no. 5 (September/October 1976), p. 485.
31. Martin Diamond, "The Declaration and the Constitution: Liberty, Democracy, and the Founders," *The Public Interest* (Fall 1975), p. 39.

CHAPTER THREE

"Chinking in" a Temporary American State (and the Strange Administrative Theory It Created)

The Administrative power in the United States presents nothing either centralized or hierarchical in its constitution; this accounts for its passing unperceived. The power exists, but its representative is no where to be seen.

ALEXIS DE TOCQUEVILLE
Democracy in America

Public administration has been practiced since the dawn of civilization, yet America's peculiar "stateless" origins made the self-conscious study of the subject not only unnecessary but unwanted as well. Americans had sought to stamp out state machinery, not nurture it, and certainly not educate themselves in exercising it wisely or well, efficiently or effectively. As Chapter Two emphasizes, "the first new nation" grew up largely without a state. Instead, America was founded on "we the people" as the ultimate sovereign authority for government. Luck also conspired to allow the United States to govern itself with little or no thought about its administrative enterprise for almost a century after the U.S. Constitution was ratified. Whatever administration was required was worked out "naturally," without any artificially created public administration. The following paragraphs describe how this was possible.

No Threat to National Security

The absence of any significant external threat to the United States throughout the nineteenth century, due mainly to this nation's geographic isolation, stimulated little demand for the study of administration. Mass standing armies with highly differentiated bureaucratic structures were an essential requirement for national security in Europe during the same period. Perfecting these institutions and the trained personnel to fill their ranks required schools, institutes, courses for military education, and training for administration. Louis XV's *Ecôle Militaire* was established in 1751; Frederick the Great's *Ritter Akademie* was founded in 1765; and the English Naval Academy was founded in 1729. In contrast, and except for the Civil War, until the twentieth century the United States could rest its primary defense upon part-time, untrained, citizen soldiers used mainly for quelling Indian uprisings in the West. Geographic accident permitted the United States the luxury of not building a professional cadre of officers and advanced military educational system long after most developed European nations had done so. Even though West Point had been established in 1802, the U.S. Military Academy's training throughout the nineteenth century and well into the twentieth was directed toward producing not military managers but, rather, technicians—a corps of engineers to build roads, canals, and bridges in the West. At its beginnings, American military education was linked to promoting national development, not to enhancing administrative professionalism within the ranks. The latter was thought of as unnecessary.[1]

Agrarian Self-sufficiency

Throughout most of the 1800s, nine out of ten Americans derived their livelihoods directly or indirectly from the land. As farming was the chief national occupation, agrarian self-sufficiency prompted little support or need for governmental administrative expertise. Self-help, not public help, was the order and ethos of the day. The apparent lack of demand for public services at the federal level was characterized by the fact that for nearly a century after George Washington's Administration, only one new federal cabinet was created, the Interior Department, and even then this new department merely combined several existing agencies under one roof. Furthermore, 86 percent of the growth in federal employees (from 4,837 in 1816 to 36,872 in 1861) was within one department, the Post Office.[2]

Routine Public Tasks

Not only were few governmental functions required for society, but also what tasks were performed by public agencies required little formal training. As Leonard D. White observes, the Post Office was a system of "vast, repetitive, fixed and generally routine operations."[3] For the most part, public tasks were fairly simple operations, oriented toward single purposes. Thus they could be largely learned on the job or by following simple, commonsense rules of thumb.[4] A complexity of purposes and difficulty in undertaking tasks would have stimulated the need for advanced administrative analysis and the development of a conscious study of public administration.

Lack of Higher Educational Institutions

Even if government agencies had required trained managers and greater administrative expertise, little training or research capacity could be found in American universities of the nineteenth century. There were no university chairs in "Cameralism," which was the study of administrative science for higher civil service positions, as were found in eighteenth-century Germany or in the French *Ecôle Polytechnique* (created in 1794). During this time, the U.S. institutions were known as "colleges" and were modeled on British or Scottish prototypes; they largely offered "classical educations for gentlemen," especially training for the Protestant ministry. No American institution of higher education during this era was, by European standards, a true university, a place for the generation and diffusion of advanced knowledge. Not until 1880 was the first school of political science created at Columbia (then called Columbia College) for the study of government and politics. Its Ph.D. required research-based dissertations in political science for the first time in America. It was also at Columbia that the first serious journal of scholarship in the field was established, the *Political Science Quarterly* (1886). In general, however, the establishment of specific administrative journals and schools of administration had to await the twentieth century.

Popular Representation

Herbert Kaufman pointed out long ago that most of the nineteenth century saw the values of popular representation in government overshadow other values, such as neutral competence and executive direction.[5] In practice, this meant that political parties and patronage served as the major force for knitting society together in the nineteenth century. Stephen Skowronek indicates that "under a Constitution designed to produce institutional conflicts and riddled with jurisdictional confusions, they [parties] came to lend order, predictability, and continuity to governmental activity."[6] Parties may not have articulated clear policies and they may have been corrupt and wasteful at times, but, as Skowronek observes, they did succeed in binding together a radically decentralized society and in giving a sense of nationhood to a faction-ridden people. In this way, national political competition and cooperation via party politics operated as the essential social glue in lieu of state administrative machinery. Thus, for the most part, the Presidency counted for little in the scheme of governance. Not until the twentieth century did Theodore Roosevelt advocate a strong "stewardship role" for the American Presidency with significant activist and autonomous executive authority. Up to that time, presidents viewed themselves and were viewed as mostly creatures of the party that put them in power, not managers of the state's affairs. There was no need for them to act or think otherwise in "stateless" America. Being a good ceremonial figurehead and political animal was mostly all that was necessary to run the Presidency.

The Multiple Crises Transforming the "Old Order" in the Late Nineteenth Century

Perhaps historian Robert H. Wiebe most aptly describes the nature of the American political community as it operated throughout much of the nineteenth century:

> America during the 19th century was a society of island communities. Weak communications severely restricted the interaction among these islands and dispersed power to form opinion and enact public policy. Education, both formal and informal, inhibited specialization and discouraged the accumulation of knowledge. The heart of the American democracy was local autonomy. The century after France had developed a reasonably efficient, centralized public administration, Americans could not even conceive of a managerial government. Almost all of a community's affairs were still arranged informally.[7]

This informal, "stateless" nineteenth-century world of America is graphically depicted by Alexis de Tocqueville:

> In no other society in the world do the citizens make such exertions for the common weal. I know of no people who have

established schools so numerous and efficacious, places of public worship better suited to the wants of the inhabitants, or roads kept in better repair. Uniformity or permanence of design, the minute arrangement of details and the perfection of the administrative system must not be sought in the United States; what we find is the presence of power, which, if it is somewhat wild, is at least robust, and an existence checkered with accidents, indeed, but full of animation and effort.[8]

The breakdown of this old social order composed of cohesive, informal island communities across America came swiftly and suddenly just before the turn of the century. A dynamic process of community change occurred during roughly the years 1877–1920, and, during this time, the old community structure was radically revised by the emergence of a new American administrative state. This transformation occurred before most Americans could dimly understand what had happened, comprehend the reasons, or even cope adequately with the changes that were wrought. Today we can see clearly the following multiple forces of change at work in the late nineteenth century.

The Closing of the Frontier

Frederick Jackson Turner's famous essay, "The Significance of the Frontier in American History," prepared for the 1893 World Fair in Chicago, argues that "the existence of an area of free land, its continuous recession and the advance of American settlement westward, explain American development" up to that time. "The frontier democracy," observes Turner, "born of free land was strong in selfishness and individualism, intolerant of administration, experience and education, and pressing individual liberty beyond its proper bound."[9] The frontier, in short, gave Americans their peculiar national identity and outlook and had largely shaped the context of national development, according to Turner. But with the advancement of civilization, all this open, endless frontier had now come to an end. No longer would the frontier "furnish a new field of opportunity, a gate of escape from the bondage of the past." Americans from now on, implies Turner, would have to adjust their lives, their economy, and their society to a closed-space world. This would require a new type of psychological orientation, as well as a new social order, even a new American Dream! As Herbert Croly's *The Promise of American Life* (1909) would later suggest,[10] the closing of the frontier required Americans to look to self-made, man-made development based on governmental institutions to guide, plan, and administer community affairs. That was a jarring notion for those accustomed to an open-ended world of unexplored opportunities, free of obtrusive state intervention.

Rapid Urbanization

Historian Richard Hofstadter pointed out that "the United States was born in the country and . . . moved to the city."[11] This urbanization of America was most intense during the 1880s and 1890s, as cities grew at a more rapid rate than at any previous time. A century before, only 3.3 percent of Americans lived in towns; during the decade of the 1880s, the figure reached 33 percent. During the 1880s, Buffalo, Detroit, and Milwaukee doubled in size; Chicago, St. Paul, and Denver more than tripled in size; and New York jumped from 2 to 3½ million people. Villages grew into towns; towns into cities; cities into urban metropolises. Much of the increase was fueled by the influx of over 5 million immigrants from abroad. At home, perhaps, even larger, though unknown, numbers moved from farms into towns and quickly transformed towns into metropolitan centers. With this unprecedented influx came all the common urban problems that begged for solutions: slums, crime, poverty, environmental pollution, public sanitation, health, transportation, and unemployment. William Dean Howells, the turn of the century realistic novelist, poignantly describes the urban scene in 1896:

> But to be in it, and not have the distance, is to inhale the stenches of neglected streets, and to catch the yet fouler and dreadfuller poverty-smell which breathes from the open doorways. . . .[12]

Rapid Technological Revolution

In large part, the urbanization of America and its bleak consequences, as depicted by Howells, were spawned by the rapid technological revolution of the era. Much of the migration off the farms and into the cities was prompted by the new efficiency of farmers. They could farm more with less manpower. Widespread application of such inventions as the steel plow, the automatic baler, barbed wire, deep water wells, poultry incubators, and windmills meant vastly increased agricultural efficiency. This was an era of rapid invention and application of new technologies. In 1880 Edison began mass-producing his newly invented incandescent electric light, which not only made the cities safer at night but also allowed for evening factory production, as well as longer hours for leisure-time activities such as going to amusement parks and theaters. Edison would eventually secure more than 1,000 patents under his name alone, many that would revolutionize the American landscape. Other inventors and inventions in the 1880s also transformed America: the opening of the first telephone exchange in 1880; the making of the modern bicycle in 1884; the first skyscraper, the Home Insurance Building in Chicago in 1884; the automobile in 1886; the automatic railroad air brake in 1886, which permitted high speed train travel; and the high-voltage transformer in 1886 that allowed electricity to move over long distances. In 1886, the first electric railway transit system was built in Richmond, Virginia. In 1889, Washington, D.C., became the first city to pave most of its streets.

A Rapid Industrial Revolution with a New "Secular-Democratic-Rational Myth"

Factories multiplied in the 1880s as mechanical inventions were produced at unprecedented rates to satisfy voracious domestic and foreign consumer demand. The isolated island communities across America were swiftly linked into a cohesive whole by lines of commerce, communication, and transportation. The rapid development from self-sufficient rural communities to interdependent, industrialized populations placed new, large-scale, permanent demands on government for a vast range of heretofore unknown requirements: public roadways, city planning, community health inspection, railroad rate regulation, and requirements for public education. The old, limited set of classical Judeo-Christian beliefs that worked well for a rural, self-sufficient society would swiftly be supplemented by another, a set of secular-democratic-rational beliefs. To cope with the strains of spreading industrialism and technological changes, new roles for government were urgently needed. A new mythos would undergird the industrial revolution in America; it would be based on beliefs in progress, science, reason, and technological advancement for the benefit of all. This new mythos would also foster a positive role for government involvement in society. In this way, the written Constitution was supplemented by a new administrative state.

International Competition

Another potent force for community transformation in America and still another stimulus for the rise of an administrative state was increasing international competition. After more than a century of unique geographic isolation, America was thrust into the troubled waters of imperialistic expansionism. The United States initiated the Pan-American Union in 1889. A decade later, Americans fought the Spanish-American War, or what Theodore Roosevelt called "a splendid little war," though it was neither splendid nor much of a war. Instead, it demonstrated America's inadequacies in logistical planning, military professionalism, and military preparedness for even the most limited overseas engagement. In just a few short months, 460 Americans died in combat, but another 5,200 deaths resulted from disease, shortages of medicine, and inadequate medical care. The minuteman tradition would no longer suffice in an era in which large-scale mobilization and complex logistics and long-range planning were the order of the day for modern warfare. A generation later, the American involvement in World War I further underscored the need for improved organizational arrangements to conduct U.S. diplomatic and international security affairs, in ways never envisioned a century before by the Founding Fathers.

New Concentrations of Private Power and New Domestic Crises

In the 1880s, there was a sudden growth of enormous, powerful, monopolistic private-sector organizations, "the trusts," as they were called by their vocal progressive opponents. In 1880 there were 1,005 iron companies in the United States; by 1901 three-fifths of the steel production was controlled by J. P. Morgan's U.S. Steel Company. The same was true in other economic markets. In 1880, 115 railroad companies operated, but by the end of the decade, only one-third were still operating. Private firms grew into powerful "pools," holding companies, and monopolies. As an economic counterforce, to represent the practical economic needs and interests of laborers, Samuel Gompers and Adolph Strasser left the weak Knights of Labor and formed the powerful Organized Trades and Labor Unions (reorganized in 1886 as the American Federation of Labor). The Haymarket Riot, the Carnegie Steel strike, national railway strikes, and the Grange movement in the late nineteenth century were domestic crises precipitated primarily by the clash between the newly emerging powers of organized labor and concentrated management. New public instruments were needed for mediating and resolving these domestic disputes.

Recall that the Great Charter of 1787 had turned a blind eye to the problems of private power in the economic marketplace. In fairness to the founders, those problems were simply not perceived as problems in 1787 when mostly small farmers and small businessmen constituted the private sector economy. The founders had feared *public* power, particularly from government, not *private* power. Smashing or controlling public power, hence, was seen as the central issue in 1787. By 1887, governmental institutions were dwarfed by many private entities. The old saw that old man Rockefeller could do everything to the Pennsylvania legislature, except refine it, was probably not very far from the truth. Demand grew in the 1880s for a new role for government as a referee in the economy. A stronger public role would emerge for government as an essential mediator in the private marketplace.

The Search for a New Governing Order: Sumnerism, Bellamyism, and Wilsonianism

The closing of the frontier, urbanization, technology, industrialization, international competition, and new concentrations of private power and domestic crises caused serious erosion in political authority based on cohesive informal island communities. The old foundations of society began cracking under the stress and strains of these pressures in the 1880s and 1890s. In the words of Robert Wiebe, America became "a distended society," a nation lacking a center, without focus, authority, or a core. Thus, how to put things back together again became a central issue. Although no replacement was at hand, many alternative political arrangements were being proposed in that era. The 1880s was a decade of Grangers, Populists, the Southern Alliance, Goldbugs, Silverbugs, and Straddlebugs. All these groups, as their names implied, sought to impose a new political order through various schemes of one kind or another.

A century ago, two of the most popular writers in America who centrally addressed these issues—measured, at least in terms of book sales, size of lecture audiences, and fan clubs—were William Graham Sumner and Edward Bellamy. In many ways, they were an odd couple on which to bestow the mantle of popular fame, for they advocated schemes of social organization that were polar opposites. Yet, they found numerous followers in a period of upheaval, ceaseless change, and social disintegration, and one in search of a new basis of social authority. In the words of John L. Thomas, they sought an "alternative America."[13]

Sumnerism and Statelessness

William Graham Sumner was a prominent professor of sociology at Yale. Through his widely read books and articles, he propounded and popularized the social Darwinist doctrines in the 1880s and 1890s, which argued, in brief, that the progress of civilization depended on the natural selection process, which, in turn, depended on the workings of unrestricted social competition. Competition, according to Sumner, was a firm law of nature that, in his words, "can no more be done away with than gravitation." He thus constantly waged war against reformism, protectionism, government interventionism, or anything that stood in the way of unrestricted economic competition. "Let it be understood," thundered Sumner, "that we cannot go outside of this alternative; liberty, inequality, survival of the fittest; not liberty, equality, survival of the unfittest. The former carries society forward and favors all its best members; the latter carries society downward and favors all its worst members."[14]

Sumner's message offered a synthesis of both the radical and conservative intellectual views of the age in search of a new basis of social authority that combined three great traditions—the Protestant work ethic, classical economics, and social Darwinism. Here was a return to the "statelessness" and "naturalism" of the founders as a basis for knitting together the new order. Put simply, Sumner argued for a social organization derived wholly from natural competition and free from artificial constraints. Listen to a Yale student's dialogue in class with Sumner:

> "Professor, don't you believe in any government aid to industries?"
> "No! it's root, hog, or die."
> "Yes, but hasn't the hog got a right to root?"
> "There are no rights. The world owes nobody a living."
> "You believe then, Professor, in only one system, the contract-competitive system?"
> "That's the only sound economic system. All others are fallacies."

"Well, suppose some professor of political economy came along and took your job away from you. Wouldn't you be sore?"

"Any other professor is welcome to try. If he gets my job, it is my fault. My business is to teach the subject so well that no one can take the job away from me."[15]

Bellamyism and the Total State

Edward Bellamy, in contrast, was a novelist who wrote only one book that earned him immense fame (and fortune as well), *Looking Backward* (1886). It became a phenomenal best-seller with a record 300,000 copies sold within two years of its publication. Bellamy won such a huge audience, not because *Looking Backward* was a novel of outstanding literary qualities, but because it was a simple, logical essay about the discordant times, which proposed a straightforward plan for fundamental social reform and economic reorganization.

In *Looking Backward*, the reader of the period is transported to the year 2000 by a genteel Bostonian named Julian West, who recounts what the reader knew so well about his own day—namely, that America was verging on catastrophe because "riches debauched one class with idleness of mind and body, while poverty sapped the vitality of the masses by overwork, bad food and pestilent homes." In time, Americans would rise up and cast off this wicked, oppressive system and fashion a new rational society, based on, as Dr. Leete, West's guide to the new utopian order says, "the solidarity of the race and the brotherhood of man."[16] A new, flawless system would be erected based on social unity between workers and citizens. The capitalists, bankers, lawyers, politicians, and other villains of Bellamy would be banished from this new social order.

Bellamy saw government as "the great trust" that would replace private interests and private industry in creating and distributing goods and services. Here the administrative state thus would not only dominate society, it would *be* the society. In his world, not humans, but the machinery of government would rule. Government-imposed cooperation would replace unregulated private competition as a basis for this new social order. Government would become omnipotent and omnipresent. "The machine which [government functionaries] direct is indeed a vast one," says Dr. Leete, "but so logical in its principles and direct and simple in its workings that it all but runs itself. . . . Supply is geared to demand like an engine to the governor which regulates its speed."[17] Here all the waste, corruption, and inequities of late nineteenth-century America would disappear as society would move beyond the laws of competition into a perfect, self-regulating state. An artificial, centralized system would rule, not the uncertain law of nature.

While Bellamy's prescriptions for the ills then afflicting society were about as far removed as could be conceived from Sumner's, both men reflected the same intense preoccupation with the problems of how to knit together society that many at the time perceived as coming apart. However, both theorists tended to ignore the Constitution and proposed extraconstitutional devices to implant their ideas into the American political order. In Sumnerism, the Constitution almost evaporated entirely as a governing device. Sumner and other laissez-faire conservatives scoffed at notions of constitutionally guaranteed individual liberties, except as won on the fierce social Darwinist battlefield of survival of the fittest. They saw little or no good coming from any government checks and balance in the marketplace, or, for that matter, from any government intervention anyplace.

At the other extreme, Bellamy's vision of a centralized, efficient government, "the great trust," is far removed from the basic constitutional concepts of 1787. The founders in 1787 had not set up—nor had they wanted—any sort of powerful, centralized system. Quite the contrary, they wanted to protect their hard-won liberties by smashing public power via a complex system of checks and balances. In short, neither Sumnerism nor Bellamyism would easily be compatible with the existing constitutional order without instituting massive, indeed revolutionary, reform.

Wilsonianism and the New American State

A third alternative was proposed in 1887 (by coincidence, precisely in the year of the Constitution's centennial birthday). It sought to find a middle solution to societal crises, yet one grounded in the existing constitutional order. This alternative happened to be proposed by a young political scientist at Bryn Mawr College by the name of Woodrow Wilson. He published these ideas in an obscure essay, "The Study of Administration," in a new journal, *Political Science Quarterly*.[18]

In the beginning of his essay, Wilson argues that concerns over "constitution-operation" had begun to replace "constitution-writing." The era of constitution-making was over. The old-style politics in which "monarchy rode tilt against democracy in high warfare of principle" had ended. Speaking directly about the apparent crises of his day, he argues "that it is getting harder to run a Constitution than to frame one." In the first section of the essay, Wilson sees public administration as an instrument of the U.S. Constitution itself, as fundamental to making the Constitution operate. "Administration is," in his words, "the most obvious part of government; it is government in action, it is the executive, the operative, the most visible side of government. . . ." The organic connection between the Constitution and administration is thus immediate, practical, and direct. "The object of administrative study is to rescue executive methods from the confusion and costliness of empirical experiment and set them upon foundations laid deep in stable principle," writes Wilson.[19]

Unlike Sumner's and Bellamy's models, Wilson called for a system rooted not in some utopian design but in America's very own constitutional order. In a broad sense, one might interpret Wilson's centennial essay of 1887 as "inventing" a new institution that is compatible with existing constitutional arrangements, one called "public administration," in order to save the old order of the U.S. Constitution from more extreme solutions to social reorganization of the likes of Sumnerism or Bellamyism. His essay advocated a new type of American state that would draw the best ideas from nineteenth-century European administrative theorists, particularly the liberal reformers in England and Germany, such as Bagehot and Stein, but certainly not adopt their centralized state prescriptions. As Wilson warns at the end of his essay: "Our own politics must be the touchstone for all theories."

In Wilson's view, the new complexity of government—both in terms of widening citizen participation in democratic government and the rising problems associated with social and technological change—demanded the development of effective administrative machinery. Yet, it would be machinery, unlike Sumner's or Bellamy's, intricately connected to constitutional government. Administration would remedy apparent defects in the Constitution, so to speak, by filling in its cracks. It would be a new institution broader than the executive, than Congress, than the courts, indeed spanning all three branches, so as to ensure that the Constitution itself would continue to run. "The administrative power is considerably wider and much more inclusive than executive power," writes Wilson. It goes beyond the scope of separation of powers, bridging independent branches of government. It includes "these duties of provident protection and wise cooperation and assistance. . . ." Administration was thus viewed by Wilson as involved in all three branches, having a broad, independent life of its own, independent of statutory enactment, yet rooted within the constitutional framework. In short, it would serve to keep the American constitutional order vital, alive, and ongoing for the next century. Here was a novel call for "the middle way" of reform.

The Development of the New American State: A "Chinking" Process?

Ironically, Wilson's essay of 1887, though symbolic and prophetic, probably had little actual influence on the founding of America's administrative state or on development of public administration thought. His essay remained largely neglected until historians "rediscovered" it in the 1940s. By then, the administrative state was a fact of life in America.

What theory or ideas then prompted the administrative state's growth? To paraphrase Oliver Wendell Holmes, Jr.'s famous opening lines in *The Common Law:* "The life of administration has not been logic: it has been experience." The rise of the administrative state began largely (but not wholly) in the 1880s, again to cite Holmes, due to "the felt necessities of the time, the prevalent moral and political theories, institutions of public policy avowed or unconscious, even the prejudices . . . have a good deal more to do than the syllogism in determining the rules by which men should be governed."[20] Specifically, public administration was both an institutional response and a set of practices that emerged as piecemeal remedies to the dramatic changes. Public administration thought developed out of these experiences of state-building. It served up realistic, pragmatic answers to the turbulent times, particularly to mitigate and temper those changes. In short, theory followed practice, not vice versa.

"Chinking in," an important part of the process of building log cabins, is an appropriate metaphor to describe the growth of the American administrative state. Builders used three types of logs— round, hewn on two sides, or squared—and in each case, the logs had to be roughly the same size so that the cracks between them could be chinked, or easily filled in with moss, clay, or mud. This chinking process of filling the cracks made the log cabins warmer, better insulated, and more secure from the harsh elements outside. If we think of the frame of a log cabin as akin to the basic constitutional structure of government, chinking—or the filling in of the cracks—by creation of the administrative state made our constitutional system workable, indeed, "liveable" during its second century.

How did this chinking process occur? Compared to the written Constitution of 1787, it was not produced by great men meeting somewhere in secret to found a regime. There were no ringing preambles dedicated to promoting the general welfare. No grand national debate over the central issue of forging a new constitutional order. No fundamental law framed; only some statutes written into the law books. The administrative state began in an ad hoc fashion, more haphazardly, much less auspiciously—some might say ignominiously—beginning roughly in the 1880s with its own peculiar lines of institutional and intellectual development that were separate, distinctive, and often quite elusive.

In the process of this chinking, the development of the American administrative state would always seem half-formed and incomplete, at least by comparison to the unified and well-developed European administrative systems. In part, this is due to the fact that institutional development of the administrative state in America did not begin all at once and in the same manner as was the case in Europe; instead, its chinking led to several different lines of development, each with its own peculiar history, values, rationale, and intellectual assumptions, that have never fit neatly together. America therefore created an administrative state and a bureaucratic administrative model without a single overarching model or well-structured paradigm, as was the case in the classic continental bureaucracies of France and Germany. America's state, in contrast, comprised seven loosely fitting, partially developed, "rationalizing" elements without a clear-cut theory "to fill in" the Constitution: (1) a trained but incoherent personnel system; (2) weak regulatory machinery; (3) an uncoordinated "public fisc"; (4) partially rationalized organization and management; (5) limited and ineffective planning systems; (6) narrow clientele politics; and (7) a new "positive" but "less-than-unified" law.

To paraphrase Ralph Waldo Emerson, America's administrative ideas would emerge with "a peculiar angle of vision." As a result, our theory and practice of administration would always seem somewhat out of sync with the rest of the world's, or at least not in tune with other state machinery.

*Chinking by Adding a Trained but Incoherent
Personnel System*

On July 2, 1881, President James Garfield was about to leave Washington, D.C., for the twenty-fifth reunion of his class at Williams
College. While Garfield was standing alone at the railroad station,
a stranger stepped up and fired two pistols at him. The assassin,
Charles J. Guiteau, was arrested, tried, and hanged less than a year
later. He had shot and killed the President because Garfield pur-
portedly had not appointed him U.S. Consul in Paris. The crime
provoked a public outcry. Within two years a sympathetic Congress
enacted a new civil service law, largely in response to the tragedy.

For more than a decade immediately after the Civil War,
reformers lobbied for civil service reform. The momentum for civil
service reform increased during Rutherford B. Hayes's administration. President Hayes requested that Dorman B. Eaton, a New York
lawyer and reformer, study and report on the British experience
with civil service reform. Eaton submitted his report in 1879,
Report Concerning Civil Service in Great Britain,[21] and it was later
commercially published and widely distributed. Essentially, Eaton
advocated a similar system for America. Eaton drew heavily on the
British model in developing a plan for the U.S. Civil Service. Much
of his proposal was enacted in the Civil Service Act of 1883.

The U.S. Constitution, as Chapter Two suggests, says nothing
about government personnel, but the new act added a profoundly
important element and outlook that, as Frederick C. Mosher points
out, sought to establish the merit criteria in place of patronage politics as the basis for selecting and promoting government employees.[22] Merit, along with depoliticization and political neutrality,
became via the Civil Service Act of 1883 the dominant theory governing personnel selection. Today these merit criteria permeate
our government, so that now professional, scientific, and technical
experts control many functions within public agencies, claiming
more specialized expertise and greater knowledge than that of
elected politicians and the lay public.

The Civil Service Act, though imitative of the British system in
that it replaced patronage with the merit principle for personnel
appointment, also departed from it in several ways. For example, at
first it only applied to a small minority of the public employees in
the federal service (approximately 10 percent), but, later, this was
slowly expanded to cover most offices. Also, it avoided the British
model of creating an elitist, generalist corps with a distinctive uni-

versity background, "an Oxbridge education" (although later scholars like Leonard White and those supporting the 1978 Civil Service Reform Act would continue to try hard to enact that idea in the United States). The Pendleton Act was highly egalitarian by contrast. It prevented the creation of an elitist class of public executives by allowing candidates for office to compete for any job opening at any level at any age. Meeting the functional and legal requirements of the specific job opening, not a general educational background, counted most in determining selection. It thus thwarted the establishment of "high-toned" educational requirements, except for professional and scientific categories.

By the enactment of the U.S. Civil Service Act, the core of America's administrative state gained over time a vital infusion of trained technical and professional expertise that was necessary for carrying out the new responsibilities of government in the late nineteenth century, but its theory clung always to egalitarian, specialized, and legalistic values. The egalitarian values of the U.S. Civil Service Act makes our civil service perhaps the most open and diverse in the world; yet, in turn, this very openness and diversity often inhibits development of common outlooks, cohesiveness of purpose, and direction in the system. The specialist emphases give the civil service enormous breadth and depths of expertise, but, at the same time, they also serve to fragment overall policy development and coordination due to the wide diversity of experts and expertise that enter into the public service. This attribute makes the American civil service system, as a whole often hard to control and direct by elected officials. For the most part, the legalistic qualities connected with our civil service ensures public accountability, but, at times, this also impedes program flexibility and integration because the practical exercise of real life administration depends heavily on informal flexibility and willing cooperation between diverse parties. Recent increased reliance in the past two decades on temporary amateur politicians to staff upper levels of department management only compounds the difficulties of programmatic integration and control.

Chinking through Weak Regulatory Machinery

The written U.S. Constitution, as Chapter Two suggests, focused largely inward, on smashing public power, not on extending public control over the influence of private power. An important element in the rise of the administrative state was the extension of public power over private economy. Passage of a weak, but vital piece of legislation, the Interstate Commerce Act, was the first attempt to regulate private firms by remedying specific problems of unfair railroad rates.

Federal regulation began as an indigenous reform that more or less bubbled up from more than a decade of grass-roots experimentation at the state level, particularly through the work of Francis Adams in Massachusetts and elsewhere. It was almost a product of the classic Marxist contest between the "haves" and the "have nots." The unfair, gouging rates railroads charged midwestern and southern farmers, combined with the incapacity of state regulation to cope with the dilemma, led to the passage of the Interstate Commerce Act on February 4, 1887. As its main congressional sponsor, Republican Shelby M. Cullom of Illinois had argued that the act was necessary "to curb the reckless strife" of railroad competition as well as "their unjust discrimination between persons, places, [and] commodities. . . ." In Cullom's view, the Interstate Commerce Commission (ICC) offered "a potential to secure stability and uniformity in the industry."[23]

Initially, the ICC was granted weak powers to prohibit pooling and discriminatory railroad rates. These powers were later substantially expanded by the Hepburn Act of 1907 and the Transportation Act of 1920. Modeled on the state commission design and to some extent on the Civil Service Commission, the ICC became the model for subsequent federal regulatory agencies such as the Federal Trade Commission, Federal Commerce Commission, and Federal Aeronautics Administration.

Congress ostensibly placed the ICC outside the traditional executive agencies to permit its independence (though during its first two years the ICC was actually housed within the Interior Department). The values of neutrality were thus paramount, but the ICC was not without problems. Its semi-autonomous status served to develop the ICC into what some have criticized as the fourth branch of government. The very autonomy of the ICC and other independent regulatory units led to problems of executive oversight and accountability. As commissions multipled outside the traditional executive departments to regulate various sectors of the economy, presidents increasingly found it difficult to provide any coordinated political control over the broad range of economic policies they promulgated. Independent commissions were easy targets to be picked off one by one by the powerful interest groups they regulated or by the powerful congressional subcommittees that determined their budgets, personnel ceilings, and enabling statutes. Further, these commissions became staffed largely by lawyers who viewed the issues they dealt with on a case-by-case basis, only exacerbating the design of any coherent national policies. In short, the initial pattern of development with regard to economic oversight established by the ICC model in 1887 allowed independence, diversity, and flexibility but little in the way of long-term coherence, effective coordination, and decisive executive control over the economy.

Chinking via an Uncoordinated "Public Fisc"

Direction and control of financial resources in the public sector—the public fisc—are some of the most powerful roles exercised by modern nation-states. Yet, how to control the public fisc is not spelled out in the written Constitution of 1787. By and large, the founders did not foresee critical fiscal or monetary roles that the national government must play in contemporary society in order to provide for individual and general welfare. In essence, they did not embrace the expansion of the concept of liberty to include *economic welfare* of citizens as essential to their exercising *political freedom*.

Despite Alexander Hamilton's pleas in the 1790s for a strong, central financial authority with ample funding sources via a National Bank, Congress in the 1800s eliminated the bank. Largely at the urging of Treasury Secretary Albert Gallatin, Congress was prodded to use the line-item method of appropriation in order to control the details of public finances. Congressional committees rather than centralized executive agencies thus took charge of public finances. The nineteenth-century congressional practice of dividing fiscal processes into two steps of appropriation and authorization further served to fragment and weaken overall fiscal policy development and make it prey to particular special interests. Until well into the twentieth century neither presidents nor Congress had a method for overall control of public monies.

Like the civil service, America looked to Britain for models to improve its budgetary practices beginning in the 1880s. Prime Minister William Gladstone's budgetary reforms were viewed as especially appropriate examples for America to follow. Billion-dollar budgets in the late nineteenth century, generated by healthy trade surpluses, led to urgent needs to reform federal budgetary practices. It was not until 1911, however, that President William Howard Taft's Commission on Economy and Efficiency, filled with the enthusiasm to promote scientific management and efficiency in government à la Frederick Taylor, actually proposed the creation of an executive budget. Yet, even then, it took a decade to enact into law the Budget and Accounting Act of 1921.[24]

While "efficiency" via the Taft Commission served as a powerful rationale for creating a national budget and the Bureau of the Budget (later the Office of Management and Budget, OMB) to integrate the public fisc, as we know all too well today, in America, unlike many European nations, fragmentation in shaping fiscal policy abounds. Largely this is due to different institutions—OMB, Treasury, "the Fed," the Council of Economic Advisors, Congress and its committees—sharing responsibilities for these chores. As a result, the right hand in this wide dispersal of budgetary authority, often does not know what the left hand is doing, and even the fingers on the same hand are not seemingly knowledgeable that *they are on the same hand!* The rise of "off-budget" items such as Social Security and the use of public tax exemptions today also contribute to further fragmentation and unquestionably are a major source of our current problems of federal deficit and trade imbalance.

But the lack of efficiency in budgeting that we witness today may also be the result of the original emphasis on the formal top-down aspects of fiscal policy development over the informal bottom-up aspects. The executive budget was devised to strengthen the hand of general policy formulation in the presidency vis-à-vis Congress, yet budgets in reality almost always bubble up from a myriad of other forces surrounding the budget process. The nineteenth- and early twentieth-century budget reformers, believers in norms of efficiency, never really addressed the organic political problems of the "normal" tendency to package budgets within a comparatively tight triangle of agencies, interest groups, and congressional subcommittees. Even recent innovations such as the Congressional Budget Reform and Impoundment Act of 1974 and the Gramm-Rudman-Hollings law have not significantly altered these organic, "bottom-up" dynamics of American budget making.

Chinking with Partially Rationalized Organization and Management

"Executive leadership" was indeed something of a dirty word in the minds of the framers, a notion associated with the strong monarchical rule that they fought to escape. With the rare exceptions of Andrew Jackson and Abraham Lincoln, presidents in nineteenth-century America largely tended to ceremonial duties of their office and played politics by dispensing favors and patronage. President Garfield could list all his duties without mentioning "management." As long as authority was lodged in island communities across the nation, imbued with an intense volunteer spirit, who needed better managed or more efficient organizations for getting things accomplished either at the top or at the bottom?

The process of wresting greater executive autonomy, independence, and organizational authority came fitfully and grudgingly. Crises had much to do with the impetus for expanding public executive roles and for creating new forms of autonomous executive organizations. The military crisis generated by the logistical nightmares of the Spanish-American War, for instance, forced changes within the military. Thanks largely to Secretary of War Elihu Root's efforts, the creation of the General Staff in 1902 gave enhanced roles for military planning and professionalism.[25] This reform spread to other government agencies as well. Creation of government corporations, beginning with the first one to expedite the digging of the Panama Canal in 1905, was an effort to design government "like a business" to promote administrative effectiveness that was free from congressional meddling and interference.

The initiation and spread of the city-manager plans that enhanced the local executive's role beginning in 1909 at Staunton, Virginia, was provoked likewise by crises at the grass roots.[26] The incapacity of informal community associations (that Tocqueville saw and praised in 1830) to solve vexing problems posed by new technical innovations, namely the automobile, telephone, and electricity, encouraged cities throughout America to adopt this new *formal type* of local organization with enhanced managerial capabilities. Stronger executive capacity in the form of council-manager plans pushed by their founder, Richard Childs, was not merely desirable but urgently needed if communities were to cope effectively *and survive* given the fundamental urban-industrial-technological transformations. The rise of the public executive focused responsibility for public action that had been missing under the old, informally coordinated system of legislatively dominated administration (the style of U.S. Government that Woodrow Wilson had forcefully criticized in *Congressional Government*, his popular book of 1885).

Again, note the new values of expanding executive effectiveness being added to the old constitutional order via these institutional reforms after the turn of the century. Our Constitution says nothing about an executive branch, a cabinet, government management, public organization or bureacracy, and yet these are essential instruments to make the older constitutional forms work in the modern age.[27]

Nevertheless, despite the strong drive for differentiated, centralized, and more autonomous executive departments after the turn of the century, these reforms were always halfway at best. Executive control over subordinate units of government and subordinate personnel at all levels of government have always been temporary "victories." Like the budget, public executives share authority with multiple outside forces of interest groups, courts, and congressional committees. Formal statutory arrangements in terms of clear rational lines of hierarchy and control, unlike European administrative systems, often mean much less in America than does informal distribution of power within or outside agencies. Indeed, only a brief perusal of *The United States Government Manual* today will show how fragmentation abounds throughout U.S. governmental structures with fourteen formally established executive departments but several hundred diverse organizations outside formal executive departments. These include foundations, institutes, independent agencies, government corporations, advisory bodies, boards, councils, intergovernmental units, and so on. And where do bodies like the Rand Corporation fit in—given that Rand is a private think tank but is mostly publicly funded? Or, is a private company like McDonnell Douglas really public given its largely public support? Our partially rationalized organizations and management in government tend to fuzz and confuse the boundaries of what is "public" and "private," not to mention what is "political" or what properly belongs to "administration."

Chinking by Limited and Ineffective Planning Systems

Over the weekend of May 31 and June 1, 1886, the entire 13,000 miles of Southern Railroad tracks were moved just three inches—from 5 feet to 4 feet 9 inches—to correspond to the track gauge of the rest of the nation. For the first time in history the U.S. had a common track gauge that united a nation and created a uniform railway system. Time zones had been standardized throughout the country just the year before.

In the late nineteenth century, we began to speak of the notion of "administrative systems," first in business and later in government. In other words, we started to view government much differently, assuming that it contained integrated elements of personnel, resources, organization, and technologies for carrying out the duties of government, for efficiently organizing work, for providing uniform practices, for planning for tomorrow, and for adapting to new events and circumstances.[28] Today, of course, we take for granted ideas like public school systems, health systems, library systems, road systems, water systems, and university systems, but a century ago this idea of "systems" was a novel one. Negative government based on the Constitution of 1787 still predominated; public organizations were meant to be reactive and passive, not complex, forward-thinking systems for achieving results. The state-building process ushered in fundamentally different values and perspectives on time itself, a "future-orientedness"—namely, the necessity for public entities, individually and collectively, to think ahead, plan for tomorrow, and anticipate change.

The development of what W. Ross Ashby would later call "a design for a brain"[29] to deal with the future was first proposed in 1880 by a relatively obscure U.S. Army General, Emory Upton. At age 41, after a short but brilliant military career, Upton committed suicide, despondent over his future professional career. He left in his possession, however, an uncompleted manuscript, *The Military Policy of the United States*. The manuscript was passed around to military reform friends but did not see the light of print until almost twenty years later, after the Spanish-American War, when Elihu Root seized Upton's ideas drawn from the Prussian and French military systems and used them as a basis for promulgating fundamental military reforms.[30]

Upton's introduction begins: "The purpose is to treat historically and statistically, our military policy . . . and to show the enormous and unnecessary sacrifice of life and treasure which attend armed struggles." The message, simply put, was that all American wars were substantially prolonged due to lack of preparation, professional manpower, trained leadership, and political interference. His famous line was: "twenty thousand regular troops at Bull Run would have routed the insurgents, settled the question of military resistance, and relieved us from the pain and suspense of four years of war."[31] Upton proposed designing a military system with a central planning staff, a strong cadre of professional soldiers, tight federal controls over state militia, and strict limits on political interference in military policies. Elihu Root, as indicated before, instituted many of Upton's proposals in 1902 in the War Department, perhaps creating the first integrated, forward-thinking, public policy–planning system in the United States.

Despite the creation of the General Staff, and subsequent civilian units like the Executive Office of the President, patterned after
the Root reforms, system-wide public planning has always been a
weak element within the United States government. Ideological
opposition, partisan politics, short-range thinking, institutional
fragmentation, and interbureaucratic rivalry can all be blamed for
making the American state more reactive than forward thinking.
On the eve of World War I and later World War II, for example, the
General Staff had no war mobilization plans. The National Planning
Board that had been created in 1939 was phased out in 1943. Planning has mostly held an uncertain, problematic, and far less than
fully developed role in American government, even though its conception can be traced back to more than a century ago.

Chinking with Narrow Clientele Politics

The development of the administrative state in America also
brought a new style of national politics with new values and outlooks. The Constitution, of course, does not speak of politics or
parties, but a party system had developed quickly after the Constitution's ratification based on rivalries between Federalists and Anti-
Federalists.[32] The old politics had been party-based, focused on win-
ning elections and patronage for sectional and local interests. But
a new one, aptly termed by Richard L. Schott as "clientele politics,"
grew up in the late nineteenth and early twentieth centuries. Schott
writes that "whereas earlier federal government departments had
been formed around specialized government functions (Foreign
Affairs, War, Finance and the like), the new departments of this
period—Agriculture, Labor and Commerce—were devoted to the
interests and aspirations of particular economic groups."[33] The
original purpose of these clientele departments was not to subsidize
or regulate economic interests, but to aid research and collect data.
This, too, changed as distinctive economic groups clustered around
their respective clientele agencies and pressed for distribution of
goods and services on behalf of their interests. In the process of
pressuring for their particular group interests, they served also to
develop, sustain, and expand the administrative state.

The Pension Office is a good case in point. Originally created
in 1833, it became one of the largest bureaus after the Civil War as
thousands of veterans were given benefits for permanent war-
related disabilities. As time passed, however, the Grand Army of the
Republic effectively exerted pressure for even more generous ben-

efits. By 1890, a law was enacted that gave a claim to a pension to any Civil War veteran who acquired a disability by any reason other than "through his own vicious habits." By 1891 the Commissioner of Pensions could assert that his was "the largest executive agency in the world." Clientele politics not only shifted politics toward administration and thereby expanded it, but fundamentally changed the nature of politics into an increasingly narrow technocratic game played by those privileged insiders who knew agency programs, services, rules, routines, and budgets. The lay public was left to watch on the sidelines, increasingly replaced by those experts in the know. In the process, this new clientele politics served to further isolate and fragment administrative institutions.

Chinking by Adding New "Positive" but "Less-than Unified" Administrative Law

The Constitution creates the fundamental law of the land in terms of defining the legal rights of citizens, the limits on public authority, and the organization and responsibilities of governing institutions. The Constitution based on the traditions of fundamental law coupled with common law operated satisfactorily as the legal foundation for American government for more than a century. But with the advent of the modern administrative state in the 1880s also came a new kind of "positive" or "man-made" law, administrative law.

The discovery of administrative law as a unique and important segment of public law was made in the 1880s when Frank J. Goodnow published the first essay on the topic, "Judicial Remedies against Administrative Actions," in the first volume of *Political Science Quarterly* (1886). He apologized for his discovery of administrative law by writing:

> Perhaps an apology and explanation should be made for the use of a term for which there is so little authority in the United States. I am trying to obtain a general classification of national public law applicable to any nation. If this classification—which is generally adopted at present in Europe—is correct, then, unless our law differs fundamentally from the law of every other state, we must on examination find in our law the rules which we have placed under the head of administrative law.[34]

Note Goodnow's emphasis upon finding a "classification" that is "adopted at present in Europe" to comprehend "national public law." His use of European, especially continental national categories, to understand and classify American administrative law was evident seven years later when Goodnow published the first U.S. textbook on the subject, his two-volume treatise, *Comparative Administrative Law* (1893). In this text, he defines the subject as "that part of public law which fixes the organization and determines the competencies of administrative authorities and indicates to the individual remedies for the violation of his rights."[35] Here was law that was "constructed" by man's reasoning, not divinely inspired (as was the case of the Constitution) or acquired by experience (as was common law), to deal with the new realities of "an administered society." It would be different from constitutional or common law.

Goodnow ideally sought to construct a unified *national* system of administrative law as distinct and separable from constitutional law and even separable from politics itself. His thinking also cast administration as narrow, legalistic action. His classic text, *Politics and Administration* (1900), argued for hard and fast separation of politics from administration in that elected representatives ought to make policies while administrators should be concerned with the largely legal and technical aspects of carrying out these policies. Goodnow envisioned administration as essentially legal offices in a unified and uniform administrative system that would efficiently carry out the political policies set by the legislatures.[36]

Indeed, administrative law would soon become a distinct field of study, separate from constitutional law with its own special courts, judges, experts, and legal scholarship, even with a separate codification in the form of the *Federal Register*, which was established in 1935. Particularly in the 1930s, administrative law grew in its role when the federal government delegated quasi-judicial powers to numerous public agencies. But the reality has never quite lived up to Goodnow's original ideal. The case method used by lawyers often serves to confuse and fragment, not unify, public policies. Furthermore, the delineation between administrative law and constitutional law has never been sharply fixed. The two fields overlap extensively, depending on the issue at hand, which often serves further to complicate, not clarify, public policies.

Administrative law today exists as a highly fragmented, specialized, even arcane system, hardly a unified national system used to impose greater overall efficiency and responsibility in government, as its founders had envisioned. Certainly, it is not the uniform, efficient system that the Europeans practiced and which Goodnow envisioned for America; at best it was a "half-formed" arrangement. Or, as two prominent administrative scholars observed recently of this field: "administrative law should not be seen as a unified body of law but rather as a variety of administrative procedures and regulations whose content depends, to some extent, on the agencies and departments involved."[37]

The Consequences of "Chinking in" a Temporary American State for Modern Public Administration Theory and Practice

A nineteenth-century European political theorist, Georg Friedrich Hegel, refused to believe America was "a real state" because it had not developed national government forms or organizations as distinguished in European states.[38] Similarly, Karl Marx thought America was "a fictive state," one of merely abstract institutions without permanent content.[39] Tocqueville considered that it was an "invisible machine" because, in his words, "so feeble and so restricted is the share [of authority] left to the administration. . . ."[40] Indeed, America was unique among nineteenth-century Western nations because, as Stephen Skowronek recently observed, its constitutional order was based on a written Constitution with a highly developed sense of national community but without any highly developed, differentiated, centralized instruments of government.[41] But, as this chapter describes, the shocks of the late nineteenth century—the closing of the frontier, rapid urbanization, technological change, industrialization, international involvement, and new domestic crises—suddenly forced America to do things differently.

In the 1880s, America as a nation faced a serious crisis—the decay and disintegration of social authority. In contrast to Europe, our administrative system grew piecemeal, attempting to cope with the shocks of change in an ad hoc manner and without any one grand design. Rather, it was designed through chinking, or filling in the cracks. As a result, the administrative state, its practices and ideas, in America would seem to many to be only half-formed, or maybe only halfway finished. America, in practice, followed neither Sumnerism nor Bellamyism, but, rather, willy-nilly, without plan, the Wilsonian middle way. By the 1880s it had a civil service, but one with only limited professionalization, scope, and influence. America adopted regulatory machinery by 1887, but machinery with very limited fragmentary powers. Its direction of the public fisc was also uncoordinated and limited. Its organization and management processes were only partially rationalized and differentiated from political influences. Its planning systems were few, fragmentary, and largely ineffective. Its administrative law procedures grew increasingly remote and specialized from the governing processes. We fostered no "Oxbridge class" as in Britain, no "grand corps" as in France, no elite Prussian officialdom to direct or give policy direction and coherence to the state. Instead, we drew our political direction of the administrative state from an increasingly narrow and isolated type of clientele politics. Ours was an American original—like no other in the world. We coped with problems but did not correct them in any fundamental way. We fashioned temporary solutions and therefore in the process constructed a "temporary" administrative state.

The consequences of this "temporary" state for public administration thought is that its ideas and practices remain hard to understand, even harder to replicate outside America. Foreigners do not comprehend this system; for the most part, they see it as too messy, too confusing, and impossible to direct. Even most Americans are confused by their own bureaucratic system. Often the very complexity of its design makes public responsibility for actions hard to pin down and even harder to evaluate. Its temporizing qualities also give the American state peculiar difficulties in follow-through. Problems are raised and discussed, generally without any relationship to creating systems for their solution. Or, if systems *are* designed, they run a great risk of being redesigned before they are tried. Americans are continuously tinkering with and tearing up their administrative machinery to the point nothing is ever given much of a chance at working—or working for very long. This, of course, is the price we pay for building such an ad hoc, jerry-built arrangement; its very complexity and temporal qualities often obscure who's in charge, who's to blame when things go wrong, and whether or not things work right at all. This temporary "chinked-in" state also sometimes frustrates effective generation of adequate political power that is necessary for decisive executive leadership—or even *any* executive direction. It even frustrates American citizens who constantly "damn that bureaucracy." President Reagan captured this ingrained American hostility aptly in his first inaugural address, when he stated, "Government is the problem." Ironically, the very openness to change that is such an intrinsic quality of the American administrative state makes it an easy, if not compelling, target for scapegoating. It forms what Charles Goodsell recently observed is a "splendid hate object" in our minds precisely because we seem never to be able to "get a handle on it" or to make it work as we want.[42]

And another negative: because the administrative state developed by patching the formal constitutional structure—filling in between the cracks—it never has seemed quite a legitimate enterprise. Periodic public debates therefore erupt—even today—about whether or not public regulation or public planning is a legitimate constitutional activity. Of course *it is*, if you believe we operate with an administrative state; of course *it is not*, if you think of America as governed *only* by America's Great Charter of 1787. It all depends, as Harvey Sherman once pithily remarked.

But there are some pluses from having this kind of temporary administrative state. It creates a highly innovative and open system, one that can readily change and adapt to new circumstances. Or, in the words of Wallace Sayre: "The Europeans have produced a more orderly and symmetrical, a more prudent, a more articulate, a more cohesive and more powerful state bureaucracy"; in contrast, he says, America has "a more internally competitive, more experimental, a noisier and less coherent, less powerful bureaucracy within its own governmental system, but a more dynamic one."[43] As a result, we have created, perhaps unwittingly, a state that Woodrow Wilson argued prophetically for a century ago, one that fits well within the framework of our "stateless" constitutional design, and which by 1887 was essential "to run a Constitution." And maybe even that is being somewhat modest about its achievements.

The American administrative state did not merely run a Constitution, but in this century successfully fought two world wars and numerous smaller conflicts as well as helped cure the Great Depression, secure prosperity for millions, and lead America to world power and free-world leadership. Indeed, civilized life within our constitutional democracy would be hard to comprehend without the services of an administrative state that performs in some highly innovative ways, from space exploration to providing video rentals in the county library. It is also hard to imagine how freedom—*real freedom*—would continue in America without the administrative safeguards of child labor laws, welfare payments, fire safety codes, public education, or police protection. The record of our chinking in a temporary administrative state is therefore not all that bad, but whether or not it will be all that good for the future survival of the United States is another matter.

Ultimately, this "temporary" state with its new variety of administration arrangements is probably the only kind Americans could have opted for, given our special intense devotion to the original "stateless" condition founded by our American Constitution as well as given our mobile, prosperous, dynamically changing society with individuals so dedicated to individual freedom. Belief in the value of individual liberty washes throughout American society— especially throughout its administrative state. An ordered, cohesive, unified, and uniform administrative state would never work on these shores. It simply does not fit the American character or our democratic ways of doing things. In the long run, this temporal quality gives our state not only its uniqueness but also its longevity by its unobtrusive adaptability to respond flexibly to the immediate public demands of the moment.

And so, too, public administration theory has followed practice. A succession of American theorists have attempted to impose the "correct" or "efficient" administrative models on the American state, but with little or only partial success—not to mention with considerable frustration. Their ideas have come and gone but never quite lived up to the original promise throughout the twentieth century. They seem like a parade of passing fads—the "efficiency techniques" of Frederick Taylor's scientific management; the British Generalist Civil Service ideals of Dorman Eaton and Leonard White; the "neutral regulatory commission" models of Shelby Cullom and Francis Adams; General Staff planning drawn from the Prussian experience by Elihu Root and Emory Upton; the city management plan of Richard Childs and Louis Brownlow; and effective administrative law as an instrument of state-building by Frank Goodnow. No idea ever quite lived up to the hopes of its founders, or stayed around long enough in the original design of its founders, but ideas were being constantly adapted and redesigned to suit the needs of the moment.

Ideas about public administration theory also never had much longevity in the United States, but were, for the most part, themselves a product of the chinking-in process—to be used for a time when needed and then discarded when unnecessary. Administrative ideas, like the practices themselves, thus seem to be in a perpetual whirl without much continuity, history, or consistency. They have always lacked firmness and a central core; hence, to this day, they are labeled "public," not "state" administration. The word "public" implies an open-endedness to tasks of administration. It even can infer that there is "no there there." Thus, modern administrative scholars—such as Luther Gulick, Max Weber, Herbert Simon, and others—have been unsuccessful at finding "an overarching theory" or a "scientific paradigm" to fully explain the American state simply because it is so changeable, pragmatic, and elusive. Their chore is much like seeking after the Holy Grail or the Fountain of Youth, an impossibility because it just does not exist.

But, as titles of modern texts attest, the search for it remains a vital, alive, and continuing endeavor—*and* frustration—for many scholars. What makes their task even more complicated, as the next chapter outlines, is the rise of the professional technocracy in a global society in the twentieth century.

Notes

1. For an excellent discussion of the American military tradition of technicism, see Samuel P. Huntington, *The Soldier and the State: The Theory and Politics of Civil-Miltary Relations* (Cambridge, Massachusetts: Harvard University Press, 1957), pp. 195–203.
2. Leonard D. White, *The Jacksonians* (New York: Macmillan, 1954), p. 46.
3. Ibid.
4. For a good description of this process, see Matthew A. Crenson, chapter V, *The Federal Machine: Beginnings of Bureaucracy in Jacksonian America* (Baltimore: Johns Hopkins University Press, 1975).
5. Herbert Kaufman, "Emerging Conflicts in the Doctrines of Public Administration," *American Political Science Review* (December 1956), pp. 1057–1073.
6. Stephen Skowronek, *Building a New American State: The Expansion of National Administrative Capacities, 1877–1920* (New York: Cambridge University Press, 1982), p. 26.
7. Robert H. Wiebe, *The Search for Order, 1877–1920* (New York: Hill & Wang, 1967), pp. xiii–xiv.
8. Alexis de Tocqueville, *Democracy in America*, vol. 1 (New York: Vintage, 1945), pp. 95–96.
9. Frederick Jackson Turner, "The Significance of the Frontier in American History," *The Frontier in American History* (New York: Macmillan, 1920), p. 1.
10. Herbert Croly, *The Promise of American Life* (originally published in 1909 and currently available through New York: Da Capo Press, 1986). The literature on this so-called "neo-Hamiltonian" view is voluminous and can be found extensively in the writings associated with authors appearing in the New Republic such as Walter Lippmann and Walter Weyl.
11. As cited in John M. Blum, et al., *The National Experience: The History of the United States Since 1865*, 4th ed. (New York: Harcourt Brace Jovanovich, 1977), p. 443.
12. Ibid., p. 447.
13. John L. Thomas, *Alternative America: Henry George, Edward Bellamy, Henry Demarest and the Adversary Tradition* (Cambridge, Massachusetts: Harvard University Press, 1983).

14. As cited in Richard Hofstadter, *Social Darwinism in American Thought* (Boston: Beacon Press, 1955), p. 51.
15. Ibid., p. 54.
16. Edward Bellamy, *Looking Backward 2000–1887* (New York: Doubleday, 1955), p. 43.
17. Ibid.
18. Woodrow Wilson, "The Study of Administration," *Political Science Quarterly*, vol. 2 (June 1887), pp. 197–222.
19. Ibid.
20. Oliver Wendell Holmes, *The Common Law* (Boston: Little, Brown, 1881), p. 5.
21. *Report Concerning Civil Service in Great Britain* (U.S. Congress, H.R. Ex. Doc. 1, part 7, 46th Congress, 2d Session, 1879).
22. Frederick C. Mosher, *Democracy and the Public Service*, 2d ed. (New York: Oxford University Press, 1982), pp. 66–73.
23. As cited in Skowronek, p. 146.
24. For an excellent account of this development, read Frederick C. Mosher, *The GAO: The Quest for Accountability in American Government* (Boulder, Colorado: Westview, 1979) or by the same author, *A Tale of Two Agencies: A Comparative Analysis of the General Accounting Office and the Office of Management and Budget* (Baton Rouge: Louisiana State University Press, 1984).
25. For a discussion of the General Staff concept, see Huntington, chapter 9, and particularly the theories of Emery Upton on which Root based his reforms, as discussed in Stephen E. Ambrose, chapter 6, *Upton and the Army* (Baton Rouge: Louisiana State University Press, 1964).
26. The history of council-manager government in the United States is outlined in Richard J. Stillman II, *The Rise of the City Manager* (Albuquerque: University of New Mexico Press, 1974).
27. Don K. Price, *America's Unwritten Constitution: Science, Religion and Political Responsibility* (Baton Rouge: Louisiana State University Press, 1983), p. 86.
28. Alfred D. Chandler, Jr., *The Visible Hand: The Managerial Revolution in American Business* (Cambridge, Massachusetts: Harvard University Press, 1977), see especially chapter 5.
29. W. Ross Ashby, *Design for a Brain: The Origin of Adaptive Behavior* (New York: Wiley, 1960).
30. As Huntington notes, "Virtually all the institutions of American military professionalism, except the service academies, originated between the Civil War and the First World War. The common theme in their emergence was the replacement of technicism and politics by military professionalism" (p. 237). It was, however, largely the Root Reforms initiated after the Spanish-American War that created the central professional institutions of the military system, such as advanced education for officers, a General Staff system, and a unified professional system of personnel promotion based on merit. All these professionalizing

ideas had been argued for by Emery Upton's *The Armies of Asia and Europe* (New York: Appleton, 1877) and *The Military Policy of the United States*, uncompleted at his death in 1881 (published in 1904 by the War Department, Washington, D.C.). Upton's remarkable ideas, life, and career are outlined in Stephen E. Ambrose, *Upton and the Army* (Baton Rouge: Louisiana State University, 1964).

31. Upton, *The Military Policy of the United States*, p. 428.

32. The whole idea of a party system was certainly not foreign to the Founding Fathers, but they did everything possible to stall its development by creating an elaborate set of checks and balances in the U.S. Constitution. Nonetheless, it evolved quickly after the Constitution's ratification based on Anti-Federalist and Federalist rivalries, and this complex story is outlined in several studies, especially Richard Hofstadter, *The Idea of a Party System* (Berkeley, California: University of California Press, 1969).

33. Richard L. Schott, *The Bureaucratic State: The Evolution and Scope of the American Federal Bureaucracy* (Morristown, New Jersey: General Learning Press, 1972), p. 9.

34. Frank J. Goodnow, "Judicial Remedies against Administrative Actions," *Political Science Quarterly*, vol. 1, no. 1 (1886), p. 1.

35. Frank J. Goodnow, *Comparative Administrative Law*, 2 vols. (New York: Putnam, 1893), p. 46.

36. Frank J. Goodnow, *Politics and Administration* (New York: Macmillan, 1900).

37. Donald D. Barry and Howard R. Whitcomb, *The Legal Foundations of Public Administration*, 2d ed. (St. Paul, Minnesota: West Publishing, 1987), p. 3.

38. Georg Friedrich Hegel, *The Philosophy of History* (New York: Dover, 1956), pp. 84–87.

39. Karl Marx and Frederick Engels, *The Germany Ideology*, ed. C. J. Arthur (New York: International Publishers, 1970), p. 80.

40. Tocqueville, vol. 1, p. 59.

41. Skowronek, chapters one and two.

42. Charles Goodsell, *The Case for Bureaucracy* (Chatham, New Jersey: Chatham House, 1983), p. 14.

43. Wallace Sayre, "Bureaucracies: Some Contrasts in Systems," *Indian Journal of Public Administration*, vol. 10, no. 2 (1964), p. 228.

CHAPTER FOUR

The Rise of a Global Professional Technocracy: A New Postwar American State System?

There is no point that serves as a center to the radii of the administration.

ALEXIS DE TOCQUEVILLE
Democracy in America

The space shuttle Challenger flight began at Kennedy Space Center, Florida, 11:38 a.m. EST, January 29, 1986, and lasted for 73 seconds. During that time, no flight controller observed any sign of trouble. The shuttle's main engines had first throttled down to limit the maximum dynamic pressure and then throttled up to full thrust as required for lift-off. Voice communications with the crew were normal. At 57 seconds after launch, the shuttle began to roll due east and Mission Control in Houston, Texas, told the crew: "Challenger, go at throttle up."

The Commander, Dick Scobee, acknowledged, "Roger, go at throttle up."

At 73 seconds after lift-off, this was the last communication with Mission 51-L. No alarms sounded in the cockpit. The crew apparently had no anticipation of any problem. The first sign of damage came from live TV coverage of the event on the ground, and then radar began tracking multiple objects flying back to the ocean. The rapid breakup of the space shuttle ensued. No escape routes for the crew were available. The range safety officer reported the vehicle had exploded and immediately sent a destruct order to the solid rocket boosters. The explosion left wreckage along several miles of the Florida coastline waters.

After an extensive investigation of the catastrophe, the Presidential Commission on the Space Shuttle Challenger Accident (the Rogers Commission) concluded on June 6, 1986: "The immediate cause of the Challenger accident was the failure of the pressure seal in the aft field joint of the right solid rocket motor. The failure was due to a faulty design unacceptably sensitive to a number of factors. These factors were the effects of temperature, physical dimensions, the character of material, the effects of reusability, processing, and the reaction of the joint to dynamic loading."[1] In plain language, the critical rocket O-ring joint did not seal properly due to extreme cold, overuse, and faulty installation.

But beyond this specific technical flaw, the Rogers report argued that "the decision to launch the Challenger was flawed." The complex, far-flung NASA management systems had broken down. Vast and complicated networks of professional experts overseeing this intricate technology around the globe from Utah to Alabama, to Florida, to Casablanca, to Dakar, to Edwards Air Force Base in California and beyond had failed to function as an effective integrated system. Possibly it was the scheduling pressures, too many sleepless nights, the intensity of media attention, or the geographic distance between key decision makers that led to overlooking the obscure O-ring problem.

As the Rogers report suggested, "the need [was] for Marshall Space Flight Center [in Huntsville, Alabama] to function as part of a system working toward successful flight missions, interfacing and communicating with other parts of the system that work to the same end."[2] In plain language again, Marshall had tried to "go it alone," ignoring necessary advice from the engineers in the field. They had not properly communicated or cooperated with each other.

"The commission is troubled also," said the report, "by what appears to be a propensity of management at Marshall to contain serious problems and to attempt to resolve them internally rather than communicate them forward."[3] "The Commission concluded," finally stated the report, "that the Thiokol management reversed its position and recommended the launch of 51-L at the urging of Marshall and contrary to the view of its engineers in order to accommodate a major customer."[4] Again, in plain language, the contractor (Morton Thiokol in Utah, maker of the solid rocket booster's O-ring) was too eager to comply with the customer's (NASA) immediate needs to launch 51-L.

Except for the faulty O-ring, there were no villains or heroes in this story. A distant, complicated system, consisting of many thousands of components of advanced technologies and professional experts and responding to complex media-political-administrative pressures, failed to function properly, all leading to the disaster.

The New Core System of Modern Public Administration: A Global Professional Technocracy

Our modern society—for better or worse, or better *and* worse—like Mission 51-L, depends on a large, complex, administrative state system composed of integrated operations of unseen professional and technological systems for virtually all of its essential services—for delivering a glass of pure drinking water free of lead and toxic contents into the homes of county residents; for protecting the national security; for educating our children; for delivering our mail; and for transporting us safely by road, rail, and air. No area of civilized society that we know of seems to be exempt from such interdependence today. All of us, like the crew aboard the space shuttle Challenger, rely throughout our lives on the rapidly moving juggernaut of impersonal, professionally run, technological systems, at times spanning the entire globe. We are governed today, in other words, by a professional technocracy that is interconnected globally for its resources and requirements as the core system of modern public administration. While often hidden from view, this professional technocracy has become an inescapable necessity for maintaining the requisites of what we call our civilized modern life today. It is what Daniel Boorstin has termed "a republic of technology";[5] Don K. Price has called "the scientific estate";[6] Zbigniew Brzezinski, "the technotronic society";[7] Daniel Bell, the "post-industrial society";[8] or Guy Benveniste, "the politics of expertise."[9] This author envisions our governing system in the late twentieth century as "a professional technocracy within a global community." In virtually all aspects, the global professional technocracy of the twentieth century has radically altered—"transfigured" may be a more appropriate word—the original U.S. government, largely in this century, and with profound consequences for reshaping how we think about public administration theory. In brief, the contours of this new American administrative system are as follows.

Sheer Size and Technical Complexity

The notion of a small, limited government, an isolated republic, has given way to a federal government of trillion-dollar budgets, with 2.8 million civilian workers, 2.5 million military personnel, 10.8 million local and state employees, and many millions more indirectly employed through contractual arrangements, accounting for 60 percent of an average agency's operating budgets (Morton Thiokol as a case in point). Government machinery now seems to touch every aspect of American life. Indeed, 66 million people in 36 million households, or about one-third of the U.S. population, now depend on some kind of federal assistance or employment. Government's activities and influence run even well beyond the borders of the United States into all nations and into the far-flung reaches of space. Public bureaucracies are in constant motion, using a wide variety of technologies to daily educate 46 million schoolchildren, pass out 3 million unemployment checks every week, deliver 10 million Social Security checks every month, maintain 4 million miles of public roads, run 172 veterans hospitals, staff 142 U.S. embassies abroad, annually handle 100 billion packages and letters, license 12 million autos and trucks—and much more!

Transitory Professionals—Inside and Outside Government—in Charge of Critical Policy-Making Machinery

While the Constitution's preamble stresses, "we, the people" as the new source of public authority in creating the *novus ordo seclorum*—a new cycle of the ages—in 1787, professionals in all fields—science, law, engineering, medicine, military, and every other arena of policy-making—now play the key roles in governing America and shaping society. In 1987, 22 percent of full-time federal workers were classed as professionals, 26 percent as administrators, and 23 percent as technical personnel. On the federal level these included 5,521 economists, 35,529 nurses, 20,115 electronics engineers, 17,118 attorneys, and 242 museum curators. Thus, over one-third of public employees were classed as "professional-technical" workers (and this would probably be a much higher percentage if we included contract employees). In contrast, only 10.8 percent of the private-sector employees were classed as professional-technical. These "pros" not only move in and out of government with ease, or between the various branches, to influence policy-making, but the global reach of these professionals is staggering. They know no national boundaries, nor do they respect any organizational or national bounds in their ceaseless, rapid quest for marshalling knowledge, resources, expertise, and talent. They are our modern-day explorers on an endless, open frontier— from finding a cure for AIDS to creating a "Star Wars" defense initiative (SDI).

The Ever-Widening Spread of New Global Technology

Our eighteenth-century Constitution had as its cornerstone the limits on government as the federal principle delegated specific powers to the federal government and reserved the rest to the states and people. Federalist principles have been quite reversed in the twentieth century: now the states have few powers that are not infringed upon, or are capable of being infringed upon, by the federal government. Modern technology has reshaped and is continually reshaping the allocation of governmental responsibilities and authority. The speed and reach of such technology as computers and information systems, as well as local demands for federal involvement in most aspects of local and national life, have made eighteenth-century Federalist limitations unworkable and obsolete, despite the rhetoric and efforts of the Reagan Revolution to the contrary in the 1980s. Take, for example, the FBI: the Bureau has developed innovative uses for behavioral research through its behavioral science research unit at the FBI Academy in Quantico, Virginia, which can profile psychological portraits of serial killers with amazing accuracy and, thereby, in cooperation with state and local police across the nation, speed up arrests. Nearby, the Defense Advanced Research Planning Agency (DARPA) is designing the fifth generation of supercomputers with profound global and local economic spin-offs. Scientific revolutions in the twentieth century, therefore, have made such a simple, static "layer-cake" division of federalism with clearly enumerated powers archaic. The old limits and restraints are gone, smashed by the unending technological revolutions of modern life.

Meshing of Powers Once Separated

Article I of the U.S. Constitution provided that the deliberative body, the legislature, should be checked and balanced, as described in Articles II and III, by coequal executive and judicial branches. This cherished Montesquieuian concept of separation of powers has been transformed into "separated institutions sharing powers" (to use the apt phrase of Richard Neustadt). Again, the press of technology and flood of professionals has meant that, in reality, the executive, legislative, and judicial branches must "mesh"—mingle and mix their three powers in order to operate effectively as a government. No *one* branch can go it alone; they must work together to get anything accomplished. Once separated branches are now made both fluid and porous, thanks to the rise of the global professional technocracy. For instance, the executive branch is deeply involved in the messy realities of legislative and judicial activities, as well as vice versa, across a wide spectrum of activities from nuclear disarmament to local welfare policies.

A New Amorphous "Fifth" Estate of Government

The press is often called "the fourth estate" of government, and now a new "fifth estate" has emerged as a potent force in the governance of American society. Today our government is composed of not only the legislative, executive, and judicial branches but also a rich mixture of informal and transitory hierarchies of policy intellectuals in universities who research problems; media publicists in various fields who inform the public; policy analysts in think tanks who gather and analyze data; "hired gun" technicians and private contractors who do the work in the field; and "issue networks,"[10] a term coined by Hugh Heclo, fluid groups in specialized fields who help establish agendas, programs, and budgets.

Congress itself is no longer the small, stable, deliberative body of thoughtful legislators who had plenty of time to legislate, as envisioned by the founders in 1787. Both the House and the Senate are in reality governed by fleeting clusters of "20,000 technocrats"— i.e., the staffers on key committees, in members' offices, or in large legislative units with acronyms such as GAO (General Accounting Office), OST (Office of Science and Technology), CRS (Congressional Research Service), and CBO (Congressional Budget Office) who research the legislation, as well as well as expert outside lobbyists who help write the legislation, lobby for it, and in many cases, then see to its passage and implementation. Presidents, like congressmen, are prisoners today of a vast array of outside ephemeral professional technologists: pollsters, media specialists, policy experts, fund raisers, and speech writers, not to mention the armies of bureaucrats housed in the various agencies and departments of the executive branch. Even the judiciary, the most tradition-bound of the three branches due to its own continued reliance upon case law and judicial precedent as a fundamental modus operandi, finds itself bound up by rapid technological change and therefore a prisoner of professional technocrats. Judges today confront the critical dilemmas on the technological frontiers such as: When does life begin? When does it end? Can biotechnology, such as a new gene-splicing techniques, be patented? And, until recently, who ever heard of the new experts who call themselves "jury consultants," charging fees of $2,000 per day? Hardly the stuff of the judicial processes of a century ago. So here, too, courts, like the rest of the U.S. government, now rely on outside specialists to aid and ultimately influence their judging.

Invention of New Human Liberties and Public Purposes

The U.S. Constitution was designed as a remarkably durable instrument for protecting citizen rights, particularly through the addition of the Bill of Rights in 1791, the first ten amendments to the Constitution. Though our political equality was ensured by those written rights of free speech, press, religion, and due process, they have been supplemented by others, again largely a result of technological inventions. Technical revolutions and social inventions in the twentieth century make the right to an education, welfare checks, unemployment compensation, a driver's license, Social Security payment, copyright protection, and regulatory monopoly far more valuable and pressing everyday concerns for Americans in all walks of life. Technological revolutions have changed our whole notion of *how we define and value human rights as well as establish public purposes.* More often than not, the professional technocrat, frequently outside government, "invents" new human liberties and defines our public agendas, implements these goals, and then is asked to safeguard them for society. Professor Samuel H. Beer sums it up well:

> I would remark how rarely additions to the public agenda
> have been initiated by the demands of voters or the advocacy

of pressure groups or the platforms of political parties. On the contrary, in the fields of health, housing, urban renewal, transportation, welfare, education, poverty, and energy, it has been in very great measure, people in government service or closely associated with it acting on the basis of their specialties and technical knowledge who first perceived the problem, conceived the program, initially urged it on the President and Congress, went on to help lobby it through to enactment and then saw to its administration.[11]

Technocracy, Professionals, and Globalism Defined

Much like the crew members aboard the ill-fated Challenger Mission 51-L, our lives today are governed in the twentieth century by highly sophisticated technologies, controlled by clusters of transitory professional experts in many fields of knowledge, operating both inside and outside the formal boundaries of government, whose decisions know no traditional national boundaries, and who depend on and are interconnected with the broader global community. The modern core system of American administrative state machinery in reality is a vastly different one from the past due to the infusion of three critical components in the mid-twentieth century: (1) technocracy, (2) professionals, and (3) globalism. Given their importance, each deserves a brief definition.

Technocracy

"Technocracy" does not simply denote applied science, the practical or industrial arts, or the hard processes or methods used by science and industries. It is something broader and is used to describe a governing system of technical experts that initiates, decides, and implements actions by using hard and soft techniques in order to provide society and its members with those things needed or desired—or even not needed or not desired!

Professionals

Simply stated, "professionals" are those individuals who govern the technocracy. They generally have a higher education, often beyond the undergraduate baccalaureate, as the necessary credential for holding a position in the technocracy. Most have fairly clear-cut occupational fields that permit not only full-time work but also afford a lifetime career. Professionals today, however, are not housed in one massive organization, but are composed of clusters or associations of specialists inside formal public institutions, as well as in profit and nonprofit enterprises such as think tanks, businesses, research firms, and universities. Sometimes they simply free-lance on their own. They are often mobile, free-floating experts who frequently remain nameless, faceless individuals to the general public, yet they exercise enormous influence through the application of their expertise across a wide array of organizations by deciding vital, even life and death, issues confronting society. They belong to what Corinne L. Gilb once referred to as the "hidden hierarchies"[12] of government or what Frederick C. Mosher called the "professional state."[13]

Globalism

The professional technocracy operates increasingly as part and parcel of the world order and, hence, is subject to pressures and trends of "globalism," not merely those within our national borders. Governance is shaped by and itself shapes the entire world, the oceans, even the frontiers of space. International economics, politics, and social and ecological forces are today of vast and profound importance to the scope, substance, and directions of America's professional technocracy. Globalism also encompasses what the French call, *l'informatisation de la société* (the informing of society). In a nutshell, this term denotes that it is not the production of goods that is changing the global context, but the production of information by the brains of people who are generating new ideas, services, and data as primary resources, intricately connected to the entire global community.[14]

Five mini-cases illustrate the point:

- A penny increase or decrease in the cost of a barrel of oil from a distant Middle Eastern nation affects by $1 million the U.S. Postal System's daily costs for delivering the mail.
- The annual influx of 1½ million illegal immigrants, largely from Mexico and Central America, dramatically transforms the social, economic, and political makeup of American society.
- The invention of a new auto design or microchip in Japan, combined, perhaps, with a new advertising media campaign created in Europe, radically changes the nature of U.S. auto,

steel, and other basic industries as well as the jobs of American workers.

- A new disease spread initially from Africa and Haiti to America and first identified in 1981 as AIDS creates a serious American epidemic causing 5,000 deaths annually.

- The development of SDI, the new "star wars" defense initiative, stimulates unprecedented international debate and controversy, not to mention the pooling of expertise and technologies from around the world.

Twin Historic Forces: The Technological Explosion and Rise of Professions

What gave rise to this new state system for governing the administrative enterprise in America? As Chapter Two explains, the original "stateless" system worked, and worked tolerably well, as the basic governing arrangement for the United States without much change for nearly a century. Accidents of birth—geographic isolation, economic plenty, cohesive island rural communities knit together by self-sufficient economic volunteerism and shielded from external military threats—made this unique constitutional order viable. In short, we did not need a European-style state for almost a century because of American exceptionalism. We were different.

But all that changed in the late nineteenth century. As Chapter Three outlines, numerous crises rocked America during this era and profoundly reshaped our fundamental constitutional order— these included the closing of the frontier, urbanization, industrialism, technological inventions, international involvement, and domestic crises. We could govern ourselves no longer via a formal written document minus a state, but increasingly "the first new nation," to remain viable, necessitated chinking in a new "temporary" administrative state. This grew piecemeal by statute, custom, executive order, and institutional practices, largely hidden from public view. The civil service, regulation, budgets, rational organization and management, administrative planning systems, clientele politics, and administrative law were chinked into the older "stateless" constitutional order, in the famous words of Woodrow Wilson, in order "to run a Constitution." In the process, the United States, as Chapter Three suggests, developed a state like no other in the world, a "temporary" state.

Another radical transformation rocked American society in

the twentieth century, however—one that forged a global professional technocracy: a vast technological explosion that began at the end of the nineteenth century and continues to this day. Just as the "stateless" eighteenth-century system easily gave way without revolution to a nineteenth-century "temporary" state, so, too, the twentieth-century global professional technocracy emerged without major social or political upheaval. It came out of necessity to adapt to the imperatives of technological change.

Up to the late nineteenth century Americans lived in a nation of island communities, in geographic isolation, with limited and comparatively homogeneous population, mainly subsisting from the land. Until this century, four out of five Americans made their living off the land and lived in rural settings. Many could walk for miles in the American wilderness or float down its rivers for days without seeing another person. It was America's manifest destiny to explore, take, use, and build on the land. If the Indians lived *with* the land, Americans actively sought to exploit it.

As historian Frederick Jackson Turner writes in "The Significance of the Frontier in American History" (1893) and we discuss in Chapter Three, the closing of the frontier changed all that at the turn of the century. In this century, the new frontier Americans turned to and pursued with equal vigor and intensity became the endless technological frontier. The machine in this century became for Americans what the land had been in the last century—the unique force shaping the national character, defining our lives, and, in the process, creating our new governing order. The explosion of revolutionary technological inventions that occurred largely in this century decisively and permanently restructured U.S. society and its government. There was the automobile, airplane, nuclear energy, jet propulsion, air conditioning, refrigeration, mechanized farming, telecommunications, computerization, the space shuttle, and much, much more. What did these technologies do for and to America just in this century?

- *Gave a new mastery of the environment* Man would no longer have to be a slave to farming the land or the weather or even bound to the earth itself, because machines invented artificial worlds apart from the land and its seasons.

- *Altered geographic distance* The flip of a switch, a ring of the phone, or the boarding of a plane profoundly changed physical distances into instantaneous (or near instantaneous) connections among people.

- *Changed time itself* In this century, Americans left behind a concept of time that was governed by the natural rhythm of seasons. Time regulated by sunrise and sunset was replaced by a clock, the wristwatch, and now the "beeper."

- *Expanded leisure time significantly* The machine freed many humans from the slavery of work, for it radically expanded and amplified opportunities for leisure time in ways never conceived of before in human history. Recall that the 8-hour day coincided with the coming of the machine age, and so did the golf cart, TV dinner, and the favorite American pastime, baseball.

- *Offered mass satisfaction and instant gratification* Through the efficiency and standardization afforded by the machine, the good life could be brought to the masses for the first time, not just the basics like pure drinking water and indoor plumbing, but the auto, a home, good diets, and travel. These became luxuries, not for the few, but within reach of most Americans.

With the coming of the machine age, as we all too vividly know, we purchased a packet of problems as well as technology:

- *Created new unsolvable, life-threatening problems* No one heard of nuclear waste until nuclear technology appeared. So far, no solutions seem easily to be found for many of what economists term "externalities" caused by the machine. Will we find a method to remove lead from drinking water or a way to prevent the destruction of the ozone layer by fluorocarbons before it is too late? Scientists tell us that time is quickly running out.

- *Created its own irreversible momentum* Once the phone and automobile were invented, they could not be "uninvented" but took on lives of their own—with relentless developments far beyond the visions of Alexander Graham Bell, Gottlieb Daimler, and Karl Benz.

- *Uprooted and isolated individuals* It is no coincidence that the great French sociologist Emile Durkheim coined the term *anomie*, defining the rootless, isolated, "alienated" individual in society, just at the dawn of the machine age. The unrelenting advance of technology destroys stable human communities and groups. It continually changes and uproots individuals with profound moral, psychological, and economic consequences. Was not that the central lesson the Hawthorne studies "proved" more than a half century ago?

- *Cheapened individual life itself* With the advent of technology, masses, not individuals, become important. In the machine age, individuals become replaceable, even discardable, parts in the machine in order to cater to the needs of masses. People turn into mere statistics—i.e., "masses" and "classes." Mass production of goods and services becomes an end in and of itself in the machine age. Remember, "efficiency" is by and large a twentieth-century word. So is "inefficiency."

As Daniel Boorstin writes in his *Republic of Technology:*

Just as the American love affair with his land produced pioneering adventures and unceasing excitement in the conquest of the continent, so too his latter-day romantic love with machinery produced pioneering adventures—of a new kind. There seemed to have been an end to the exploration of the landed continent—an end to the traversing of uncharted deserts, the climbing of unscaled mountains. But there were no boundaries to a machine-made world. The New World of Machines was of man's own making. No one could predict where the boundaries might be or what his technology might make plausible. To keep the machine going, Americans advanced from the horse power to steam power to electrical power to internal-combustion power to nuclear power to who could guess what.[15]

It is therefore no small wonder that, given their love affair with machine technology and the existence of a minimal "temporary" state, Americans should fashion a new twentieth-century state system based on machine technology and the work of professional technocrats. The very openness—looseness?—of the "temporary" state design allowed a new core for America's state system to emerge in this century, shaped according to the driving global imperatives of machine technology.

Professionals grew up as an important by-product to the ceaseless technological revolutions in this century, for professionals served to knit American society together, as well as to govern the technologies in a society that was rapidly being torn apart by technological changes. In essence, professionals were the creatures of the modern technological explosion, for they were functionaries "invented" precisely to cope with technological challenges, changes, and impacts on modern society. The reach of professionals' authority, however, over the dynamics of U.S. government came slowly and in piecemeal fashion, with little clusters of experts scattered here and there, mostly in the twentieth century in response to very specific challenges arising from technological change. Some agencies, such as the U.S. Department of Justice, have always been dominated by lawyers. But professionally trained lawyers with LL.B. degrees, steeped in learning and specialized expertise and responsive to American Bar Association policies, did not appear at the Department of Justice in any sizable numbers until the rapid expansion of legal activities that required specialized investigative, regulatory, and litigating skills to cope with the shocks of sociotechnological changes during the New Deal in the 1930s and World War II in the 1940s. Military officers held top U.S. Army posts from the time the War Department was created in 1789, but the modern professional cadre of officers did not appear until after 1900. The Spanish-American War, as we learned in Chapter Three, taught Americans that warfare was too technologically difficult, demanding, and important to be left to amateurs. Through the 1902 reforms of Secretary of War Elihu Root, who pushed for the creation of the Army's General Staff, a unified personnel system, as well as an advanced education program for officers, professionalization of the Army began in earnest after the turn of the century. The Rogers Act of 1924 started similar processes of professionalization within the ranks of the Foreign Service. Expanding international responsibilities in twentieth-century America required a cadre of trained experts such as George Kennan, "Chip" Bohlen, and other professionals to conduct diplomacy, which formerly had been the domain of the politically well-connected and wealthy gentlemen.

Likewise, control of state and local agencies yielded bit by bit throughout the United States to professionals due to specific socioeconomic and technological crises in law enforcement, welfare, planning, education, health, housing, and other local policy fields. Professionals in America developed from particular events. The need for passable streets and sidewalks, after the old ones had been turned into quagmire with the appearance of the new automobile, led Staunton, Virginia, to hire the first city manager, Charles Ashburner. Thus, a new profession began quite literally out of potholes in roads created by cars.

Similar events prompted by technological change caused fledgling professional associations in the public sector to be established and grow: International Association of Chiefs of Police (1893), International Association of Fire Chiefs (1893), American Society of Municipal Engineers (1894), Municipal Financial Officers Association (1906), National Recreation Association (1906),

National Association of Public School Business Officials (1910), National Association for Public Health Nursing (1912), and City Managers' Association (1914). For the most part, until after World War II, these professional groups were small, weak, and ineffective voluntary associations that exercised little control over the inner dynamics of government. The postwar era, however, brought into both grass-roots and higher-level federal offices a hidden revolution in the conduct of American government by an influx of university-educated specialists with a wide assortment of technical skills. The postwar era saw these armies of specialists grow in numbers and influence in order to cope with a myriad of new technical tasks—from constructing high-speed freeways, cleaning air and water, administering social security programs, enforcing complex industrial regulations, and overseeing virtually every public policy endeavor. At times professionals coped well with technological challenges, at other times poorly; but, increasingly, Americans listened to, even desired and respected their authority. The mid-twentieth century America saw what Burton J. Bledstein calls "a culture of professionalism" in which "regard for professional expertise compels people to believe the voices of authority unquestionably."[16] Professionals commanded new authority in postwar America based on advanced knowledge and specialized skills essential to invent technologies, to manage them, and to adjust to technological change in society.

After World War II, the growth of professionals through all levels of U.S. government meant that now, as Mosher notes:

- A rising percentage of the public work force is made up of clusters of professionals in various public policy fields.
- Increasingly key professionals provide a considerable share of the leadership within most agencies and units of government.
- By their education, examination, accreditation, and licensing practices, professions control the content and direction of their own professional activities.
- Professions, due to their size and leadership abilities inside government, substantially influence public policy and the definition of public purposes.
- In turn, professions serve to spawn other professional groups in government by subdividing their activities or inventing new activities.
- Professionals decisively influence the distribution of power

and status within organizations where they work and, as a consequence, the direction and quality of work, both their own as well as others'.[17]

Other Historic Factors: America's Postwar Supremacy and the Growth of Higher Education

The rise of a global professional technocracy after World War II as the new state system for the United States was also a product of two other factors. First, America's sudden emergence to unrivaled dominance in world affairs brought its peculiar state system to the front and center of the world stage. The rise of America as a great world power came by default. In the immediate postwar era the United States was clearly the most economically and politically influential power in world affairs. America's major wartime rivals as well as its allies—the USSR, Britain, Germany, and France—were left economically devastated by the war, whereas the productivity of the American economy was at its peak performance and surpassed all other nations. For example, in 1938 U.S. per capita income was roughly about the same individually as that in Great Britain, Sweden, or Switzerland. By 1948, just a decade later, America's was higher than all of these countries' per capita income combined. America's superior wealth, efficient economic productivity, and unchallenged leadership of the free world, pushed the United States willy-nilly into new global international roles, rapidly broadening and expanding the scope and responsibilities of the American government. Through the establishment of the United Nations, the Marshall Plan, NATO, and other foreign assistance programs, as well as through its private business connections abroad, suddenly America's state system had a global reach heretofore inconceivable in the prewar days of United States' isolationism and limited world involvement. America's professional technocracy was pulled— often haphazardly and without choice—into every corner of the globe due to America's unsurpassed postwar economic power and unrivaled political influence. In Henry Luce's words, this century became "the American century."[18]

Another key factor that fueled the growth of America's global professional technocracy state system was the expansion of higher education. The professional technocracy in a global society would not have been possible to construct without creating world-class universities. Professional manpower, technological inventiveness, and a vast array of skilled talent were essential to run this new administrative enterprise. Only a well-supported, quality university system, open to all talent, could produce such "products." The postwar era saw an unprecedented growth in support of American higher education, public and private, at all levels, from junior college to advanced graduate degree–granting institutions.

Scientific and professional education at these institutions was also significantly enhanced by the influx of foreign scholars and students from abroad, as well as American educators and students who were encouraged to go abroad as part of their degree programs through Fulbright scholarships and other exchange programs. New funding sources through government programs, such as the National Science Foundation, private businesses, and nonprofit foundations, spurred the growth of science education, technological innovation, and specialization in American higher education. The global professional technocracy was in many ways a creature of this vastly expanded, enriched, and highly productive American university system. Universities, indeed, became the primary beneficiaries of the growth of a global professional technocracy. From where else could the system draw the essential skills, talent, and technologies required for its operation? Thus, the university-technocracy relationship was both mutually supportive and synergistic.

Contemporary Governance by Clusters of Professionals: "The Core of the Core"

At the core of the core of the new postwar American state system are various clusters of professionals, themselves products of technological changes in America, who control much of the policy direction and implementation. It is an organic, evolutionary, largely invisible process that can only be sketched here in brief.[19] Following, then, are the means by which professionals control policy.

Marking off Exclusive Arenas over Public Policy

The various clusters of professionals inside and outside government—be they established professionals like lawyers or doctors or newer professional groups such as computer specialists and risk managers—seek to gain influence and authority over specifically defined policy arenas. Sometimes professionals achieve control chiefly from within government—such as military professionals who are employed within the Department of Defense. On the other hand, they may attain authority from the outside—such as medical doctors in health policy fields or investors, bankers, and economists over monetary and fiscal matters who are mostly employed in the private sector.

Professionals tend to want to establish clear-cut boundaries where they can operate relatively free from outside pressures and set policy agendas, so they can maintain exclusive privileges. Various informal and formal techniques are used to mark off these policy boundaries and secure their "rights" through licensing procedures, educational requirements, professional experience, and provisions for control through promotion boards, as well as pay and status distinction.[20]

As a result, large patches of government policy-making processes have been handed over to clusters of professional groups in various fields, many of whom have allegiance to no particular organization but float among public, private, and nonprofit sectors. They also move easily within government from legislative staffs into executive departments and independent judicial agencies. At times their policy turfs overlap and can create heated controversies, such as the turf fights among the U.S. Army, Navy, and Air Force over control of the United States' defense policy. Periodically such battles are publicized in the media, but more often than not the boundaries between professional groups are relatively well established and relatively free of controversy.

Application of Specialized Expertise

Professionals also influence policy choices by, as Max Weber observed about bureaucratic expertise many years ago,[21] claiming to know more about a particular subject than others. They lay claim to special privileges and prerogatives for setting public policies in specialized fields because they are more in the know than are mere lay citizens. Their professional education and experience is aimed entirely at doing a specific line of work—properly and well—and attaining more knowledge about its substance and practices than outsiders—hence, the specific concern for educational achievement exhibited by most professionals. Their depth of training for specialized professional roles, as well as their often lengthy apprenticeship requirements, are focused almost exclusively on enhancing the skills and expertise recognized by society to do a particular line of work. Status, pay, and prestige are also derived by professionals through gaining such expertise. Professionals not only must appear to know more than the uninitiated but also are granted special recognition by society by virtue of their singular claims to monopolizing such expertise. Concentration on work performed, attainment of technical competency, and proficiency in doing a task are the modern hallmarks of professionalism, as well as the chief source for their claim to influence the policy processes in any particular field.

Belief in "a Correct Way"

Professionals influence policy because they also profess more strongly than others to claim to know more about the policy or policies within their discretionary purview. They often hold a deep faith, which is similar to religious zeal, that they alone understand the correct way both to view and to solve problems. They are convinced by their own dogma, much like religious believers, that they have the right and proper way of seeing the world, accomplishing tasks, and defining the public good. The devout are anointed in professional faith in order to preach and follow their "calling." It is hard for the "unanointed" to argue with "the anointed." Through such beliefs, professions acquire membership, gain status, and claim control over policy issues. No profession is without such a set of articles of faith often embodied in codes of conduct, ethical statements, and pronouncements by recognized leaders and professional associations. Through such avenues, professional beliefs are fostered that explain the world and the correct view of it throughout the profession. Much like a church, the corporate body of a profession is held together and proselytized by doctrinal creeds. Nevertheless, such professional "professions of faith" always tend to be partial faiths. Wholistic views of the world are rare among professionals. A generalist philosophy is often missing because professional specialization, by its very nature, induces myopia. Larger claims of society, needs of the nation, and concerns for the general public welfare are frequently absent because professionals, to be professional, must specialize in a narrow subject matter. Few professionals often see or grow beyond their own professional dogma. Like a submariner who continuously views the ocean through the limited confines of a periscope, fixed in a particular direction and focused on one object, the professional to be professional chooses to fix his or her sights on one narrow aspect of life. In so doing, professionals believe that not only can they advance knowledge, but they gain self-confidence that they know "the truth," as well as the way to get to it (often without realizing what is sacrificed in the process). Lawyers, for example, *believe* as gospel in the case method for handling issues and resolving disputes, even though the reductionist case-by-case approach sacrifices the whole for remedying a particular legal problem. Engineers are dedicated to the goal of building on time and within costs "the completed project" without reference to the broader effects on the general welfare or the environment.

A Sense of Shared Corporate Identity

The strength of professionals today in controlling pieces of public policy-making throughout government is also founded on a strong sense of shared organic unity and group identity. Professional size, expertise, and commitment to a professional dogma or faith are critical in acquiring such influence, but also informal personal ties are important. Professionals know each other—and through their long personal relationships they share knowledge, experiences, and wisdom. The corporate identity has its origins in the professional training programs, apprenticeship opportunities, common career tracks, and shared work responsibilities. Professional associations and organizations dedicated to furthering the profession are also important sources for creating and sustaining the bonds between individual professional practitioners. Here informal networks of pros who have sweated over similar issues and fought together in the trenches are established. These networks, maintained over lunches, phone calls, and social events, allow individuals to talk more freely and openly in thinking through their problems and advancing the art and science of their respective fields. In turn, such interpersonal contacts help solidify the common bonds, shared purposes, and overall aims of a profession. At state or national bar association meetings, medical societies, teachers' conferences, and other professional organizations of various sorts, these face-to-face contacts so vital to professional bonding are nurtured and strengthened in ways the public never sees nor students of government little appreciate.

Informal Hierarchy and Elites

Professional associations normally have clearly established, if often informal, pecking orders from the novice apprenticeships to the top elites within the profession. In some professional callings, such rankings are obvious—military officers wear their bars and stars on their shoulders—but in many professions the pecking order is much less apparent. Who are the respected teachers, economists, or nurses within professional peer groups is not always easily discernable. Gradations often depend upon such intangibles as recognized competence, leadership skills, and experience with handling critical problems, at least problems considered critical to the professional field in order to win the respect of colleagues and "earn your spurs." Elites set the priorities for the profession, chart its future, exercise the most vital leadership roles in policy-making, establish standards for conduct, serve as role models for career development, and set rules for entrance and achievement within the ranks.

Max Weber's comment is relevant here: "The discipline of the army gives birth to all discipline."[22] It is true that professional hierarchies can ultimately trace their discipline back to military discipline. This internal discipline, depending on its strength and application, is imposed by a professional hierarchy and elite and gives direction, coherence, and influence to every profession's public policy-making roles.

Older and more established professions, like medicine and law, generally can impose stronger hierarchical elite control over their ranks. In contrast, frequently the newer professions find it much harder to do so, although professional hierarchy elite controls vary considerably from agency to agency and from field to field within government. A social worker with a master's degree in social work may be an "elite" in a welfare department but not in a general hospital where medical doctors are in charge. A research scientist can be a member of an elite within a research institute but not in a U.S. Army weapons development installation where the military command is in charge.

The Continuous Drive for Freedom from Political Controls

Professions generally profess a hostility toward politics and desire as much freedom and autonomy as possible from political oversight and external accountability. Their aim is generally to exercise the greatest latitude of control that is possible over their particular realm of expertise. By and large, professionals hold a built-in antagonism toward government, which they view as akin to red-tape, bureaucracy, amateurism, politics, and incompetence. In short, professional animus primarily is directed against meddling by the nonexpert in what is regarded as their own turf. Professionals thus strive for self-government of their affairs and prefer internal controls through their own professional elites and associations, rather than controls exercised by outsiders. What they do, professionals repeatedly contend, is too important and complex to be understood or compromised by lay citizen involvement. Even those professionals who are employed entirely by government agencies—such as military, educational, and diplomatic professionals—often view themselves and their work from this perspective—that is, as individuals: they do not consider themselves a party to the governmental enterprise of public accountability, but, rather, as separate entities devoted to advancing their own callings. An unspoken professional motto is, bluntly put: "We professionals profess to know more than others."

Links to Scientific and University Enterprises

If professionals seek independence from government oversight and broad political accountability, they look to association with universities and scientific bodies to give them status, recognition, and independence. Professionals gain authority and influence by means of appeals to science and the scientific method, as well as more widely "knowledge-creation" processes prescribed by universities, especially prestige universities. Over the long haul, universities, particularly in their professional programs, science departments, and advanced research endeavors, shape the ranks of professions by defining the specializations, content, and skills required to enter a profession and to exercise progressively advanced positions of authority in a professional field as well as by setting research agendas for what is considered important to the entire profession's advancement. Governments, in turn, rely on universities for licensing and establishing credentials and for training programs for professional personnel. Increasingly, government yields to universities in defining the nature, scope, and requirements for public employment through their degree requirements and specialized credentials. Universities act as the profession's gatekeepers. Professionals, universities, and government are now so interconnected that it is often impossible to tell the three apart.

To sum up the chief methods by which professionals influence the direction of policy and administration within the contemporary American state system:

- Professionals stake out territory within a particular policy field and governmental activity, sometimes with boundaries similar to the agency but more likely spanning across various private, public, and nonprofit enterprises.

- Professionals apply their expertise based on length of experience and specialized training that serves to legitimize their claims for dominance and influence within specific policy arenas.

- Professionals create "dogmas" for correct views of the world and ways of doing their work that provide the essential ideological glue to knit together a profession and give it distinctiveness and claims to influence in public affairs.

- Professional associations, hierarchies, and elites provide a significant degree of shared corporate identification, policy direction, and control over their members' activities through the discipline they impose and the ideals they articulate.

- Professionals strive continuously for freedom from external control over their activities and value internal accountability through peer-imposed codes of ethics or licensing processes.

- Professionals aim to link up to scientific and university bodies outside government in order to enhance their knowledge base, prestige, and status as "authoritative experts" within public policy arenas.

The Fallout for Contemporary Public Administration Theory

Given the emergence of a global professional technocracy as dominating postwar American state governance, what are the implications for modern public administration theory? This reconfiguration of the administrative enterprise in the United States today indicates the following for theorizing about the field of public administration.

Definition by Little Clusters of Professional Experts

If professionals today significantly influence the direction of policy within various policy arenas, so, too, do they define what is the "good" or "correct" administration within specific policy fields. The military model with its strict discipline, steep hierarchies, clearly delineated ranks, well-established lines of authority, and strong elite controls offers the ideal form of administration within the Defense Department. At the State Department, good administration is measured by different standards, primarily imposed by Foreign Service Office professionals, in which collegiality is prized, diplomatic skills are stressed, compromise is valued, informal discussion and negotiation are considered vital, and personal ties and friendship are seen as important for maintaining good relationships. Among local government professionals, such as those in law enforcement, city management, or education, proper administration may be defined even more differently according to the particular professional association values and professional norms. Public administration theory thus becomes no longer one best way but, rather, a creature of many best ways as defined by the specific profession "in charge."

Hyperimpermanence and Complexity

If a chinking process, which emerged out of the peculiar national crises of the late nineteenth century, forged a "temporary" state, the late twentieth-century state system is even more ambiguous and impermanent by being shaped and reshaped continuously by an endless stream of advanced, sophisticated technologies and governed by highly mobile clusters of skilled professionals, responding to the socioeconomic and political forces of today's global environment. Public administration theory within specific policy arenas controlled by professionals thus becomes ever more elusive and complex, without easily understandable forms, clear-cut purposes, or a stable substance. Moreover, it is an ongoing process of discovery and invention, rather than an immutable set of principles or concepts.

The Blurring of Boundaries between Public and Private Sectors

The global professional technocracy supplies an unending stream of goods, information, and services demanded by society, for which there are seemingly no limits to the possibilities or potentialities. The professional technocracy's presence is felt everywhere throughout society. Thus the old distinctions in public administration theory between what is private and public or what is political and administrative blur. Also, distinctions between the local and national or national and international realms become more ambiguous and elusive. Mobile clusters of professionals move easily across organizations and fuzz such old boundaries for the study and practice of public administration.

A Commitment to Values of Specialization, Expertise, and Meritocracy

The dominant class that shaped America's "temporary" administrative state and public administration theory in the late nineteenth century was largely the white, male, upper-class, Protestant reformers such as Dorman Eaton and Richard Childs. Many tended to be learned and affluent, with wealth derived from corporate family connections, whose reform ideals were shaped by an ardent belief in saving constitutional democracy of the eighteenth century through chinking in new bureaucratic forms of administration. Thus, often they attached strong ethical ideals to the administrative reform prescriptions they proposed. In contrast, the global professional technocracy is governed by a belief in specialization, expertise, and meritocracy, free of ethical reformist zeal. In other words, it is governed largely by individuals who are products of universities, think tanks, and private industry research firms, with advanced degrees and skilled at manipulating and applying technologies to public issues without necessarily a commitment to constitutional democracy. Professional specialization, merit, and expertise, rather than land, race, economic class, sex, or family background, decides individual power, position, and status in professional hierarchies. Public administration theory has had to accommodate the fact that professional meritocratic elites operate in a democracy without much understanding, attachment, or commitment to constitutional, public, or democratic values.

Dilemma of Knitting Together Technical Change with Public Purposes

The global professional technocracy draws on a rich, diverse, and highly fluid mixture of private business, nonprofit, and governmental enterprises here and abroad to achieve its ends. This mutable amalgam is blended and reblended in new ways, frequently through contracting out for services at home and overseas, and is shaped by the need both to solve immediate technological problems and to maintain accountability to the public. Balancing the specifics with public goals is often complicated by rapidly shifting global technologies, particularly information systems, computers, and telecommunications, which allow our modern institutional arrangements new flexibility, versatility, and geographic spread. They also foster constant change and confusion that can serve to confound understanding both details and the "big view" (as overlooking the O-ring problem in the space shuttle Challenger pointed up all too well). How to knit everything together for public purposes therefore becomes a central dilemma for public administration theory.

The Driving Technological Imperatives

The global professional technocracy's aim might best be succinctly captured by Burger King's TV slogan—"have it your way." It is a system driven by hard and soft technologies—computers, communications, electronics, management systems, automation, robotics, and so on. These not only allow mass production of information, wealth, goods, and services for society that were previously unknown in human history but also permit a degree of individualization of these goods and services heretofore unknown at any time or anywhere in the world. The new administrative system satisfies masses, classes, and individuals all at once. It thus breaks down old distinctions, but also continually extends and fragments the state enterprise, making it constantly difficult to define and identify ends and purposes in administration theory and practice.

Higher Education as Key "Legitimizer" and "Theory-Maker"

University training, professional expertise, and professional skills serve as the chief "legitimizer" of authority and mode of entrance into the professional meritocracy. Thus, expert knowledge derived mainly from university education becomes the basis of defining direction and authority within this system. Since universities are the source of the skilled professional manpower in virtually every field today, the professional technocracy is intricately bound up with the particular fate and future of university academic departments and professional schools around the world. The authority of the professionals is defined in theory and practice by (1) the credentials accorded by the universities, (2) the status within professional hierarchies based on these university degrees, (3) the delegation of authority flowing from legislative mandates to these elite bodies, and (4) the specific utility and the applications of knowledge generated by professionals.

Faith in Sciences and Professional and Technological Inventiveness

The global professional technocracy flourishes due to its inordinate American faith in science and the capacities of technologies of all kinds to provide mass material satisfaction for mankind, combined with an efficient distribution capability to individualize these goods and services. It is thus rooted in both intense faith in technology and in expertise to expand material benefits, economic opportunity, and values of "the good life." Ultimately, the global professional technocracy is dedicated to no fixed ends, but only the promotion of endless frontiers of science, technology, and knowledge and one involving constant change, turmoil, inventiveness, discovery, and flux, without history or a seemingly stable set of values. In short, public administration theory—like the state according to Marxian interpretation—seems to wither away as professional technocracy looks toward exploring endless technological frontiers. Thus, not stable doctrine, but rates of technological invention, global socioeconomic-military-political developments, applications of scientific expertise, standards of professional associations, selection of professional elites, opportunities for university education, and professional licensing and credentialing processes become critical aspects in defining the future directions of the theory and practice of public administration. Public administration thought itself, therefore, becomes a creature of global professional-technological revolution, which makes it a less and less comprehensible subject, though nonetheless central to the governance of America and mankind. As Jeffrey S. Luke and Gerald E. Caiden sum it up well:

> In the last twenty years, public administration has been transformed by an increasingly complex globalized environment. Characteristic of this new international order are spreading networks of subtle and direct interconnection and interdependence that enmesh public officials at all levels of government, from one part of the planet to another. Such networks have always existed, although for the most part they have been weak, temporary, and insignificant. But since World War II

and particularly in recent years, global interdependence has gained strength, permanence, and significance.[23]

To Sum Up, of Sorts

The "stateless" origins of America offered an open invitation to the growth of the global professional technocracy in the twentieth century. From birth, America's lack of state gave its society a porousness, unlike most other nations, and allowed the administrative enterprise in the United States to be shaped—and reshaped—indefinitely by external forces—namely, in the twentieth century by technological change, professional expertise, and global influences. Unique compared to other nations, America's administration is held hostage to largely outside forces, and, thus, to many it seems without a centerpoint or focus. As Tocqueville observed 150 years ago, "There is no point that serves as a center to the radii of administration." In contrast, if an established state system had existed at the birth of "the first new nation," not only would there have been a greater likelihood for a center for the administrative enterprise but strong hierarchies, purposeful direction, and clear boundaries as well. A strong state would have, to a much greater degree, inhibited the widespread impact of the modern technological explosion, by erecting barriers that would have moderated the effects of technological change. Similarly, the pervasive influence of professionals and professions and the wider global involvement would have been curtailed or limited sharply. The global professional technocracy took root, grew, and is now in charge of America's state system precisely because there was never much of a state system from the outset to impede its development. All this had important consequences for American public administration theoretical doctrines, as we shall see in the next chapter.

Notes

1. *Report of the Presidential Commission on the Space Shuttle Challenger Accident* (Washington, D.C.: U.S. Government Printing Office, June, 6, 1986), p. 72.
2. Ibid., p. 104.
3. Ibid.
4. Ibid.
5. Daniel Boorstin, *The Republic of Technology: Reflections on Our Future Community* (New York: Harper & Row, 1978).

6. Don K. Price, *The Scientific Estate* (Cambridge, Massachusetts: Harvard University Press, 1965).
7. Zbigniew Brzezinski, *Between Two Ages: America's Role in the Technotronic Era* (New York: Viking, 1970).
8. Daniel Bell, "Notes on the Post-Industrial Society," *The Public Interest*, vol. 6, no. 1 (Winter 1967), pp. 24–35.
9. Guy Benveniste, *The Politics of Expertise*, 2d ed. (San Franciso: Jossey-Bass, 1983).
10. Hugh Heclo, "Issue Networks and the Executive Establishment," in Anthony King, ed., *The New Political System* (Washington, D.C.: American Enterprise Institute for Public Policy Research, 1978), pp. 8–124.
11. Samuel H. Beer, "Federalism, Nationalism, and Democracy in America," *American Political Science Review*, vol. 72, no. 1 (March 1978), p. 9.
12. Corinne L. Gilb, *Hidden Hierarchies: The Professions and Government* (New York: Harper & Row, 1966).
13. Frederick C. Mosher, *Democracy and the Public Service*, 2d ed. (New York: Oxford University Press, 1982), see especially chapter 5.
14. For a useful discussion of this subject, read Harlan Cleveland, *The Knowledge Executive: Leadership in an Information Society* (New York: Truman Talley Books, 1985).
15. Boorstin, p. 47.
16. Burton J. Bledstein, *The Culture of Professionalism: The Middle Class and the Development of Higher Education in America* (New York: Norton, 1976).
17. Mosher, p. 114.
18. For a highly readable recent account of this postwar growth of the American global influence, see Walter Isaacson and Evan Thomas, *The Wise Men: Six Friends and the World They Made* (New York: Simon & Schuster, 1986); for Henry Luce in particular, read W. A. Swanberg, *Luce and His Empire* (New York: Scribner's, 1972).
19. Much of the following information is summarized from Frederick C. Mosher and Richard J. Stillman II, *Professions in Government* (New Brunswick, New Jersey: Transaction Books, 1982).
20. James W. Fesler's comment that "professional licensing boards are virtually the creatures of the professional societies" is probably still accurate, as reported in his 1942 study, *The Independence of State Regulatory Agencies* (Chicago: Public Administration Service, 1942), pp. 60–61.
21. Max Weber, "Bureaucracy," in H. H. Gerth and C. Wright Mills, eds., *From Max Weber: Essays in Sociology* (New York: Oxford University Press, 1946), pp. 196–244.
22. Max Weber, "The Meaning of Discipline," in ibid., p. 261.
23. Jeffrey S. Luke and Gerald E. Caiden, "Coping with Global Interdependence," in James L. Perry, ed., *Handbook of Public Administration* (San Francisco: Jossey-Bass, 1989), p. 83.

CHAPTER FIVE

Shifting Doctrines in Twentieth-Century American Public Administration Thought— One, Two, Many

At different periods dogmatic belief is more or less common. It arises in different ways and it may change its object and form; but under no circumstances will dogmatic belief cease to exist, or, in other words, men will never cease to entertain some opinions on trust and without discussion.

ALEXIS DE TOCQUEVILLE
Democracy in America

Some of the major aspects involving the intellectual development of American public administration in this century have already been touched on in Chapters Two, Three, and Four as related to the evolving concept of the American state. Now it is important to look more directly at the topic of public administration doctrines, specifically what they are and how they have evolved in the twentieth century. Such an examination can provide clearer and broader perspectives on the prominent ideas that have shaped the content of the field. This chapter outlines these influential theories, their sources and substance, that created modern public administration thought in America.

Twentieth-Century American Public Administration Doctrines as Reflections of the Changing American State

Major trends in American public administration thought that are accepted as truths and doctrines over the last century can be understood only against the backdrop of the rise and evolution of the American state. Ideas about public administration that jelled into an identifiable field of study have, by and large, reflected the peculiar contours of state development in the United States. Overall administrative theory served mainly to echo major lines of institutional development in America.

As suggested in Chapter Two, at its birth America missed the development of a state, and so until the twentieth century conscious thought about public administration largely was unnecessary. Rules of thumb, common sense, and on-the-job experience could suffice as practical guidelines for conducting administrative affairs in America.[1] Agrarian self-sufficiency, geographic isolation, lack of external threats, rapid technological change and urbanization made large-scale public organizations and their formal study unessential. Grass-roots cooperative efforts based on a strong sense of community largely organized and directed what later became called public administration. The American community was informal, democratic, energetic, and adequate to meet the organizational needs of Americans for roughly a century after the ratification of the U.S. Constitution. Hence, without a state, not only was formal study of state administration unnecessary,[2] but also it was impossible to educate for and Americans were smart enough not to even try. Anyway, Americans were actually successful at administration without realizing they were accomplished in the art and science of administration, at least in any formal sense.

All this changed in the late nineteenth and early twentieth centuries, as Chapter Three outlines, with the chinking in of the "temporary" American administrative state. The Wilsonian middle way devised limited, temporary institutional arrangements to cope with the crises and challenges of that era. The formal conscious study of public administration, symbolized by Wilson's famous centennial essay in 1887, emerged in this period and prophetically reflected the rise of and need for formalized and refined state institutions. The growth and dominance of the new state, a global professional technocracy in post–World War II America, as Chapter Four points out, reshaped and significantly revised American administrative practices and doctrines based on the new influential roles of professionals, technology, and globalism.

Much of the difficulty and debates over sorting out public administration doctrines in the twentieth century derive from the shifting historic traditions of state development in America: i.e., "statelessness," the "temporary" administrative state, and the global professional technocracy. How did these three systems throughout the twentieth century shape the identity of American public administration theory? Why do they continue to exert powerful forces even today, defining what the field "is" and "ought to become"? How did three clashing views of the nature of the American state harden in doctrines and dogma? Why do these dogmas still persist and influence the minds of Americans with various degrees of intensity and emphasis? Why does the place of administration in politics become such a difficult, recurring, and central focus of doctrinal debates over the years? Such questions will be the primary focus of discussion in this chapter.

American Administrative Doctrines before World World II: Reflections of State-building

Many of the basic doctrines of the field that first appeared and gained popularity in this century coincided with the rise of the administrative state. With maturing of the administrative state in the 1920s and 1930s, the first introductory text appeared—Leonard D. White's *The Study of Public Administration* (1926); the first school of public administration was founded—the Maxwell School of Citizenship and Public Affairs at Syracuse University (1924); and early professional associations of public administrations were formed—such as the International City Management Association (first formed in 1914 as the City Managers' Association in Springfield, Ohio). Later journals like *Public Management* (1927) and the *Public Administration Review* (1940) built on and elaborated these doctrines, often into authoritative dogmas and fixed scientific truths, even "laws" akin to the physical sciences. A synthesis jelled by the 1930s and was based on the following five critical doctrines.

Politics versus Administration

Perhaps the most critical doctrine that led to the rise of the prewar synthesis was proposed by Frank Goodnow's *Politics and Adminis-*

tration (1900). As its title implies, the book argues that government activities can, indeed should be, divided between politics and administration. Or, in Goodnow's language, politics defines "the will of the state" whereas the execution of that will involves "administration." Goodnow sees the problem as the achievement of harmony between expression and execution of the state's will, as opposed to stalemate or conflict between the two. As Goodnow writes: "There are, then, in all governmental systems two primary or ultimate functions of government, viz. the expression of the will of the state and the execution of that will. . . . These functions are, respectively, politics and administration."[3]

Goodnow's dichotomy between politics and administration was widely influential among the twentieth-century founders of American public administration, for it justified the development of a distinct sphere for administrative development and discretion—often rather wide—free from the meddling and interference of politics. The dichotomy, which became an important instrument for Progressive reforms, allowed room for a new criterion for public action, based on the insertion of professionalization, expertise, and merit values into the active direction of governmental affairs. In practice, too, the dichotomy served to justify the institutional developments of such basic features of the administrative state of the civil service system, personnel classification, and planning systems, as well as the introduction of public budgets.

Goodnow's dichotomy became a fundamental element in pre–World War II administrative thinking for it allowed public administration, as a whole, to emerge as a self-conscious field of study, intellectually and institutionally differentiated from politics. As Frederick C. Mosher observes,[4] a neutral administration free of "spoils" became something of a moral crusade for many of the early reformers associated with promoting public administration in the United States. However, this moral cause also presented knotty intellectual problems: namely, to what degree should administration be separated from politics *and how?* And was it possible and constitutionally proper to conceive of American government in such a fashion? After all, had not the Founding Fathers divided the federal and later every state government along the lines of a tripartite division of power (legislative, executive, and judicial), not between simply politics and administration? Can one, in other words, logically advocate and constitutionally justify a dichotomy when the Constitution was founded on a trichotomy?

Scientific Processes

A second doctrine in pre–World War II public administration, the belief in science and scientific processes, also served to buttress the rise of the American administrative state. However, this doctrine had different origins. As Chapter Three suggests, the late nineteenth and early twentieth centuries were the age of inventors and rapid inventions, which spawned the need for new administrative systems such as regulation and planning to cope with the profound technological changes in society. These flourishing ideas of science and the methods of science were also deeply infused into the administrative beliefs of that era. The early founders of the field held strong beliefs that administration could ultimately achieve the status of a science and that the good and correct "principles" of administration akin to scientific laws in the physical sciences could ultimately be discovered. If only enough data was gathered, proper analysis performed, information correlated, and objective methods utilized, permanent scientific "truths" or "principles" would be revealed in public administration that were beyond debate or discussion. The cool, calculating, rational spirit of science, in other words, would guide the field's development to discovery of a set of unchanging principles of administration.

The founders posited a stable Newtonian universe. Books, such as the second textbook in the field, written by W. F. Willoughby, even appeared confidently propounding the "principles" in their titles: *The Principles of Public Administration* (1927). Early writers boldly declared the discovery of "the basic principles" of public administration. Henri Fayol, one of the early saints of the field, dogmatically asserted that there were no more or no less than fourteen such principles that included "unity of command" and "unity of direction."[5] Of course, many—even other founders— were not quite so certain there were exactly fourteen; the number seemed to vary from founder to founder. Yet, whatever the number of "discovered principles," the faith in science fit neatly with the notion of separating politics from administration in order to support Goodnow's development of the administrative state in America. If politics was normally associated with passion, disorder, and irrationality, administration could claim the opposite attributes of a science: rationality, calculation, objectivity, and reason. This was certainly popular in an era of hero inventors like Henry Ford and Thomas Edison. By embracing the scientific mindset so stoutly, public administration thus could avoid the messy problems of dealing with values and human purposes. These could be—ought?—left to "politics" to define, at least according to many founders. Administrators could then be left with the "serious tasks" of state-building and maintenance; with "doing," not talk![6]

Economy and Efficiency

Another important doctrine emerged from yet another quarter, from the scientific management movement that stressed values of economy and efficiency. Scientific management grew out of business experiences largely associated with the work of one man, Frederick W. Taylor, who was a foreman in the Pennsylvania Steel Company at the turn of the century. Taylor had performed elaborate experiments with steel-cutting methods. He came to believe that the personal, informal hit-and-miss methods of work should be replaced by the most efficient and effective one best way to perform a task. Empirical experimentation, according to Taylor and his followers, would objectively reveal the one best way. Furthermore, if the one most-efficient way could be found for cutting steel or loading pig iron, so, too, for larger group operations in business or government could the one best way be discovered as well. The ultimate aim was not for capitalistic profit but, rather, for increased prosperity for all, or as Taylor put it: "Maximum output, in place of restricted output. The development of each man to his greatest efficiency and prosperity."[7]

Taylorism spread into government via such influential sources as the New York Bureau of Municipal Research, founded in 1907 by a reform-mind civic group to reform municipal government, as well as the Taft Commission on Economy and Efficiency (1910–1912). The Taft Commission first recommended the establishment of a national budget and other efficiency reforms at the federal level. By the 1920s, the doctrine of economy and efficiency was deeply imbedded into the core of public administration theory. Indeed, it would be hard to overestimate the critical importance of Taylorism to this era of public administration. Simply getting good people into government, as earlier nineteenth-century civic reformers had advocated, was not enough to improve government; goodness can come and go, and maybe it was even of questionable value. Rather, what was critical to the conduct of government was creating a system, *the system*, predicated on economical and efficient performance.[8] These ends, according to much of public administration doctrine of that era, could be achieved through creating a sound system, based on scientific study and investigation, free from political interference. In other words, it all fit neatly together: a strong, effective administrative system could flourish if politics was restricted to its proper sphere, if scientific methods were applied, and if economy and efficiency were societal goals.

Top-down Hierarchy

Along with the business values of economy and efficiency, models of business corporations captivated the minds of administrative students of this era. While there were debates in the literature over the virtues of decentralization versus centralization, the dominant view within the prewar public administration favored arranging government along the lines of a business corporation, with one designated chief executive officer (CEO) and clear lines of authority running up and down the organizational hierarchy. Policy, then, it was believed, should be determined, just as in business, by a small, cohesive board of directors and implemented by the CEO, from the top down. Much of the literature supporting the council-manager plan emphasizes its value because of its similarity to the business model for conducting every city's affairs. For example, Richard S. Childs, one of the prime advocates of the council-manager plan, argues that "the advantages of having a city manager are obvious to any businessman. For counsel, many minds are needed; for execution, a single head is required. Universal business practices demonstrate this. . . ."[9] In fairness to Childs and other reformers, all this was a means to an end, namely fostering and furthering democracy. "Democratics" was the term Childs coined to stress the basic values he ultimately sought. In this respect, Childs shared the Progressive faith with the other early administrative reformers.

Advocates of the corporate model sought the same plan for even larger entities, so that wholesale revamping of the entire state or federal government was urged along business lines. Although popular, such revamping was never achieved. Partial adoption of the business model in the form of government corporations at the state and federal levels, however, spawned widespread support. Certainly there were some sharp critics of this top-down organizational model based on private enterprise, such as Francis Coker, Mary Parker Follett, and Ordway Tead, but they were then very much considered out of step with the Progressive spirit of the era, since everyone else seemed to be so impressed with the potential benefits of sound business practices applied to the conduct of government.

Expert Public Administrators

Finally, the pre–World War II doctrines of public administration favored a much stronger, more visible role for public administrators in governing and directing public enterprises. It was obvious, at least to the early founders of public administration, that those who are competent to administer, according to pre–World War II doctrines of the field, should be in charge. Who else could be? Establishment of the new state system would require a new cadre of public managers who justified their positions on the basis of knowledge, proven experience, and professional abilities. Certainly the old rulers in world history now were incompetent to govern in this new order: neither kings ruling by divine right, Platonic philosophers governing by virtue of wisdom, nor princes seizing power by strength of arms à la Machiavelli was acceptable—or feasible—to rule in this new state system. Rather, an administrative class would be in charge who were not simply experts or bureaucrats but people who were much broader in background and vision: public administrators!

Louis Brownlow expresses it in "The New Role of the Public Administrator":

> The task of the public administrator above all else . . . is to concern himself with human relations, with human values, with those deeper economic, social and spiritual needs of human beings whose government in its administrative branch, he represents. . . . He will not merely represent one government agency or be a legal or technical specialist but rather be a center of social cooperation and able to command and utilize broad knowledge, deep understanding, and human sympathy in a synthesis of social wisdom.[10]

Implicit in Brownlow's vision was an abiding Progressive faith in an administrator's capacity to govern with an ethical consciousness and to solve problems better and more efficaciously than others. This belief was held, often unconsciously, by many of the pre–World War II founders of the field, Progressives and Post-Progressive leaders such as Leonard D. White, Frederick A. Cleveland, W. F. Willoughby, William E. Mosher, Richard Childs, Henry Bruere, and Charles A. Beard. They were keenly convinced that good organization with able administrators at the helm would solve many of the ills afflicting urban, industrial society in the twentieth century. Much of what they collectively viewed as "the enemy" to the advance of civilization and "the good society" were notions such as laissez-faire that limited the role and constrained influence of public administrators. Here was an optimistic faith in mankind and their organizational capacities. It was this bright optimism about mankind's potential that created the driving force for the emergence of a self-conscious field of public administration as well as the new American state.

Toward a Temporary POSDCORB Synthesis: White, Gulick, and Brownlow as State-builders

In practice, pre–World War II public administration doctrines evolved piecemeal, from varied sources, in fragmented, partial forms, often through trial and error of experimentation at the grass roots. The formation of the American administrative state—and its doctrines—literally bubbled up from below and were not imposed from the top down. They came via local civic reform movements, various academic and intellectual proponents, diverse business initiatives, research bureau studies, and various government commissions. As a result of its diverse local sources, American administrative doctrines, like the formation of the state system in America, never quite fit together neatly as an ordered whole. Yet somehow these doctrines did jell, or seemed to jell. By the 1930s, more than at any time before or since, scholars of the field seemed to arrive at an agreed intellectual synthesis. In many respects, this was at best a temporary compromise among competing viewpoints. Some would also contend it was the golden age of public administration in terms of its visibility and prominence in the United States.[11]

White

More than any other academic text, Leonard D. White's *Introduction to Public Administration*, a basic text that went through four editions, must be credited as being one of the major intellectual achievements to unify the field. White's *Introduction* was the first published text in 1926 but especially his second edition in 1939 espoused the clearest and most forceful synthesis of public administration, which then became accepted as "the gospel" for many. In his view, public administration was "a process which is common to all organized human effort."[12] It meant building, doing, creating, making a better society via effective public or state action. Indeed the word "state" features prominently in White's text. Public administration, however, was not something concerned with a specialized activity in a state—such as military administration or municipal administration—but, rather, a generalizable and generalized field "concerned with the management of men and materials for the accomplishment of the purposes of the state."[13] The keys to White's synthesis can be discovered by examining its basic four premises, which were both new and old. They were new in the sense that they provided a workable synthesis, a concise methodological framework of administrative management for public administration. They were old in the sense that each premise attempted to draw on past doctrines of public administration thought.

White's first assumption was that there is a single process of administration; he envisioned "an essential unity in the process of administration, whether it be observed in the city, state, or federal governments."[14] It was not enough for White to observe that there *is* "unity of administration"—throughout his text, he repeatedly stresses the normative value that there *should* be "unity in administration" to achieve effective government action. For White, building strong, centralized, executive-centered administration was equated with good government. As White writes: "the concept in the administrative system at all levels . . . now prevails as the ideal either to be achieved or progressively approximated. The role of unity is essential in the long run both to secure efficiency and responsibility."[15] Whether discussing chapter headings labeled "The Chief Executive," "Middle Management," "Headquarter–Field Relationships," "Independent Regulatory Commissions," or "Government Corporations," White over and over again admonishes the worth of maintaining and achieving executive unity in the administrative structures. Indeed, the bulk of his text deals with the tools and methods of securing integration of executive activities through reorganization, budgeting, and personnel controls. In short, state-building, or, more precisely, building an effective administrative system, was White's prime goal.

His second assumption was that administration is equated with management, and it envisions both the study of public administration and the processes of administration based on management rather than the law. White clearly saw administration as an executive function, unlike Willoughby, who saw public administration as shared with other branches. White does not deny the dependence of public administration on legal statute and rules, but his book emphasizes the managerial components of administration and minimizes its legal and formal aspects. The ends of public administration may be set by law, but the achievement of these ends rests with management (or one could substitute the words, "an energetic chief executive"). He idealizes strong executives, be they strong presidents like the two Roosevelts, effective cabinet officers like Alexander Hamilton, or professional local managers like city managers. The good administrative manager, "the doer," not the good lawyer, is clearly his ideal for government service.

White's third assumption was that administration is an art in transformation to a science, which incorporates the older scientific management search for placing the processes of government on secure foundations of principles of administration. Scientifically tested and arrived at, this system would be above petty politics and personal whim and caprice. Here, the older values of scientific management are evidenced. Each succeeding edition of White's text after 1939 contains fewer references to scientific principles and seems to be less certain about what principles are "correct" to propound, like "the correct span of control" or "administrative responsibility should always be equated with authority." By his fourth and final edition, these principles eventually turn into rules of thumb, but White never gives up his quest to place the study and practice of administration on the solid ground of science with the end goal of achieving effective government. As White writes: "The very great influence of the scientific management movement in government has been due, not to its specialized procedures, but to the ideas that administration is subject to constant improvement, that some ways of organizing are better than others, and that it is the duty of top management to find the best way for arranging staff under given conditions. . . ."[16] Thus the older technical, scientific values of Taylorism's one best way fade in White's writings as they are qualified as significant core values over succeeding editions of his text.

Finally, White's fourth assumption was that administration is the central problem of government. He assumes "that administration has become, and will continue to be the heart of the problem of modern government."[17] Here, too, White showed his preference for the view that the legislative body should be increasingly supplanted by effective executive management in order to cope with the vast new complexities of governing an industrialized nation. White writes:

> The problems which crowd upon legislative bodies are often entangled with, or become exclusively technical questions which the layman can handle only by utilizing the services of the expert. . . . These [experts] are not merely useful to legis-

lators overwhelmed by the increasing flood of bills; they are simply indispensable. They are the government. One may indeed suggest that the traditional assignment of the legislature as the pivotal agency in the governmental triumvirate is destined at no distant date to be replaced by a more realistic analysis which will establish government as the task of administration.[18]

Here the implication is clear: the work of legislatures is being taken over by experts, who "are the government," in White's view. Administration is the place where the *real* issues of government are decided and the *real* work is accomplished. This is the place where, also according to White, such problems *ought best be decided and accomplished.*

Students of public administration for more than two generations were strongly attracted to White's text, for its fundamental values were the values of state-building and state-making that dominated the American landscape in the pre–World War II era. And White was perhaps the most articulate, forceful, and thoughtful champion of its cause.

Gulick and Urwick

Along with White's text, *Papers on the Science of Administration,* edited by Luther Gulick and Lyndall Urwick in 1937 provided a second important intellectual effort to synthesize pre–World War II public administration. In the opening essay of the book, Gulick poses the questions: "What is the work of the chief executive? What does he do?" Gulick made up the acronym, POSDCORB, to emphasize those universal functions every administrator presumably ought to accomplish in the following logical sequence of steps:

Planning: "working out in broad outline the things that need to be done and the methods for doing them to accomplish the purpose set for the enterprise";

Organizing: "establishment of the formal structure of authority through which work subdivisions are arranged, defined and co-ordinated for the defined objective";

Staffing: "the whole personnel function of bringing in and training the staff and maintaining favorable conditions of work";

Directing: "the continuous task of making decisions and embodying them in specific and general orders and instructions and serving as the leader of the enterprise";

Coordinating: "the all-important duty of interrelating the various parts of the work";

Reporting: "keeping those to whom the executive is responsible informed as to what is going on, which thus includes keeping himself and his subordinates informed through records, research and inspection";

Budgeting: "all that goes with budgeting in the form of fiscal planning, accounting and control."[19]

In laying these functions out, Gulick goes on to note that "this has been recognized in many of our larger governmental units, though there has been until recently no very clear philosophy laying back of the arrangements which have been made." He points to some separate institutions performing these various roles, such as planning activities by the National Resources Committee and budgeting by the Bureau of the Budget. For the most part, however, POSDCORB functions in government, in Gulick's view, remain "not institutionalized, but undifferentiated and unimplemented in the hands of the President." Thus the President is now swamped and "needs help," according to Gulick, and it therefore must be recognized "the job of the Chief Executive is POSDCORB." Hence, according to Gulick:

> Each one of these managerial establishments should be a part of the executive office. Their budgets should be brought together, and as far as possible they should be in the White House itself. It should be as natural and easy for the President to turn to the chairman of the planning board, or to the civil service commissioner when confronted by problems in their fields as it is now to call in the budget director before deciding a matter of finance.[20]

At the root of Gulick's POSDCORB synthesis was a cogent plea for building an effective, efficient administrative system right up into the very highest governmental levels, the Executive Office of the President. Gulick's synthesis shared the same four doctrinaire premises as White's, especially the premise that public administration is (1) a single process, (2) not law but management, (3) an art in transition to scientific principles, and (4) the central business of government.

The Brownlow Commission

POSDCORB ideas ultimately served as the basis for fashioning the Brownlow Commission Report. Early in the last year of his first term, on March 22, 1936, President Franklin Roosevelt appointed a three-member committee, the President's Committee on Administrative Management, to study and make recommendations on the overall management of the executive branch. That committee became known as the Brownlow Committee, after the name of its chair, Louis Brownlow, but the ideas of the committee and the authorship of the final report in reality reflected Gulick's thinking (he was one of the three committee members). The central idea expressed in the 1937 Brownlow report was that "the President needs help" and thus greater administrative capacity is required for that office. Indeed, the President should become the manager of the executive branch, fulfilling the duties of POSDCORB. His office should be better empowered, staffed, and organized according to the principles of POSDCORB. Specifically, POSDCORB served as the framing idea for the first major reconceptualization of the Presidency since 1789 by the Brownlow Committee, which included such key recommendations as:

1. Expand the White House staff so that the President may have a sufficient group of able assistants in his own office to keep him in closer and easier touch with the widespread affairs of administration and to make a speedier clearance of the knowledge needed for executive decision.

2. Strengthen and develop the managerial agencies of the government, particularly those dealing with the budget, efficiency research, personnel, and planning, as management arms of the Chief Executive.

3. Extend the merit system upward, outward, and downward to cover all nonpolicy-determining posts; reorganize the civil service as a part of management under a single responsible Administrator.

4. Overhaul the 100 independent agencies, administrations, authorities, boards, and commissions, and place them by executive order within twelve major executive departments.

5. Establish accountability of the executive branch to the Congress by providing a genuine independent post-audit of all financial transactions by an auditor general.[21]

Legislation to implement the Brownlow recommendations was proposed in 1937 at the high point of the New Deal's popularity after Roosevelt's landslide reelection. But the proposed legislation was tagged as "the dictator bill" and became tangled in bitter fights over Roosevelt's "court-packing scheme." Though bits and pieces of the Brownlow report were enacted by the Reorganization Act of 1939, the Reorganization Plan No. 1 (1939), and Executive Order No. 8248 (1939), Americans seemed to reject the vision of a strong, managed administrative state based on POSDCORB. Instead, they continued to chink in an administrative state in bits and pieces, as they had done since the late nineteenth century—more out of necessity than from any grand, academic design.

Powerful Postwar Attacks on POSDCORB: Simon, Waldo, and Appleby as POSDCORB Challengers

The dramatic increase in government social services during the New Deal combined with successfully fighting a global world war, then coping with the aftershocks of industrial conversion to a peacetime economy, as well as the new worldwide responsibilities exercised by America in the Cold War, meant that, for many students of public administration, POSDCORB suddenly seemed a less compelling idea for organizing the complex tasks facing postwar American government. Within a decade after the end of World War II, attacks by prominent administrative scholars of that era saw POSDCORB and other prescriptive state-building doctrines less influential as dominant dogmas. Soon other new competing doctrines flooded into the field which offered up other possible replacements. They came from many sources, but especially from the university world where powerful new analytical approaches were invented for the field of public administration. What they offered were important alternative visions to the one best way in public administration.

Simon

Perhaps the best known and most effective attack upon POSDCORB came from the pen of Herbert Simon in his book, *Administrative Behavior* (1947),[22] which was originally his doctoral dissertation at the University of Chicago. Simon introduced to the literature of public administration a radically new philosophic doctrine of logical positivism, drawn from continental European philosophy. Logical positivism via Simon had four important effects on the field. First, it was a tough-minded, no-nonsense approach which asserted that philosophy should—or can—only deal with what *is* and not what "ought to be." As a belief system it dismissed values, ethics, even ideas, and emphasized analysis, empiricism, and logic, hence the name, "logical positivism." Like science, logical positivism, particularly in the hands of Simon, saw that public administration should deal only with questions of "facts" that can be empirically verified (though ironically his book contains few facts and data on administration per se). Value questions and normative statements about the principles of administration were labeled as proverbs, contradictory, and fuzzy, thus unworthy of serious attention. Sharp distinctions between "fact" and "value" were therefore introduced through Simon's writings into the field of public administration.

Second, Simon differentiated between theoretical and practical science. Theoretical science is interested in the abstract, establishing causal linkages between phenomena and using complex analytical techniques, with results that are not always of immediate use. Practical science is concerned with application to concrete affairs and, by definition, is not abstract, often mingling "is" and "ought" questions. It was Simon's assertion that public administration as a field should become more theoretically abstract and more consciously scientific. The older applied POSDCORB ideas that were directly related to administrative practice were deemed by implication less suitable or worthy for organizing research.

Third, Simon's *Administrative Behavior* argued that the appropriate focus of the theoretical study of administration, as the title of the book implied, should be on the "behavior" of administrators, or what they actually do, and, more specifically, how they make decisions and choices. These aspects of a job can be analyzed and measured; models can be developed and empirically tested. Simon thus defined administrators and their world narrowly, involving only questions of choice, not broader institutional roles or the historical, philosophical, and moral dilemmas they faced. The world of Simon's public administration became apolitical in the sense that it avoided messy problems of institutional development, political controversy, ideological challenges, policy issues, and partisan questions. In certain respects, as several scholars noted at the time, Simon revitalized the old Goodnow politics-administrative dichotomy by defining administrators' roles as merely "choice mechanisms."[23] "Politics," in the Simonian world as in Goodnow's, were left to others, or *ought* to be let to others.

Finally, at the root of Simon's thinking was the introduction of a new view of administrative rationality, "bounded rationality." The Simonian world was not made up of *public* organizations but merely *organizations*, that included private, public, and nonprofit. In other words, he introduced a generic focus for the field based upon "the organization." Organizations in his view are instruments created to enhance human rationality. In his instrumentalist concept, humans are limited in their capability to respond to complex problems and solve them, for as Simon writes, "The capacity of the human mind for formulating and solving complex problems is very small in comparison with the size of the problems whose solution is required for objectively rational behavior in the real world—or even for a reasonable approximation to such objective rationality."[24] Thus, because men are limited in their individual rationality, they must link together in organizations to enhance their rationality and to deal effectively with the world. Public administration, in a Simonian view, was the means for creating such linkages within organizations with the ultimate aim of producing "efficient decisions." Ironically, while Simon attacked the principles of Gulick and Taylor as "mere proverbs," he ultimately shared their faith in achieving a better world for mankind by introducing a new, tough-minded, scientific rationality for the field. Through the generic study of organizations, Simon aimed to find fundamentally technical solutions to human problems. Clearly, the central decision-making role of administrators was to be efficient technical decision-makers. They were little more than instruments for operating a vast, impersonal administrative machine. They were faceless, life-less automatons without political, moral, or social choices. Simon's tight embrace of logical positivism made his work *appear* a radical departure from the past. Though his language and logic differed dramatically from pre–World War II authors, one did not have to dig too deeply into Simon to find the continuation of many administrative doctrines of the politics-administrative dichotomy, instrumentalism, professionalism, science, rationality, reductionism, and technical problem-solving.

However, by smashing the belief in an applied POSDCORB synthesis and at the same time raising abstract scientific methodology to the forefront of public administration's intellectual priorities, Simon effectively, if unwittingly, displaced the central pre–World War II administrative state-building focus of the field. At the very least, the prewar doctrines were rooted in values and purposes that were intricately connected to the practical betterment of American society. Simon sought to smash once and for all such linkages between the "normative" and the "scientific." His intense preoccupation was on "what is" not "what ought to be." Values were something "out there;" "mere things" beyond the bounds of serious analysis and discussion and without connection to "what is." The "is" became disconnected from "ought," with the result that everything seemed to become unrelated to ends, without purpose, and freely floated in the void of the random here and now in the Simonian world. Logical positivism's only ends, ultimately, were logical positivism. Methods, not substance or purpose, of administration became goals in themselves, and, ironically, this led, in turn, to new ruling dogmas and doctrines of methodology for postwar public administration. Here was, above all, a methodology in accordance with the needs and necessities of the postwar new American state, that is: technocratic, professional, instrumentalist, and free of normative, political, or value concerns.

Waldo

Other voices also attacked the old POSDCORB proverbs of White, Gulick, and Brownlow, but in different ways. Another prominent postwar scholar, Dwight Waldo, effectively demonstrated the serious shortcomings of POSDCORB doctrines in his book, prepared as a doctoral dissertation at Yale University, *The Administrative State* (1948).[25] But Waldo viewed the subject from an entirely different direction. If Simon had subjected POSDCORB doctrines to the intense technocratic, reductionist, microscopic analysis of logical positivism and found the doctrines wanting, Waldo looked at POSDCORB through the long-range telescope of 3,000 years of political history and philosophy and discovered that POSDCORB was not a neutral administrative doctrine, as many of its adherents had pretended it to be. Rather, it was very much infused with complex values involving ancient political and philosophic issues, like the ones Plato and other political theorists in the West had wrestled with in the great dialogue: Who should rule? What is the meaning of the good life? What are the ends of government? How should governments be organized—centralized or decentralized?

Waldo so effectively challenged prewar administrative ideas and elaborated on the normative foundations in the context of contemporary administrative writings that POSDCORB suddenly seemed no longer *the* faith but *a* faith among many competing ideas for constructing a good state system. Waldo brought a healthy skepticism and a more balanced perspective to a field inhabited, particularly in the first half century, by numerous "true believers." By revealing the value premises upon which POSDCORB doctrines had been constructed, Waldo turned POSDCORB into posdcorb, or one point of view among many. He placed the development of the American administrative state in historical context, and, for the first time, identified its broad intellectual and institutional significance in America. Though also he so effectively attacked POSDCORB, Waldo was criticized by some as being too good a critic: that is, he destroyed POSDCORB but offered no replacement vision for the field, other than a plea for heterodoxy.[26] His faith was ultimately a faith in democratic administration with a small *d*. For a field predicated on action taken in relationship to some goal or objective, heterodoxy seemed in reality to some to provide an extraordinarily difficult basic guide or criterion for action. Most people understand "ambiguity" to mean frustration and confusion, even an excuse for inaction. Or, to paraphrase another philosopher, "men will die for the orthodox but hardly notice the heterodox." The historical sophistication and philosophical wisdom, moreover, that Waldo sought in comprehending the complexities of modern administration would be no match to the instrumentalist, technocratic vision offered by Simon. Simon provided the field not *a* way but *the* way, which fit hand in glove to the requirements of the new American global professional technocracy. Could this account for the relative neglect of Waldo's *Administrative State*, at least compared to Simon's work, by most postwar students of the field? Waldo had failed to offer *the way?*

Appleby

Paul H. Appleby's *Policy and Administration* (1949)[27] provided a third powerful critique of POSDCORB doctrines, from yet another perspective, that of an institutional insider. Appleby, unlike Simon and Waldo, was not an academic by training, nor did he write primarily for an academic audience. Rather, he was a seasoned journalist who entered public service at mid-career in the New Deal, serving throughout Roosevelt's administration in high policy-making posts, first as Under Secretary of Agriculture and later as Assistant Director of the Bureau of the Budget. After World War II, at age 56, Appleby became Dean of the Maxwell School, Syracuse University, where he wrote six books in rapid order that were highly readable and influential within the field. They were hardly scientific, nor, for that matter, did they offer serious philosophy; rather, they were based on a mix of personal insight, seasoned wisdom, and astute observation about the modern administrative enterprise.[28]

Particularly in *Policy and Administration*, Appleby made a convincing case that public administration was not something apart from politics. Rather, it was at the center of the political life of America. No sharp lines of demarcation could be drawn between what was administration as opposed to politics. In his view, administration was infused with policy choices and thus politics. As he writes: "Executives do not sit at two different desks treating policy at one and administration at the other. Even intellectually, they more often deal with whole problems than they deal with them as exclusive problems of policy or problems of administration."[29] For Appleby, "administration here is treated, therefore, as a broad term involving policy-making as well as execution."[30] Like Waldo's, the Applebian vision of the administrative enterprise became an organic and highly relativistic world, where there was no longer one best way of administering but rather many best ways. It depends on the situation, not on the correct doctrine. Nothing about administration, even by implication, in the Applebian view, then remained distinctive or clear for public administration as a process, purpose, or set of beliefs. The field became so intertwined with politics and so freed from the rigidities of POSDCORB that it also became a much more difficult and complicated subject for study and practice. In the end, it became hard to define what "it" actually was. Was it merely politics? What indeed was the new definition and institutional reality for the field? Had Appleby simply spent so much of his government career as a man at the top that he had mistaken his personal experiences as a policymaker and politician in the Roosevelt cabinet with the entire world of public administration? Appleby begged off from answering such questions.

From Orthodoxy to Heterodoxy: New Multidisciplinary Resources for the Postwar Global Professional Technocracy

Under the withering crossfire of Simon, Waldo, and Appleby, as well as other university-based intellectual leaders in the field such as Norton Long, James Fesler, and Robert Dahl, POSDCORB rapidly faded as an accepted overarching paradigm for the field, at least in the academic world. POSDCORB orthodoxy lingered on for many years, however, in the world of government practitioners. The two Hoover Commission Reports, *Report of the Commission on Organization of the Executive Branch* (1949 and 1955), were referred to, for example by James W. Fesler, as "Mr. Brownlow's children"[31] because both were predicated on the POSDCORB doctrine, as was true of other major governmental reports published still later, the Price report, *Report of the President's Task Force on Government Reorganization* (1964), and *Reorganization Plan No. 2* (the Ash Commission report of 1970).

Indeed, the POSDCORB framework did not even die out right

away as a guiding doctrine for the academic enterprise of public administration. At the dawn of the postwar era, POSDCORB remained a vital force for defining the essential subject matter taught in masters programs in public administration (MPA). Typical MPA programs included coursework in organization and management, personnel administration, and budgeting and planning—that is, fundamental bread-and-butter classes that remain common in MPA programs even to this day. POSDCORB also continued to guide mainline topics for dissertation research in the field. Dissertation titles for the doctor of public administration (DPA) written throughout the 1940s and the 1950s reflect POSDCORB thinking: "Recent Developments in Philippine Budgeting"; "Program Budgeting: Theory and Practice with Special Reference to the U.S. Department of the Army"; "Program Management in the Department of the Army"; "City Manager-Hospital Administrator Relationships"; "Social Security Legislation in the United States"; "An Analysis of Performance Budgeting in the City of Los Angeles"; and "A Century of Service: An Historical Analysis of the Service Function of a State University."[32]

Therefore, if Simon, Waldo, Appleby, and other name theorists sought alternative visions that would shift away from, or even displace, the POSDCORB ideal as the central doctrine for public administration, they were not entirely successful. POSDCORB left slowly, if not completely, in theory and practice. In the postwar era, however, the field certainly expanded into a wide array of new alternative methodologies and approaches due to the requirements for running and sustaining a vast, complex, global professional technocracy. The rise of this new state system meant no one best way orthodoxy could possibly define the entire intellectual scope and substance of public administration. Nor was it reasonable to expect that one could be found. The global professional technocracy that emerged in the United States as the governing state system after World War II was so diffuse, so complicated, and so involved with every facet of American life that one paradigm, or even a few, was insufficient to define, comprehend, and operate the new state system.

For some serious scholars like Dwight Waldo, there was a sense of an increasing frustration at an inability to define what "it" (public administration) is if "it" is everywhere and so central to society and government. By the 1960s Waldo began arguing that the field was facing "an identity crisis" as a result of an inability to define the scope and substance of the field.[33] For others, like Herbert Simon, the effort to comprehend the whole became less and less interesting or revelant to research interests. Simon, like many other scholars in the global professional technocracy, became increasingly attracted to more specialized, technical, and arcane topics of investigation such as computer simulation of "efficient" decision-making models. Did they become the new soldiers in the new state system? Certainly Simon and his followers unwittingly seemed to fit in well with its primary imperatives.

From the late 1940s onward, public administration was transformed into a vastly broader, more enriched, and more dynamic field, infused with multiple doctrines, ideas, and subject matter, particularly generated from the university, for comprehending and running the new, multifaceted, immense global professional-technocratic state system. As a result, there could no longer be one agreed-upon set of norms or one orthodoxy for the field. If the prewar administrative scholarship was largely devoted to the normative values of state-building through promulgating principles such as POSDCORB, the postwar theorists could, for the most part, no longer hope for a general synthesis, such as POSDCORB, intricately connected to the state-building enterprise. Rather, administrative students and scholars were attracted to enhancing more specialized, narrow subject matter as defined by professionals and technicians, largely in universities, as *important subjects for research and analysis.* To a greater or lesser extent, they shared a faith, albeit a more sophisticated and a less explicit faith, in the bright promise and efficacy of specialization, and in a science that would build valid models, testable theories, and empirical approaches that would comprehend, explain, and analyze aspects of the new state. But there could be no *one* best way. When the dichotomy between politics and administration proved to be untenable and when the scientific management approaches withered under pounding, postwar criticisms, there simply was no other viable, broad-ranging paradigm to take their place. There were many pretenders to the throne of public administration theory—such as, systems theory, cybernetics, decision models, and public choices—but all failed to become *the* way; they only turned out to be *a* way.

In one important respect, the global professional technocracy served to push the field in that direction by defining the scope and substance of postwar public administration in a much narrower, more segmented, empirical, and analytic manner. In response to the professional technocracy's diverse interests and needs, public administration theory itself became a creature of the global professional technocracy as vast, diverse, technical, specialized, and professionalized as the new postwar American state system itself. Thus, if there could no longer be a grand synthesis, such as POSDCORB, a new heterodoxy emerged to comprehend, to operate, and to explain bits and pieces of the professional technocracy as defined by experts within various academic specialties. In short, the field itself became captive to its own specialization, subspecializations, and professionalization, fashioning a conceptual heterodoxy fed by diverse university disciplines.

"New Political Realism" and "Policy Science" from Political Science

From Woodrow Wilson to the present, the academic discipline of political science made strong, consistent contributions to public administration thinking. For many years public administration was political science, or was considered a significant portion of this field. The intellectual and disciplinary linkages between the two were so close that they were often viewed as indistinguishable and inseparable. The names of pre–World War II leaders of political science, such as Woodrow Wilson, Charles Beard, Leonard White, and Luther Gulick, were also academic leaders of public administration.

In the postwar era, political science became much larger, more specialized, compartmentalized, and professionalized. The behavioral revolution in the field via Simon and others brought more emphasis to methodology, science, and technical specialization, which resulted in tougher, more empirical, and more neutral approaches by political scientists interested in many topics broader than public administration issues. Several illustrious figures from political science, such as Norton Long, V. O. Key, Robert Dahl, Charles Hyneman, David Truman, James Fesler, Marshall Dimock, John Gaus, Emmette Redford, and Carl Friedrich, thought, wrote, and researched at least a portion of their scholarly works in public administration.

On the whole, the emphasis in postwar political science—when it did address public administration—was to bring a new political realism to understanding administrative processes. Many political scientists had had first-hand experience in administration during the depression of the 1930s or in wartime agencies of the 1940s. The neutral application of techniques such as efficiency and effectiveness measures attracted little interest for them, nor did POSDCORB doctrines seem realistic for explaining the postwar world. Rather, as Norton Long puts it: "Administrative rationality requires a critical evaluation of the whole range of complex and shifting forces on whose support, acquiescence, or temporary impotence the power to act depends."[34] Long and other postwar political scientists brought a frank and fresh recognition of the realities of power as the basis for all administrative action, or as Long writes, "The budgeting of power is a basic subject matter of a realistic science of administration."[35] For some, like Long, administration became wholly a question of power; other administrative issues or technicalities mattered little, if at all.

Some political scientists not only studied administration from the vantage point of power, but also conceived of their research in terms of influencing the choices and directions of public policy, particularly from the top echelons of government. The call for the study of policy-making, policy science, and policy analysis attracted many talented students of political science. Policy studies began in the mid-1950s at Harvard, Berkeley, and Yale and other major departments of political science by focusing on making, shaping, and implementing good, correct, and wise public policies in various fields.[36] In the postwar era, therefore, political scientists brought not only new realism about political power to the field but also new definitions of roles and responsibilities for career and appointed administrators, particularly those at the top, in the policy-making realm. By the late 1960s and early 1970s new schools and departments devoted to studying policy emerged, mainly stimulated by leading figures from political science such as Aaron Wildavsky, Yehezkel Dror, Graham Allison, Amitai Etzioni, and Harold Lasswell. For many leading political scientists, administration became entirely subsumed under the new categories of policy and power.

"Bureaucracy," "Systems Theory," and "Organization Theory" from Sociology

Sociologists were equally influential in enriching postwar public administration literature in many areas. In its broadest sense, sociology concerns all the general problems of human existence: the causes and effects of social change, as well as the narrower concerns of class, power, status, roles, caste, occupations, and community. For public administration after World War II, sociologists fundamentally offered a new lens from which to view, analyze, and define the world of public administration. Max Weber's concept of bureaucracy was translated from the German and spread throughout American universities by writers such as H. H. Gerth, C. Wright

Mills, Reinhard Bendix, Peter M. Blau, Marshall W. Meyer, Talcott Parsons, and Michel Crozier.[37] The concept of bureaucracy became widely accepted throughout public administration circles as a significant advance for understanding both the whole of bureaucracy as well as the elements of modern government. While not without its critics, Weberian analysis became accepted as a true, correct, and fundamental conceptual building block pertaining to defining basic features of modern government, its structure, and its historical and cultural contexts.

Systems theory, as a conceptual tool for understanding administrative actions and activities, also found widespread appeal within the ranks of academic administrative scholars. Developed from sociological studies, systems models became a useful methodology for conceptualizing about public administration. Especially the writings of Philip Selznick were seminal in thinking about systems in connection with his study of the role of the Tennessee Valley Authority as a public institution with the Tennessee Valley Region and relationship to the total social system within that region.[38] Selznick's work visualized this formal public organization as a system in shaping the adaptive responsive to its own survival and development. Selznick coined the term "cooptation" as one type of adaptive response for ensuring organizational maintenence and growth. Increasingly, sociologists developed more sophisticated and more complex theories of organizational systems and their behavior that enriched and broadened the literature of public administration. As these theories multiplied, organization theory often became a standard required subject for graduate students in public administration that emphasized the diversity of models and approaches drawn largely, if not exclusively, from sociological research.

"Case Studies" from History

History has long served as a fruitful source for understanding administrative institutions, their development, and their dynamics. Indeed, many of the early American academic studies of administration were essentially case studies of various agencies or units of government and their practices, such as "capture and record" efforts in the 1930s. In the postwar era, a more conscious, systematic, and deliberate utilization of historical case studies was made for training professionals for the public service. Along the lines of business, law, or medical schools, public administration cases were developed for preparing professional students for public service careers. The aim was to bring into the classroom more "realistic" professionalized training for public administrations.

By the late 1940s, Harvard began a large-scale, systematic case-writing program focused on specific historical episodes of administration, objectively described, and normally focusing on a decision or choice involving some significant administrative event. The Inter-University Case Program (ICP) was founded in 1951 with Ford Foundation support and through the effective leadership of Harold Stein, who edited the first ICP text, *Public Administration and Policy Development* (1952).[39] It brought fresh, well-written, and realistic cases to public administration classrooms. The Stein text, as well as the more than 200 ICP cases generated since World War II, offered students a slice of administrative reality by means of a close description of the complexities, dilemmas, and options confronting administrators in actual working situations.

The case method became an important creative innovation in the field and demonstrated the diversity and complexity of modern-day administration activities. No easy solutions were often given or apparent in these cases, thus inviting the complaint that cases were "messages without a moral." However, in the hands of some of the ablest students of the field, such as Arthur Maass, Frederick C. Mosher, and Graham Allison,[40] the case method was used for theory building in such diverse administrative topics as decision making, governmental reorganizations, and budgeting.

"Decision Sciences," "Management Processes," and "Computer Technologies" from Business

As outlined earlier in this chapter, public administration in the twentieth century drew for its original doctrines on a rich heritage of business administration through scientific management doctrines à la Frederick Taylor and his followers. Postwar public administration for the development of the global professional technocracy continued to draw on this vital strand of influence. The older prewar three Es—efficiency, economy, and effectiveness—that had dominated early business management thinking gave way to much broader, more sophisticated analyses of managerial processes. Indeed, interest in the first two Es tended to fade as the accent by scholars in this field was placed increasingly on the third E of effectiveness in both public and business administration by writers, particularly Peter Drucker in his popular text, *The Effective Executive* and Fred E. Fiedler in *A Theory of Leadership Effectiveness*.[41]

Conceptual terms like principles of management also declined in popular usage in business management circles and sounded old-fashioned and dated. Newer scholars spoke of managerial processes and decision sciences. Herbert Simon's ideas became especially popular and influential in both business and public administration in stressing the application and validity of scientific decision methodologies to generic administration issues. His decision-making schema, which emphasized a generic approach for understanding and conceptualizing about public and private sector decision making, found widespread appeal. Simon was an early and highly visible proponent of the use of computer technologies in administration. Computer use fundamentally changed the way administrators thought about public sector administration and the way they conducted administrative affairs in government. By the 1970s computers and information technology classes became common in most public administration programs, as did work in decision sciences and management.

Public Finance, Budgeting, and Fiscal Policy from Economics

Postwar public administration looked toward the discipline of economics for research, training, and skill development involving a wide range of topics associated especially in matters concerning public finance, budgeting, and fiscal administration. The Keynesian Revolution in the 1930s and the passage of the Employment Act (1946) brought economics and economists into prominent and permanent relationships with the American public administration community.

Public administrators in the postwar era increasingly turned to economists and economic thinking for answers to such issues as how to administer taxes fairly, efficiently, and equitably; how to put together budgets in order to manage, direct, and control public organizations and to use wisely and well scarce community resources; determining the appropriate methods for forecasting future revenues and expenditures in government; and determining the alternatives for raising revenues and reducing costs in public sector operations. As public revenues and expenditures took over increasing shares of the gross national product, as well as determining state and local economic growth rates, public administration students and scholars were increasingly attracted to writings by economists such as Arthur Smithies, Jesse Burkhead, Charles

Schultze, Charles Hitch, Walter Heller, Arthur Okun, and Richard Musgrave, who attempted to wrestle with such questions.

In a much broader sense, economics as a discipline provided public administration as a field of study with a far better comprehension of notions of the exchange of scarce economic resources throughout society and the seminal roles government plays in shaping such exchanges. The various editions of Paul Samuelson's basic text, *Economics*, as well as such works as Arthur Smithies' *The Budgetary Process in the United States*, Jesse Burkhead's *Government Budgeting*, and Robert Dahl's and Charles E. Lindblom's *Politics, Economics and Welfare*, demonstrated for students in administration the critical importance of the links between economics and politics for setting public agendas.[42]

The "Informal Group," "The Individual in Organizations," and "Human Relations Skills" from Social Psychology Disciplines

The study of individuals, groups inside organizations, and human relations skills was infused into public administration largely from psychology and social psychology disciplines. Research on this subject began before World War II. The Hawthorne studies in the 1920s and 1930s, conducted by the Harvard Business School at the Western Electric Plant at Hawthorne, Illinois, near Chicago and directed by Elton Mayo and a team of prominent researchers, began large-scale research into this field.[43] Their intensive investigations into topics of personnel morale and motivation conclusively demonstrated for both business and public administration students that there were clear limits to the effectiveness of the application of rational approaches of scientific management. In brief, these researchers discovered, in the words of Fritz Roethlisberger, Mayo's principal associate throughout the Hawthorne experiments, the "great illumination"—namely, that the feelings, sentiments, and beliefs of humans and informal groups within organizations affected productivity and performance, as much, if not more so, than did rational, scientific approaches to management. In short, informal groups and human sentiments were real and powerful forces that managers, public or private, had to recognize and deal with inside organizations.

The human relations movement infused postwar public administration with numerous new concepts, ideas, and theories that directly and indirectly shaped thinking about public personnel, human resources planning, and public service management. The general emphasis of these approaches, when applied to public administration, placed priorities on understanding human problems of complex organization and the effective use of people, human groups, and public service personnel for enhancing overall organizational effectiveness and performance. Writings by scholars in the 1950s and 1960s, some who were involved with the Hawthorne research, such as Chris Argyris, Frederick Herzberg, Douglas McGregor, George Homans, and Rensis Likert, enriched public administration's knowledge base in such diverse topics as how leadership can be effectively exercised in government; what the relationship is between morale and productivity in the workplace; what factors encourage positive human relationships within organizations; why informal groups are formed and how they influence the formal administrative system; what generates conflicts and promotes cooperation within organizations; and what stimulates personal growth or stagnation on the job.

Comparative Public Administration and New Global Perspectives

The broadening and enrichment of American public administration came from the outside as well during the postwar era. The new powerful leadership roles that the United States exerted after World War II suddenly thrust Americans willy-nilly overseas through assignments in the military, the United Nations, foreign assistance programs, business, private foundation, and nonprofit work. Prewar public administration, both academics and practitioners, had largely focused their work and study at home, but postwar students of the field quickly found themselves engaged by the thousands in work and travel abroad. Many were woefully unprepared from their backgrounds and training in the United States for their new international roles, but most were eager to learn from these foreign experiences. And they did learn a great deal that fundamentally changed the way they looked at and practiced public administration.

One of the most impressive lessons for public administration scholars was the need for greater knowledge and research in comparative public administration as a basis for undertaking new international responsibilities. The comparative administration research movement, which actually began in World War II with postwar military occupation of enemy territories, accelerated particularly with postwar technical assistance programs such as Point Four and later

Third World foreign-aid programs through the U.S. Agency for International Development. Especially, with initial funding from the Ford Foundation in the late 1950s, a Comparative Administration Group was formed (which lasted until 1973) with its own journal, conferences, and an identifiable group of distinguished scholars led by Fred Riggs, Ferrel Heady, and others.[44] The lasting significance of such widespread interest in comparative administration by prominent administrative scholars fostered new perspectives and knowledge about public administration throughout postwar academic American public administration. The infusion of comparative ideas into American public administration theory and practice stimulated new questions and raised important issues about America's own administrative theories and practice. Questions were raised particularly about the feasibility and appropriateness of transferring American administrative ideas and techniques overseas. The comparative movement encouraged the field of public administration within the United States to take an inventory and make a self-examination of its own central values and methodologies which optimistically many believed to be applicable *everywhere*.

New Professional Technologies, Techniques, and Specialties

Public administration in the postwar era was significantly enhanced as well by the work of various professional programs, scientific schools, and professional associations in many fields: business, law, social work, accounting, information sciences, engineering, medical, public health, and education. These and other advanced graduate academic programs and career specializations spawned numerous new technologies and techniques—both hard and soft—which emerged from research for advancing these professional fields. Such technologies profoundly changed the way America conducted its public administration in the postwar decades. The innovation and application of the computer alone transformed the way administrative work was performed in government: data manipulation, record keeping, information sorting, storage, and retrieval. The computer opened up new ways of arranging and using the work force, the workplace, and even thinking about the fundamental nature of public programs and their problems through model building, testing, and data analysis. The creation and application of the computer can also be credited with stimulating the growth of new fields of study such as operations research, statistical analysis, decision making, systems research, game theory, and simulation techniques—all of which today are fundamental analytical methodologies widely utilized and studied by public administration students and practitioners in the United States. Other breakthrough technologies and techniques were invented in the postwar era by professionals in numerous fields unrelated to public administration, such as the discovery of the Salk vaccine, which virtually ended the dreaded threat of crippling poliomyelitis, or the fluoridation of public water systems, which reduced tooth decay dramatically by the 1980s. These also profoundly changed administrative practices and priorities for society.

The Sixties and Seventies: "Anti-State" and "Stateless" Doctrines in Public Administration Thought

If the acronym POSDCORB symbolized pre–World War II state-building doctrines, postwar American public administration was characterized by a loose heterodoxy of various multidisciplinary university studies. This heterodoxy emerged and flourished by the 1960s, responding to the governing necessities of the global professional technocracy. A vast global professional technocracy required a diversity of talent, tools, and techniques to make it function. The postwar field of public administration therefore became shaped in the very image of the new state—the global professional technocracy—it served and sustained. The expert who knew and applied diverse skills of computers, systems analysis, program budgets, PPBS (planning, programming, budgeting systems), or policy science became the hero in this new state system.

However, the late 1960s and early 1970s witnessed, in the words of Samuel P. Huntington, a "democratic surge" characteristic of past nineteenth-century historic eras of Jeffersonian-Jacksonian democracy and Progressive reform where there was a vital reassertion in all phases of American life of democratic idealism. As Huntington notes, the era reflected:

> a general challenge to the existing system of authority, public and private. In one form or another, this challenge manifested itself in the family, the university, business, public and private associations, politics, the governmental bureaucracy and the military service. People no longer felt the same compulsion to obey those whom they had previously considered superior to themselves in age, rank, status, expertise, character or talents.

Within most organizations, discipline eased and differences in status became blurred. Each group claimed its rights to participate equally—and perhaps more equally in the decision making which affected itself. More precisely, in American society, authority had been commonly based on: organizational position, economic wealth, specialized expertise, legal competence, or electoral representation. Authority based on hierarchy, expertise and wealth all obviously ran counter to the democratic and equalitarian temper of the times.[45]

While the reasons for the sudden democratic surge were complex and still remain unclear, Huntington points to a number of significant consequences of the democratic surge:

1. Expansion in the size and scope of governmental activity, though with a concomitant decline in governmental authority;
2. Increased public interest and concern about government, but coupled with a sharp decline in public trust and confidence toward government;
3. Increased public activism in politics, yet with a commensurate decay in the traditional two-party system;
4. A noticeable shift away from coalitions supporting government to those in opposition to it.[46]

Characteristic of this period was a popular philosophical treatise by John Rawls, *A Theory of Justice* (1971), that defined justice in largely egalitarian terms. In the fields of history and politics, Arthur Schlesinger, Jr.'s *Imperial Presidency* (1973) found a wide and enthusiastic post-Watergate audience with an argument directed against the flagrant abuses of strong executive institutions in American government. Also, egalitarian themes found their way into economics, particularly in E. F. Schumacher's popular tract, *Small Is Beautiful* (1973), which proposed a more equitable distribution of the goods and services in society, directed toward, in the words of its subtitle, *As If People Mattered*.

Populist attacks on the administrative state and a reassertion of century-old "stateless" doctrines at the same time were evidenced in the literature of public administration. *Toward a New Public Administration: The Minnowbrook Perspective* (1971), edited by Frank Marini, consciously sought new intellectual foundations for the field.[47] These younger, mostly under-30 scholars argued for fresh beginnings for public administration largely based on ideals of participation, consensus, sharing, decentralization, trust, and even love of mankind. Their writings were implicitly and explicitly hostile toward such traditional state-building doctrines as POSDCORB and techno-professional expertise as represented in systems analysis and economic models. With varying degrees of accents and emphases, this and many other texts (such as H. George Frederickson's *Neighborhood Control in the 1970s*, 1973; Warren H. Schmidt's *Organizational Frontiers and Human Values*, 1970; Eugene P. Dworin's and Robert H. Simmons' *From Amoral to Humane Bureaucracy*, 1972; and George Berkley's *The Administrative Revolution: Notes on the Passing of Organization Man*, 1971 pressed for increased local autonomy, concern for humane values, flexibility in organizational structures, and a new focus on individual growth, human development, and personal freedom within organizations. In short, these authors sought a loosening of traditional state structures and state-building administration practices, possibly a return to the pre–twentieth-century Jeffersonian communal visionary ideals of statelessness.

The most popular, widely discussed, and controversial public administration scholarly treatise in the 1970s was probably Vincent Ostrom's *The Intellectual Crisis in American Public Administration* (1973, rev. 1974) that frontally assaulted the POSDCORB doctrines, which the author referred to as "the Wilson-Weber paradigm."[48] Ostrom proposed a replacement paradigm, which he called "democratic administration." In reality, Ostrom's democratic administration paradigm attracted broad interest from students and scholars in public administration precisely because of its forceful attacks on traditional normative state-building and state-maintenance doctrines within twentieth-century public administration. Ostrom in his treatise, *The Intellectual Crisis*, directly challenged the Weber-Wilson model of "single-centered administrative power," "hierarchical administration," and "separation of politics from administration." Instead, his democratic administration replacement paradigm favored diverse "democratic decision making centers," "popular participation in administration," and "dispersed administrative authority based upon structures of overlapping jurisdiction and fragmented organizations." Here was the revival of Jeffersonian republican enthusiasm for the village values of nineteenth-century grass-roots democracy, the New England Town Meeting, and, hence, the "stateless" society. The state dissolved as a recognizable entity in the Ostromian schema of "public choice" (which in reality was "private choice") where radical individualism replaced the state as the focal point for decision making.

In the 1970s the normative doctrines undergirding American

public administration seemed to be reverting backward toward a simpler world of the agrarian past. The question was whether American administrative theory could return to nineteenth-century anti-state and stateless thinking in the late twentieth century. Could such nostalgic romanticism reconstructed from distant American republican ideals flourish in the modern era? Would statelessness become something more permanent, an enduring feature on the landscape of American administrative theory in the contemporary era? Or was it merely a passing bit of Rousseauianism in the modern age?

By the 1970s, the world of administrative doctrines became so clouded and confused with so many competing paradigms, models, and concepts that many agreed with Ostrom's assertion that the field was facing anomie and malaise, "an intellectual crisis." Though few in public administration swallowed wholesale his prescription of "public choice," Ostrom's "crisis" diagnosis seemed convincing.

The next chapter examines the contours of modern American public administration thought from the perspective of how the accumulation of these various competing twentieth-century doctrines and dogmas look from the standpoint of contemporary texts, teaching, and training. Has the field moved beyond "crisis"? Where is "it" today?

Notes

1. For an interesting discussion of the informal rules of thumb that guided early nineteenth-century American administration, see Matthew A. Crenson, *The Federal Machine: Beginnings of Bureaucracy in Jacksonian America* (Baltimore: Johns Hopkins University Press, 1975), especially chapters five and six; or in business administration during the same era, Alfred D. Chandler, Jr., chapter 1, *The Visible Hand: The Managerial Revolution in American Business* (Cambridge, Massachusetts: Harvard University Press, 1977).
2. For a useful account of the sort of political science education dominant during this period, read Dwight Waldo, "Political Science: Tradition, Discipline, Profession, Science, Enterprise," in Fred I. Greenstein and Nelson Polsby, *Handbook of Political Science*, vol. 1 (Reading, Massachusetts: Addison-Wesley, 1968).
3. Frank J. Goodnow, *Politics and Administration* (New York: Macmillan, 1900), p. 16.
4. Frederick C. Mosher, *Democracy and the Public Service*, 2d ed. (New York: Oxford University Press, 1982), pp. 66–73.

5. Henri Fayol, "The Administrative Theory in the State," in Luther Gulick and Lyndall Urwick, *Papers on the Science of Administration* (New York: Institute of Public Administration, 1937), pp. 99–114.
6. This no-nonsense, let's-get-the-job-done attitude can be found in most of the writings of the early administrative writers, but it is especially pronounced in Frederick W. Taylor, *The Principles of Scientific Management* (New York: Norton, 1911, reprinted in 1967).
7. Ibid., p. 11.
8. For the best two accounts of this early intellectual history of public administration, see Jane S. Dahlberg, *The New York Bureau of Municipal Research: Pioneer in Government Administration* (New York: New York University Press, 1966) and Dwight Waldo, *The Administrative State: A Study of the Political Theory of American Public Administration* (New York: Ronald Press, 1948) recently republished with a new preface (New York: Holmes & Meier, 1982).
9. Richard S. Childs, "The Principles Underlying the City-Manager Plan," in Frederick C. Mosher, ed., *Basic Literature of American Public Administration, 1787–1950* (New York: Holmes & Meier, 1981), p. 97.
10. Louis Brownlow, "The New Role of the Public Administrator," *National Municipal Review*, vol. 23 (May 1934), pp. 248–251.
11. Chester A. Newland, *Public Administration and Community: Realism and Practice of Ideals* (McLean, Virginia: Public Administration Service, 1984), as well as Frederick C. Mosher, ed., *American Public Administration: Past, Present, Future* (University: University of Alabama Press, 1975). For an excellent recent discussion of this era related specifically to the birth of the American Society for Public Administration, read Darrell Pugh, *Looking Back, Moving Forward: A Half-Century Celebration of Public Administration and ASPA* (Washington, D.C.: American Society for Public Administration, 1988).
12. Leonard D. White, *Introduction to the Study of Public Administration* (New York: Macmillan, 1939), p. 6.
13. Ibid.
14. Ibid., p. ix.
15. Ibid., p. 6.
16. Ibid., p. 16.
17. Ibid., p. ix.
18. Ibid., p. 17.
19. Luther Gulick, "Notes on the Theory of Organization," in Gulick and Urwick, p. 13.
20. Ibid., p. 14.
21. "Report of the President's Committee on Administrative Management (The Brownlow Committee, 1937)," in Frederick C. Mosher, *Basic Documents of American Public Administration, 1776–1950* (New York: Holmes & Meier, 1976), p. 135. For the best history of the Brownlow report, see Barry D. Karl, *Executive Reorganization and Reform in the New Deal* (Chicago: University of Chicago Press, 1963), and for an excellent recent extended commentary, read Frederick C. Mosher, ed.,

"The President Needs Help" (Lanham, Maryland: University Press of America, 1988).

22. Herbert A. Simon, *Administrative Behavior* (New York: Macmillan, 1947).
23. James W. Fesler, "A Review," *Journal of Politics,* vol. 10 (February 1948), pp. 187–189.
24. Simon, p. 69.
25. Dwight Waldo, *The Administrative State: A Study of the Political Theory of American Public Administration* (New York: Ronald Press, 1948).
26. For an extensive commentary on Waldo's life and ideas, see Brack Brown and Richard Stillman, *A Search for Public Administration* (College Station: Texas A&M Press, 1986). Also helpful on surveying Waldo as well as Simon and other major founders' ideas is Brian R. Fry, *Mastering Public Administration: From Max Weber to Dwight Waldo* (Chatham, New Jersey: Chatham House, 1989).
27. Paul H. Appleby, *Policy and Administration* (University: University of Alabama Press, 1949).
28. Appleby's influence on the intellectual and institutional development of the field was considerable and deserves a full-length book treatment, although the introductory essay by Roscoe Martin is useful in Roscoe C. Martin, ed., *Public Administration and Democracy: Essays in Honor of Paul H. Appleby* (New York: Syracuse University Press, 1965).
29. Appleby, p. 19.
30. Ibid., p. 25.
31. James W. Fesler, "Public Administration and the Social Sciences: 1946 to 1960," in Mosher, *American Public Administration,* p. 101.
32. For a discussion of the doctoral research and the development of the Doctor of Public Administration, see Richard Stillman and Jeremy Plant, "The DPA Degree: A Source of Research Professionals or Professional Leaders," *International Journal of Public Administration,* vol. 7, no. 2 (Spring 1985), pp. 207–239.
33. Dwight Waldo, "Scope of the Theory of Public Administration," *Theory and Practice of Public Administration: Scope, Objectives and Methods,* monograph no. 8 (American Academy of Political and Social Science, 1968), pp. 1–26.
34. Norton Long, "Power and Administration," *Public Administration Review,* vol. 9, no. 3 (Autumn 1949), p. 257.
35. Ibid.
36. While "policy" was a term long in use in public administration, it began to be used by practitioners and academicians with much greater frequency in the late 1960s. Indeed, entire schools and programs at that time added "policy" to their names. Perhaps an influential essay that focused attention on this subject was Yehezkel Dror, "Policy Analysts: A New Professional Role in Government Service," *Public Administration Review,* vol. 27, no. 3 (September 1967), pp. 197–203.
37. Especially important for popularizing Weber's ideas in America were H. H. Gerth and C. Wright Mills, eds., *From Max Weber Essays in Soci-*

ology (New York: Oxford University Press, 1946); Reinhard Bendix, *Max Weber: An Intellectual Portrait* (New York: Doubleday, 1960); Peter M. Blau and Marshall W. Meyer, *Bureaucracy in Modern Society* (New York: Random House, 1956); Talcott Parsons, *The Social System* (New York: Free Press, 1951); and Michael Crozier, *The Bureaucratic Phenomenon* (Chicago: University of Chicago Press, 1964).

38. Philip Selznick, *TVA and the Grass Roots: A Study of the Sociology of Formal Organization* (Berkeley: University of California Press, 1949).

39. Harold Stein, ed., *Public Administration and Policy Development: A Case Book* (New York: Harcourt, Brace, 1952). For the background and development of the case method, see Edwin A. Bock, ed., *Essays on the Case Method* (Syracuse, New York: Inter-University Case Program, 1962).

40. Arthur Maass, *The Army Engineers and the Nation's Rivers* (Cambridge, Massachusetts: Harvard University Press, 1951); Frederick C. Mosher, *Governmental Reorganizations: Cases and Commentary* (Indianapolis: Bobbs-Merrill, 1967); and Graham Allison, *Essence of Decision: Explaining the Cuban Missile Crisis* (Boston: Little, Brown, 1971).

41. Peter Drucker, *The Effective Executive* (New York: Harper & Row, 1967) and Fred E. Fiedler, *A Theory of Leadership Effectiveness* (New York: McGraw-Hill, 1967).

42. In the 1950s and well into the 1960s, the most popular and influential budgeting texts in the field of public administration were Paul Samuelson's *Economics*, 13th ed. (New York: McGraw-Hill, 1989); Arthur Smithies, *The Budgetary Process in the United States* (New York: McGraw-Hill, 1955); Jesse Burkhead, *Government Budgeting* (New York: Wiley, 1956); and Robert Dahl and Charles E. Lindblom, *Politics, Economics and Welfare* (1953).

43. The best work summarizing the Hawthorne experiments is Fritz Roethlisberger and W. J. Dickson, *Management and the Worker* (Cambridge, Massachusetts: Harvard University Press, 1941); for an interesting retrospective on Hawthorne, refer to "An Interview with Fritz Roethlisberger," *Organizational Dynamics*, vol. 1 (Autumn 1972), pp. 31–45.

44. For a concise history of this comparative administration movement and the development of CAG, read Ferrel Heady, chapter 1, *Public Administration: A Comparative Perspective*, 3d ed. (New York: Marcel Dekker, 1985).

45. Samuel P. Huntington, "The United States," in Michael Crozier, ed., *The Crisis of Democracy* (New York: New York University Press, 1975), pp. 74–75.

46. Ibid.

47. Frank Marini, ed., *Toward a New Public Administration: The Minnowbrook Perspective* (Scranton, Pennsylvania: Chandler, 1971). Refer to Chapter One, notes no. 1, for additional citations on Minnowbrook.

48. Vincent Ostrom, *The Intellectual Crisis in American Public Administration* (University: University of Alabama Press, 1973).

CHAPTER SIX

Current Trends in American Public Administration Thought: The Drive to Specialize in Texts, Teaching, and Training

Americans always display a clear, free, original, and inventive power of mind.

ALEXIS DE TOCQUEVILLE
Democracy in America

How does public administration thought appear today in America? What are its central doctrines, ideas, and theories as taught and expressed in the contemporary setting? Have they advanced or changed significantly from previous twentieth-century doctrines outlined in the last chapter? Or are there important continuities and similarities now with themes from the past?

This chapter explores some of the prominent intellectual features of modern American public administration theory as it actually is represented by present-day basic textbooks, higher education graduate degree programs, and in-service training methods used throughout the United States. It will be argued that each of these three approaches—texts, teaching, and training—reflects important philosophical points of view, intellectual assumptions, and ways of thinking about the nature and substance of the field. They also may be seen as a useful gauge of where the field is today—and, possibly, where it may be heading tomorrow.

How Recent Basic Texts Define the Field: A Plethora of Voices

More than four dozen general public administration textbooks are now available for teaching students and practitioners about the subject according to *Books in Print, 1989–1990*. Often these textbooks are used in beginning classes as a basic introduction for further study at an advanced level. Usually the opening chapter of each of these books is devoted to defining, or attempting to identify, what the subject is all about. Even a quick glance at a few of these definitions from opening chapters in prominent introductory texts shows a lack of consensus about what is the identity of modern public administration:

> Public Administration is the production of goods and services designed to serve the needs of citizen-consumers.
>
> Marshall Dimock, Gladys Dimock, and Douglas Fox
> *Public Administration* (Fifth Edition, 1983)

> Much of the time, when "government" does something, it is the employees who really take action. They are the people who actually pick up the garbage, inspect goods, collect taxes, write traffic tickets, and perform the countless other acts involved in "the work of government"—public administration.
>
> Rayburn Barton and William L. Chappell, Jr.
> *Public Administration: The Work of Government* (1985)

> Traditionally, public administration is thought of as the accomplishing side of government. It is supposed to comprise all those activities involved in carrying out the policies of elected officials and some activities associated with the development of those policies. Public administration is . . . all that comes after the last campaign promise and election-night cheer.
>
> Grover Starling
> *Managing the Public Sector* (Third Edition, 1985)

Public Administration:
1. Is a cooperative group effort in a public setting.
2. Covers all three branches—executive, legislative, and judicial—and their interrelationships.
3. Has an important role in the formulation of public policy, and is thus part of the political process.
4. Is different in significant ways from private administration.
5. Is closely associated with numerous private groups and individuals in providing services to the community.

Felix A. Nigro and Lloyd G. Nigro
Modern Public Administration (Seventh Edition, 1989)

Public administration is the use of managerial, political, and legal theories and processes to fulfill legislative, executive, and judicial governmental mandates for the provision of regulatory and service functions for the society as a whole or for some segments of it.

David H. Rosenbloom
Public Administration (Second Edition, 1989)

Public administration is a broad-ranging and amorphous combination of theory and practice. Its purpose is to promote a superior understanding of government and its relationship with the society it governs, as well as to encourage public policies more responsive to social needs. It seeks to institute managerial practices attuned to effectiveness, efficiency, and the fulfillment of deeper human requisites of the citizenry.

Nicholas Henry
Public Administration and Public Affairs (Fourth Edition, 1989)

These attempts to define public administration by several authors of basic texts during the past decade seem to identify the field with (1) the executive branch of government (yet it is related in several ways to the legislative and judicial branches as well), (2) the formulation and implementation of public policies, (3) involvement in a considerable range of problems concerning human behavior and cooperative human effort to perform the basic tasks of government; (4) a field that can be differentiated in several ways from private administration but also overlaps with private administration; (5) concern with making "public" goods and services; and (6) concern with both theory and practice.

Note also, however, how different these six contemporary texts emphasize various aspects of the administrative enterprise in their definitions.

1. *Economic*   The first sees public administration as essentially an economic activity much like business but centering on the production of public goods and services.

2. *Institutional*   The second views the topic more or less as an institutional process, focusing on gaining cooperative group effort, largely as a means for undertaking public action(s), but different from private enterprise in significant ways.

3. *Personnel*   The third deals with public administration as largely personnel involved in "the work of government."

4. *Accomplishing*   The fourth considers the subject as virtually everything associated with the "accomplishing side of government" but also sees it as concerned with the selection of policy choices as well.

5. *Processes*   The fifth interprets the field as essentially institutional processes, or a combination of three interrelated governmental activities—managerial, political, and legal—necessary in order to fulfill formal legislative, executive, and judicial governmental mandates.

6. *Theory and Practice*   The last book sees administration as a combination of theory and practice that mixes management processes with the achievement of normative values in society.

Although they have some important similarities, these basic texts seem to reflect, at least on the surface, a staggering array of approaches to the field. They look at the same phenomenon in society, public administration, yet each text defines the topic from different angles or points of view, representing distinct value accents and specialized emphases on certain aspects of the administrative enterprise. How can one make sense out of this apparent diversity and lack of common outlook today in the field?

A Closer Look at a Comparison between a Present and a Past Popular Introductory Text

By scanning the table of contents of two popular textbooks in the field—both titled *Public Administration*, the former a present-day text and the latter five decades old—one can sense even more clearly the treatment of certain familiar themes, yet also new directions, perspectives, and approaches to this subject.

Public Administration in America, 3d ed.
by George J. Gordon[1]

PART ONE / INTRODUCTION

1 Approaching the Study of Public Administration
What Is Public Administration?
Principal Structures of the National Executive Branch
State and Local Executive Structures
Explaining the Growth of Government Bureaucracy
Public and Private Administration: Similarities and
    Differences
Dilemmas in the Study of Public Administration
A Word about This Book

2 The Context of Public Administration: The Political System, Values, and Social Change
The Political System and Government Bureaucracy
Political Values
Administrative Values
Social Change and Public Administration
The Changing Value Context and Bureaucracy under
    Pressure

PART TWO / THE POLITICAL SETTING OF PUBLIC ADMINISTRATION

3 Bureaucratic Politics and Bureaucratic Power
The Political Context of Bureaucratic Power
Foundations of Power: Political Support
Foundations of Power: Bureaucratic Expertise
The Politics of Organizational Structure
Bureaucrats As Politicians: Subsystem Politics in America
Bureaucratic Power and Political Accountability: More
    Questions Than Answers

4 Chief Executives and Bureaucratic Leadership
Chief Executive-Bureaucratic Linkages
Presidential Leadership: Strengths and Weaknesses
The Office of Governor: Continuity and Change
Mayors, City Managers, and County Executives:
    Variations on Recurring Themes
Commonalities and Differences in Leadership Resources

Both textbooks, though roughly fifty years apart, appear to have several themes in common. Both at the outset try to define public administration as a "generalizable" and "teachable" subject; outline its historic development in America; discuss the key bread-and-butter administrative processes such as organization, budgeting, management, and personnel practices; and consider contemporary issues such as collective bargaining and regulation. Note also that there seems to be agreement between the two that the field should be largely executive-centered and action-oriented. The appropriate definition and coverage of the subject according to the first text is:

> Public administration may be defined as all processes, organizations, and individuals (the latter acting in official positions and roles) associated with carrying out laws and other rules adopted or issued by legislatures, executives, and courts.[3]

Hence, much of its central focus flows from that perspective. The bulk of its chapters, especially Parts Three and Four, pertain to the various aspects of bureaucratic processes and institutions, largely within the executive branch, for "carrying out laws and rules." The first text gives considerably more attention than the second text to

150   *Preface to Public Administration*

the surrounding environmental influence on public executives within the administrative system. The author focuses, for example, on topics of normative democratic values and the socioeconomic and political impacts of the broader society on the administrative processes in Chapters 2 and 15. "The Future" is also explored as well as topics of "Leadership," "Bureaucratic Politics and Power," "Intergovernmental Relations," "Organization Theory," "Decision Making," and "Dynamics of Organization." The first text also makes a more deliberate and conscious use of recent organization and bureaucratic theory throughout the book as a basis for studying the field. Indeed, theory as *theory* per se for knowing and comprehending this field seems more prominently featured.

In contrast, the older text's definition of public administration, as discussed in the last chapter, serves up a sharper, more rigid POSDCORB orientation:

> The immediate objective of the art of public administration is the most efficient utilization of resources at the disposal of officials and employees. Good management seeks the elimination of waste, the conservation and effective use of men and materials, and the protection of the welfare and interests of employees.[4]

With this definition, the author's focus seems more applied, more instrumental, and less consciously theoretical. Chapters throughout consistently stress getting the job done. Executive action is deemed vital for using "internal institutional sources" for promoting efficient use of public resources for "state purposes." Such chapter titles as "The Quest for Unity: Departmental Organization and Management," "Budget Procedures and Practice," "Promotions, Efficiency Records and Discipline," and "Position Classification" underscore that utilitarian, prescriptive perspective. There is a marked emphasis on the *possibilities* for efficient use of internal resources as opposed to the appreciation of the *constraints* in the external political environment for building the American state. Indeed, the word "state" figures prominently in White's book, unlike Gordon's. And as a consequence, a greater attention is placed on lower "line" and "staff" personnel activities, as well as on "middle managers" and "headquarters-field" concerns in order to portray a more complete picture, top-to-bottom, of state administrative functions.

In contrast to earlier general public administration texts published in the immediate pre– and post–World War II eras, the 1980s text offers a remarkably more descriptive, analytical emphasis on how external socioeconomic and political forces shape administration. There is less emphasis on internal institutional processes and formal administrative structures for state-building purposes. There is also more tendency to view the world of administration from the top: from governor's, mayor's, county and city manager's offices.

The swift pace of change since World War II has meant that the study of administration has become more diversified, complex, and open to outside forces; particularly, it is no longer dominated by the one best way orthodoxy aimed at promoting state-building efficiency via formal, internal structural processes. Rather, a heterodoxy of specialized approaches and methods is recognized as many best ways of doing the job of public administration. The field seems to be open to a wider range of visions, to many definitions, with differing objectives, and to numerous acceptable approaches, and to be receptive to multiple external influences in a rapidly changing environment. Diversity, flexibility, fluidity of ideas, less rigidity, openness to changing arrangements, competing values, and external pressures characterize modern-day public administration textbook thinking. However, unlike the White book in which POSDCORB acts as a sort of intellectual glue in order to provide some consistency and to integrate its chapters, the Gordon text, devoid of such a clear-cut, overarching paradigm, appears more or less as merely a collection of discrete specialized chapters, perhaps individually "teachable," but not necessarily adding up to a generalizable whole. Each chapter seems to sum up distinctive knowledge skills, understandings, and terminology that could stand alone as an essay about a field of study—such as "leadership," "budgeting," "personnel," and so on.

Other Recent, More Specialized, Basic Textbooks: A Growth Industry in the Field?

Not only are there more general texts on the market today than ever before, reflecting more diversity of points of view with frequently more varied intellectual assumptions about what *is* American public administration, but also there are more specialized basic texts on the market. These more specialized introductory books are sometimes not even labeled "public administration," but, in fact, they very much describe this field but under such headings as "educational administration," "rural administration," "health management," "regulatory administration," "information systems management," "intergovernmental management," and "police supervision" or generic policy titles such as "making health policy work," "managing urban public policy," "future defense policies," "public organizations and policy," and "public policy making in America." Often such texts offer very distinctive perspectives, are sharper and more well-defined, and are especially targeted for more specialized audiences, in either a single occupational or policy field, compared with the two generalist texts by Gordon and White.

Also there are several new specialized textbooks that take a single methodological approach to the field. One text that explicitly follows a single methodology, perhaps reminiscent of White's POSDCORB-based text, is Cole Blease Graham, Jr. and Steven W. Hays, *Managing the Public Organization* (1986).[5] This book, as its title implies, is for those managing or intending to manage public organizations. In other words, it offers a useful overview for those who operate inside government, particularly line managers. The text states in its introduction that it is grounded on the generic view, that "management functions . . . are common to all organizational executives."[6] Hence, although it is explicitly about *public* administration, the authors study public administration by consciously focusing on "internal management" and by describing general managerial functions common to both business and public enterprises. Their model is the one identified many years ago by Luther Gulick's acronym POSDCORB: planning, organizing, staffing, directing, controlling, reporting, and budgeting.

Drawing on the 1937 Gulick formulation, the authors stress themes of more efficient, rational bureaucratic action but with use of contemporary examples and literature to bring the POSDCORB methodology up to date. Business values of economy and efficiency for the achievement of explicit democratic goals are underscored in this text. The emphasis is mainly on getting the job accomplished—that is, managing the mission(s) properly, efficiently and effectively—or what the authors view as the central activities and tasks of public administrators. Under each of the POSDCORB categories, there is significantly widened and updated coverage to include newer methodologies and approaches. "Planning," for example, covers the broader concepts of policy analysis; "staffing" includes human resources; and "reporting" is updated and revised to cover information management issues and problems. New chapters on leadership and evaluation are also added in this text. Thus, while the POSDCORB categories remain to structure the text, the authors fill in and expand considerably beyond the old POSDCORB content and substance.

In contrast, Jong S. Jun's *Public Administration: Design and*

Problem Solving (1986)[7] envisions public administration as rooted in an entirely different perspective. He defines the central aim of the field as follows: "Public administration in a democratic society must be concerned with ways of enhancing individual freedom, broader representation and participation, individual representation, and the improvement of the quality of working life."[8] For Jun, public administration theory is, as the subtitle indicates, "design and problem-solving," intricately interwoven within the very democratic values and fabric of modern American society with the goals of enhancing personal or individual freedom. No sharp division is made between policy and administration. The bulk of Jun's text is directed not at describing or refining the formal, rational bureaucratic instruments of state administration but, rather, seeks to integrate administration into society with chapters on "The Context of Public Bureaucracy," "Human Nature in Administration," "Administrators and the Public Interest," and "The Ethical Side of Public Problem Solving."

For Jun, the job of public administrators is not viewed so much as *institutionally* "getting the job done efficiently" but as achievement of personal and social goals interconnected with and dependent on *individual and environmental processes*. Public administration involves more the informal dimensions of design, reflection, problem solving, imagination, and sensitivity to wider democratic and humane values. Jun values openness, creativity, change, and innovation. Promoting institutional stability, clear differentiation of functions, hierarchy, integration, effective organizational capacity, rational administrative systems, or achieving clear-cut goals within defined time frames, in short "state building," are not only *not* stressed but considered unworthy aims for public administration. Rather, Jun speaks forcefully to the fulfillment of more personal, humane ends through temporary arrangements that improve the quality of working life.

A third text that projects yet another distinctive vision of public administration is E. S. Quade's *Analysis for Public Decisions*, 3d ed. (1989).[9] Here "administration" is treated almost entirely as a subject of technical analysis for making public choices, as opposed to achieving public action. Learning the appropriate analytical methods to apply to public decision making by professional experts, in other words, is what defines this text's subject matter. Administration in this text further entails mainly the process of deciding what to do by highly specialized experts, using more advanced methodologies and quantitative techniques. Very little is said about carrying out those policies. Only in one chapter, chapter twenty, does the author treat administration, almost as an after-thought, under the topic, "implementation." And here the coverage is brief and cursory. Quade acknowledges that the problems of policy implementation are "widespread," but the solutions offered are little more than exhortations for analysts to "take implementation into account as an element in the design and comparison of alternatives for policies" as well as "to help solve some problems that arise during the process of implementation itself."[10]

Quade's book is for policymakers who prefer to specialize more in the policy dimensions, or choice dimensions, of administration and leave the carrying out part of administration to others. Chapters are titled "A Basic Framework for Policy Analysis," "Objectives and the Measurement of Their Attainment," "Alternatives," "Costs," "Models," "Qualitative Methods and Computer Models," and "The Criterion Problem." Quade's approach, as reflected in these chapter titles, is to see administration in terms of, first, its rigorous commitment to a scientific-technical process of selection of the best or optimum policy direction. Not only is the carrying out of policies a secondary interest, but little or no mention is made of ethical, "ought," or value questions. Technologies and scientific methodologies drive the choice processes. Highly specialized, rational expertise, not generalized common sense, insight, or wisdom, is viewed as critical for achieving the "good" or "proper" policy solutions.

Second, there is little or no attention paid to bureaucratic institutions, their history, politics, or legal-constitutional aspects in this textbook. The author seems to consider that policy making and administration of policy operate apart from such traditional institutional factors. While the author acknowledges that "environment is critical to the implementation of programs" and urges that it "may have to be considered as part of the problem [of implementation]," relatively few pages (only 2 out of 380) are devoted to the subject. Quade begs off issues such as what is the purpose of policy analysis, what is the role of policy analysts, and where is their place in modern American government.

Finally, the author draws primarily on nonadministrative sources for his methodology. Virtually no reference is made to traditional public administration literature. Quade principally bases his book's formulations on systems analysis, mathematics, economics, and the policy sciences. The effort throughout his text is directed at devising "generalizable," harder, more quantitative foundations for policymaking, akin to the physical sciences. Quade's conceptualization therefore revives a much sharper differentiation between politics and administration, at least compared to many other current textbooks in the field. The skills, expertise, and technologies Quade advocates for making good "correct" policy choices do not permit much infusion of "normal" politics and legal considerations. Nor does he allow for American constitutional values to matter much. Rather, "policy analysis" is separated from American institutions, democratic values, and governmental politics as more or less a distinct technocratic process. One needing highly specialized professional skills and quantitative methodologies, sharply differentiated from open, representative, democratic processes. In sum, democratic values come from outside, not inside, the administration. They remain out there . . . somewhere. Just as the Graham-Hays text is written for the line manager and Jun's text is written for the creative problem solver, the Quade text seems targeted at a specific audience within public administration—that is, technical policy analysts.

Patterns of University Teaching in the Field: Subfield? Discipline? Profession? Focus of Study? or Specialization?

Before World War II, as the last chapter stressed, university training in public administration reflected a POSDCORB-dominated approach, but like textbooks, American higher education teaching practices in the field today reflect a broad diversity and many more specialized options. Here, as well, there is an enormous degree of latitude in defining the content of the field for American classroom instruction, often in highly particularized ways. No two educational programs in American colleges and universities are found today that are precisely alike in instructing public administration. Even within one university several programs and departments teach the subject under such different labels as "public policy," "public affairs," "organization theory," "implementation studies," "bureaucratic behavior," "public management," "not-for-profit administration," or administration of this or that specialized functional field such as social work, law enforcement, or education. Individualism in teaching approaches persists, and the program alternatives seem to defy simple conceptualization.

However, five major categories tend to dominate the organization of this subject matter in higher education. First, there are university programs that teach the subject as a subfield of political science or liberal arts programs in which the political or liberal arts features of administration are emphasized. Second, there are separate public administration programs or more specialized in-service training courses in which the generic subjects of administration are stressed as an applied discipline or interdiscipline drawing together an assortment of administrative methodologies such as personnel, management, and budgeting. Third, newer public policy degree programs are popular in American higher education that aim to educate policy professionals through more technical and analytical methodologies in an array of specialized policy fields. Fourth, there are comprehensive programs that define public administration broadly, something of a general focus of study, and that allow for considerable individual choice and program flexibility by combining a variety of methods of education for the public service in various configurations and combinations. Fifth and finally, public administration is increasingly taught as a particular specialization, such as law enforcement, health management, or education, frequently without any mention of a public administration label in the coursework. Let us look at actual examples of each of these five types of educational approaches to public administration.

Subfield

Where public administration is taught as a subfield of political science or the liberal arts, the dominant focus of the educational program is on what some might describe as the environmental and external aspects of public administration: its history, values, politics, institutional settings, social science philosophies, perspectives or organization, and bureaucratic role(s) in society. Generally, within these programs there are fewer requirements for quantitative, analytical, or technical expertise. When such classwork is required for the degree, such as in the fields of budgeting or financial management, the perspectives emphasized are frequently political, philosophical, and descriptive, rather than managerial or analytical and draw on such texts as Aaron Wildavsky's *The New Politics of the Budgetary Process*[12] and Allen Schick's *Congress and Money: Budgeting, Spending, and Taxing.*[13] When more specialized classes are required, students often must go off campus, to other departments, or to classes taught by part-time faculty rather than in-house offerings. Almost two-fifths of public administration programs are housed in political science departments; thus, this is the most prevalent form of program format.

The University of North Carolina at Chapel Hill provides an

example of an MPA program housed within a political science program (which itself is within the College of Arts and Sciences). The director is a member of the political science faculty, as is the bulk of the faculty who teach within the MPA program. The program consists of a basic series of core classes, which have as their aim, according to UNC's current MPA program brochure:

> Core courses acquaint all MPA students with economic, legal, political, and social institutions and processes of democratic government. They provide each student with concepts and skills for analyzing and evaluating policy options and public programs and for organizing and managing human and fiscal resources. All MPA students learn how to use computers, how to write clearly and concisely, and how to deal effectively with people. In their courses, MPA students also explore public service ethics and values guiding public policy choices.[14]

The core, taken during the first year of the two-year program (45 credits) includes politics and administration of public organizations, public management and leadership, statistics for public policy analysis, methods for policy analysis and evaluation, public budgeting and finance, and administrative writing. These core classes are combined with a requirement to select a concentration in either public policy analysis or public management, taken from more specialized faculties of law, engineering, or the nearby Institute of Government. Much of the second year is devoted to an MPA internship in various North Carolina state or local agencies, combined with periodic meetings on campus in a faculty-sponsored internship seminar that involves discussions and preparation of a major paper related to public management problem-solving issues. Many of the graduates wind up working for the state or local agencies they intern for. A final oral exam completes the MPA degree requirements.

Applied Discipline

A major variety of public administration program is often found in autonomous departments of public administration. This format treats the subject as an applied discipline or interdiscipline much like education for nursing, journalism, or social work, and the course content draws together diverse administrative skills and technologies. This free-standing program format for public administration teaching in America constitutes nearly one-third of the public administration programs in the National Association of Schools of Public Affairs and Administration (NASPAA). The design and content of these programs often place a heavy emphasis on practical line and staff administrative subjects and on the managerial technologies deemed essential for practitioners to operate effectively within government agencies. The curriculum and programatic goals are closely linked with preparing students to enter line or staff professional public service posts within government or related not-for-profit enterprises.

The Edwin O. Stene Graduate Program in Public Administration at the University of Kansas grew out of a long association with training city managers in the south-central and midwestern regions of the United States and retains a strong commitment to education for local government service and city management in particular. The program is housed in its own independent department, and its current MPA program brochure states its philosophy as follows:

> The Edwin O. Stene Graduate Program in Public Administration combines an established tradition of academic excellence with a long-standing concern for the practical aspects of public management. . . . This orientation toward professional education reflects a philosophy that well-trained public administrators should be able to apply current theories of management and analytical techniques to future challenges as well as the day-to-day problems they will face.[15]

In keeping with these objectives, MPA students at Kansas's Stene Graduate Program must take first-year core classes more directly focused on day-to-day operational facets of public management such as the public administration practicum, human resource management, public financial systems, introduction to applied decision analysis in the public sector, advanced decision analysis in the public sector, the role and context of public administration in American society, organizational analysis, and public policy and administration. The applied administrative orientation is continued in the second year in which "full-time students without professional work experience are required to complete a full-time internship, lasting nine months, following their traditional academic work." In the second-year internship, the link between theory and practice for administrative training in public administration is stressed:

> Our internship program is unique in its use of professional development seminars. Interns meet three times a year with faculty for week-long seminars designed to help them learn

from their professional experiences and to link theory with practice. Alumni and other practitioners are brought in to assist interns in this transition from academic life to professional career.[16]

Policy Profession

The Lyndon B. Johnson School of Public Affairs at the University of Texas at Austin offers an MPA and represents a third distinct type of program that is popular today in higher education for public service training—that is, as a policy profession. The LBJ School is a free-standing school with its own sizable faculty and considerable resources (which significantly enhances this program's instructional capacity compared to other programs). The School's particular emphasis is placed on learning policy and its formulation and implementation rather than on the more traditional public administration approaches, techniques, and methods. As its current catalogue outlines:

> The School's goal for individual students is to prepare them to apply their particular blend of talents and ambitions to a career that may move from public to private sectors, from one level of government to another, from one policy area to another. The School helps each student achieve his or her goals by offering a standardized core curriculum designed to teach essential managerial and analytic skills, a menu of courses offering opportunities to specialize in one or more policy areas, and constant exposure to people and issues that provide a meaningful context for all that is being taught. Opportunities for individual development and enrichment are provided throughout the program, requiring only that the student choose to take advantage of them: guest speakers, workshops, self-help programs. . . .[17]

"Policy" provides the central focus of much academic study for professional careers across the spectrum of government, business, and nonprofit fields. The curriculum emphasizes learning a common core of analytical techniques and generic methodologies in first-year classes labeled policy development, public financial management, operations research, systems analysis, political economy, applied statistics, applied econometrics, and policy research project. An internship and "extended policy project" in the second year completes the MPA degree.

Unlike the first two varieties of programs, the faculty at the LBJ School is drawn from more diverse academic fields and policy backgrounds, and their courses consciously aim to educate students with "harder" analytical skills and interdisciplinary tools, rather than more normative institutional or value subjects. The purpose is to turn students into "policy professionals" with the skills to understand, interpret, and make policy decisions at higher levels of government, nonprofit, or business organizations. Influenced by the idealism and governmental activism of the Great Society in the 1960s, the LBJ School's founders recognized "that the increasing complexity of modern government would require analysts and managers with a broader education and vision than could be acquired through traditional single-discipline graduate programs.[18]

Three assumptions in particular seem to guide public service education within this type of policy professional program. First, the mastery of a large body of interdisciplinary quantitative skills and "harder" optimalization techniques can—should?—direct the selection of the best or most-efficient policy choices from among alternative policy choices. Conversely, political, ethical, value, and historical normative questions are of lesser interest or importance for training in the public service. Second, expertise in one or more policy fields is considered to be the most suitable route for training in careers inside or outside government. Indeed, the appropriate focus for educational development is placed on "policy," wherever the job may be, not public service in government. Values of public service matter less than the policy field in which a student may specialize (and only roughly one-third of the LBJ graduates enter public service, which is significantly lower than the two previously described educational programs). Finally, "administration" per se becomes nearly invisible in the curriculum. Administration is often viewed as a subject somewhat beneath the concerns of policy students and is generally relegated to lower status within the School's program. If it is discussed at all, it is frequently under the "harder" heading of "implementation" and is addressed from largely technical and quantitative, and nonhumanistic, perspectives.

Focus of Study

Further, there are the comprehensive programs, which view public administration broadly as a general focus of study. Large public administration programs, housed in free-standing autonomous schools, such as at the University of Southern California, offer under one roof a wide range of public administration programs that combine a diversity of educational approaches in politics, management, and/or policy. Faculty size, institutional resources, student diversity, and even geographic diversity (in the case of USC) allow for the comprehensive program to offer students a variety of specializations within the MPA degree.

USC's MPA, much like other MPA degrees, ostensibly aims "to provide creative, high-quality education for public-sector personnel,"[19] but because USC runs public-service educational programs at three campuses (in Los Angeles, Sacramento, and Washington, D.C.) the USC program can draw on as well as respond to a broader type of student interests and backgrounds for an MPA degree. The USC downtown Washington Public Affairs Center offers a series of MPA classes geared directly to the functional needs of a practicing *federal* manager with class titles covering such topics as federal management systems; problems in R&D administration; seminar in intergovernmental management; from the national perspective; public financial management; project management; theory, practice and realities; acquisitions management; and defense management and national security. These topics are more directly focused on the salient issues that confront modern federal managers working in the Nation's Capital, and they are frequently taught by knowledgeable, well-respected practitioners from the Washington, D.C. government community. Furthermore, at times USC can supplement these instructors with regular faculty from its other two campuses and even offer MPA classes at locations and times convenient for busy public managers (for example, in weekend intensives).

In contrast, pre-service students (i.e., those without previous public employment experience), at the Los Angeles main campus or in Sacramento, can opt for policy or traditional administrative programs along the lines of the University of North Carolina at Chapel Hill, the University of Kansas, or the University of Texas at Austin. Pre-service students are further required to have internship experiences as well as to supplement their classwork with various electives in such specialized subfields of administration as the administration of justice, health administration, developmental administration, and so on. Considerable latitude in mixing and matching courses is allowed USC's MPA students in order to tailor programs to their individual requirements, interests, and needs. Indeed, individualization is encouraged, as the USC catalogue indicates:

A major difference distinguishing USC from many large universities is the more personal approach to education. Despite an excellent reputation as a research university, USC remains stu-

dent-oriented, continually upgrading the faculty and developing new programs to better fit the needs of today's students.
As the University of Southern California moves into its second
century, these traditions of academic excellence, innovation,
personalized education, and community involvement will
continue.[20]

Specialization

Similarities may be noted among the major four varieties of public-
service training programs, such as the use of internships for pre-
service students or requirements for some exposure to budgeting,
personnel, and management skills. In reality, as stressed before, it
should be apparent from this brief review that a wide range of diversity exists today in education for the public service. Specialization
and heterogeneity tend to be the "norm" for the format and content
of higher education instruction. Indeed, increasingly, public
administration programs simply teach the subject as a particular
specialization or set of concentrations devoted to specific public-
sector skill needs, local interests, or regional issues. For example,
the Graduate Program in Public Policy and Administration at
Columbia University offers specializations in city management,
urban planning, and not-for-profit administration, as one would
expect of a program in a large metropolitan setting. The Department of Political Science in the University of West Florida provides
an MPA with concentrations in coastal zone policy and elderly care
administration, reflecting the prime interests and concerns in that
locale. Even within the same university, the topic of administration
is often taught, as suggested before, under different labels suitable
for catering to different career clientele groups. Education administrators, health managers, and social workers frequently have their
own designated degree programs within a single higher education
institution. These programs offer classes that often have heavy components of public administration training involved in their curriculum, even though such classes are rarely tagged with these labels
or are offered as part of the formal public administration degree
programs, such as the MPA, on campus. The programs frequently
view public administration as a technical, functionally specific
subject.

A good case in point of a highly specialized degree offering
public administration without the public administration label is
seen in the School of Community and Public Affairs at Virginia

Commonwealth University, where various options are offered under the B.S. in the Administration of Justice Core.

Bachelor of Science in Administration of Justice—
Administration of Justice Core[21]

Required courses for all Administration of Justice majors (30 semester hours)

AJP 181	Justice System Survey
AJP 260	Criminal Law
AJP 324	Courts and Judicial Process
AJP 352	Crime and Delinquency Prevention
AJP 355	Foundations of Criminal Justice
AJP 380	Criminal Justice Research
AJP 432	Criminal Justice Organizations
AJP 363	Comparative Criminal Justice Systems
AJP 480	Seminar: Critical and Career Issues in Criminal Justice
AJP 492	Directed Individual Study

or

AJP 493	Internship

or

AJP 394	Field Service in Criminal Justice

Career Options Requirement—Select four courses from desired career option, including both the introductory and program courses (underlined below).

Law Enforcement Option

AJP 254	Introduction to Law Enforcement
AJP 305	Enforcement Theories and Practice
AJP 310	Industrial and Retail Security
AJP 370	Criminalistics and Crime Analysis
AJP 434	Enforcement Administration
AJP 463	Strategies for Delinquency and Crime Prevention
AJP 468	Economic Offenses and Organized Crime
AJP 475	Case Studies in Criminal Procedure
AJP 491	Topics Seminar

Juvenile Justice Option

AJP 252	Introduction to Juvenile Justice
AJP 350	Evaluation and Treatment of the Offender
AJP 351	Community-Based Correctional Programs

AJP 378   Juvenile Justice Law and Process
AJP 433   Adult/Juvenile Correctional Administration
AJP 462   Strategies for Delinquency and Crime Prevention
AJP 491   Topics Seminar

Corrections Option

AJP 253   Introduction to Corrections
AJP 350   Evaluation and Treatment of the Offender
AJP 351   Community-Based Correctional Programs
AJP 363   Correctional Law
AJP 433   Adult/Juvenile Correctional Administration
AJP 491   Topics Seminar

Legal Studies Option

AJP 255   Introduction to Legal Studies
AJP 358   Lawyer's Role in the Justice System
AJP 363   Correctional Law
AJP 378   Juvenile Justice Law and Process
AJP 475   Case Studies in Criminal Procedure
AJP 491   Topics Seminar

In-Service Training Programs, or Public Administration as Practical Training

It is also important to take note of a substantial and increasing number of in-service training programs in public administration, sometimes housed within government agencies to augment managerial expertise of their organizations. Indeed, much of what passes for public administration today is in the form of practical training programs, especially in the format of in-service training. In-service education is designed to bridge the gap between higher education degree programs such as the MPA and on-the-job experience. This in-service training can be also highly fragmentary, ad hoc education, designed to fill in missing educational experiences for on-line supervisors and managers and to provide for specific skills demanded by agencies. The federal government as well as cities and states offer internship opportunities where a candidate works for another professional or is rotated through various units of the agency to learn the ropes of that particular career. During the internship period, the student is assigned to do various tasks under the supervision of the mentor who ideally critiques the student's performance and instructs him or her in the methods and tasks of the organization during the intern's rotation period. Many types of specialized intern experiences are possible, and as a whole they offer important learning opportunities within the field today by giving practical on-the-job-training in real working situations within public administration.

Other types of in-service training, using more formal classroom work, are also found throughout government. This education can take the form of short courses offered to students via video films to longer extensive education through for-credit programs, even leading to degrees in various highly specialized aspects of administration necessary for running particular agencies. For many years, the U.S. Department of Agriculture ran such extension for-credit programs in public administration, and the International City Management Association's famous "Green Book Series," begun in 1934, has remained a major source for local government on-the-job training in diverse municipal specialties such as fire science, police administration, and municipal finance.

Many agencies and departments especially sponsor large in-house training schools that teach junior- and senior-level managerial skills. In the U.S. Armed Services nearly one-third of an average officer's career is spent in such training schools. The Naval Postgraduate School at Monterey, California, for example, provides officers an MS in management with twin objectives: first, "to provide the Naval Officer with specific functional skills required to effectively manage in a subspecialty area" and, second, "to provide the officer with a Navy Defense Systems-oriented graduate management education."[22] A student in this well-supported program follows a highly specialized training routine related closely to the in-house administrative needs of Department of Defense management by taking classes on such topics as material logistics, transportation management for defense, defense contract management, and Armed Services Systems inventory management. These classes encourage writing papers related to various subspecialties for which the candidate is being trained. Faculty at the school often retain close ties with the various segments of the Defense Department, which enhance the practical educational training aspects of students at the Naval Postgraduate School. Such in-house programs, of course, vary from agency to agency in the quality and content of the classes and course of study, but overall they tend to be highly functional, career-oriented training that is geared to the specific managerial expertise and skills needed by government.

Finally, it should be added that annual national and regional conferences sponsored by various professional associations within the public administration community provide major sources of timely, practical training in the United States today. Agencies sponsor their employees for various half-day to several day-long professional conferences on a wide variety of specialized training subjects and themes that often address relevant and important issues facing administrators. These conferences are critical sources for information, advice, and face-to-face exchanges between experts from university, government, business, and nonprofit sectors who are grappling with common policy and management issues in public administration. Sections within these conferences offer specialized topic discussions on budgets, personnel issues, human resources management, and so on. Indeed, the growth in recent years within the American Society for Public Administration has been directed toward eighteen specialized sections at national and regional conferences.[23]

Scanning the list below of Conference Themes at the American Society for Public Administration 1989 National Conference in Miami, Florida, can give one the sense of the broad range of global-managerial-policy topics, often highly technical subjects, discussed at typical national conferences today for public administrators.

1989 ASPA National Conference Themes

Theme 1—Changing Populations: Understanding, Adapting, Shaping

- Cultural/Ethnic Diversity
- Population Shifts—Age, Location, Density
- Changing Distribution of Resources
- Financing Government—Who Pays? Who Benefits?

Theme 2—Managing Human and Technological Systems

- Infrastructure, Waste, Transportation
- Management Systems: Theories and Techniques
- Decaying and Obsolete Technologies
- Implications for Social and Ecological Environments

Theme 3—Reshaping the Public Service

- Broader Definitions of "Public Service"—Nonprofits, Contractors, and Partnerships with Traditional Governments

- Changing Responsibilities and Management of State and Local Government
- Developing Management Skills for the Future
- Concern for Ethics and Individual Liberties

Theme 4—Serving in a Global Community

- Issues in Economic Development
- Institutional Cooperation and Conflict
- International Finance
- Knowledge and Technology Transfer

A Quest for Improved Educational Quality, Uniformity, and Standards: NASPAA's Role in Public Service Training

Public administration education in America reflects specialization, diversity, and lack of uniformity in education for the public service from pre-service through advanced in-service training. Many styles, approaches, and methods are being used today. Significant efforts in recent years, however, have tended to encourage a greater degree of standardization and uniformity in training for the graduate professional degrees within public administration, especially for the MPA degree. The National Association of Schools of Public Affairs and Administration (NASPAA) in 1988 was designated the accrediting body for the MPA degree by the Council on Postsecondary Education.

Until 1977 there was no general oversight of standards or curriculum design and content of MPA programs. In 1977, NASPAA established a review process for graduate-degree programs that combined a self-study of MPA programs by the faculty involved with the degree program instruction with site visitations by a team of professional teachers and administrators from the public sector. The opinions and recommendations of the site visitation team was advisory and non-binding. Successful completion of self-study and its approval by the site visitation team led to a school's program being "rostered" or officially recognized as meeting the sanctioned NASPAA standards for graduate-degree programs.[24]

NASPAA's recently established accreditation process introduces a new formality to the decades-old peer-review process. The new accreditation role for NASPAA perhaps puts more teeth into NASPAA's requirements by prescribing adequate course offerings, staffing, library support, and other conditions for effective teaching and educational requirements for public service personnel. Course content as specified by NASPAA standards, nevertheless, remains comparatively loose and flexible to accommodate a wide variety of policy, management, value, and administrative emphases found in various schools across the country. For instance, the NASPAA standards prescribe "MPA managerial requirements for tools" vaguely and leave their content open to ample interpretation. Management tools for MPA degrees are to include, according to NASPAA, such courses as human resources planning, budgeting and financial processes, information and computer literacy as well as policy development, policy and program formulation, implementation and development. As the NASPAA standards further suggest: "These area requirements do not prescribe specific course content. Neither do they imply that equal time should be spent on each area."[25]

The option for NASPAA program review and accreditation, furthermore, remains a voluntary action on the part of individual MPA university programs. Unlike the American Medical Association for medical schools or the American Bar Association for law schools, accreditation or rejection by the NASPAA accreditation body of specific MPA programs will not restrict graduates of those programs from entering the field or from practicing government administration. In short, NASPAA's accreditation process—even as open and as flexible as it is—carries no legal sanction or much weight in public. Numerous small programs and specialized public service training courses are entirely left outside NASPAA's accreditation process. Some large prestige universities, like Harvard's John F. Kennedy School of Government, a major American public service training program, choose to ignore NASPAA membership entirely. The Kennedy School's choice, indeed, may well be symbolic of the continued loose, decentralized, diverse nature of the field itself where standards cannot be imposed from above—no matter how worthy they may be for development of the field as a whole.[26]

By Way of Summary

What is the contemporary image of American public administration thought as reflected in this survey review of basic texts, teaching, and training programs in the field today? Is "it" a subfield? discipline? profession? focus of study? specialization? practical training? or what?

As John William Ellwood recently observed, "Graduate education in the United States is characterized by its diversity—a diversity required to meet the differing needs of various levels of American government and the variety of professions which dominate employment in the public sector."[27] Clearly diversity, fragmentation, and complexity—but above all increasing specialization—emerge as central, perhaps *the* central, characteristics of trends in modern American public administration. There is hardly any one best way. Unlike the French *Grand Corps* trained through a standardized program at the National School of Administration *(Ecole National d'Administration)*, multiple narrow backgrounds, specialized methodologies, and particularistic perspectives are the source for most of higher educational training for the American public service.

From one point of view, this specialized heterogeneity may seem like a confusion of purpose or "a crisis of identity." From another, such variety can be expected; indeed, it is necessary. A diversity of approaches may well be a consequence of America's lack of a strong sense of state. Without a clear definition of "state," how can Americans have a clear sense of purpose with regard to training for state administration? The development of the new state system in postwar America, the global professional technocracy, furthermore, as Chapter Four outlines, has made diverse specialized expertise increasingly valued, essential, and even the foundation for the new American postwar state's successful operation. Both operational needs and individual career advancement depend on training within narrow technical and professional career lines, without clear public purposes, frequently changing according to the shifting demands for new technologies and the need for new professional skills in the global marketplace. In this new postwar state system, such rapidly changing requirements for professional technological expertise are today prized as the engine for national progress and future material development. Further, the professions that dominate the public sector tend to foster development of their own separate and specialized education programs, distinct from a general public administration label. The decline of a generalist public administration label is the result of increasing professional control.

As the opening Tocqueville quote to this chapter suggests, "Americans always display a clear, free, original, and inventive power of mind." In recent years Americans certainly have been forced to be innovative in regard to training for public service skills and expertise. Born without a state, Americans traditionally place little stock in such education but now living in a new postwar global professional technocracy, the system fails to operate without vast numbers of highly educated talent. Hence, there is a persisting and driving demand throughout all aspects of American higher education, not only within public service training but in all areas of professional-technical education, for increasing specialization and expert training for fulfilling the varied needs of America's vast global professional technocracy.

America's new state system is everywhere and so must draw on every kind of professional expertise in order that it function. This is evidenced by the increased number of more specialized and narrowly focused texts, greater numbers and varieties of teaching programs in higher education, more emphasis on training directed at narrow, professional groups such as policy experts and practical training programs devoted to in-service career specialties within various professional and technical fields. But, again, there is no grand model or overall design for such education because Americans never have held a grand concept of state. Indeed, they have preferred to do without one. Hence, "technology," "professionals," and "globalism" have been allowed to define the American state, and, hence, the crazy-quilt patterns of texts, teaching, and training programs for state administration. This of course is all very American, and only American! In the next chapter we examine the consequences of this for public administration theory in the 1990s.

Notes

1. George J. Gordon, *Public Administration in America*, 3d ed. (New York: St. Martin's, 1986).
2. Leonard D. White, *Introduction to the Study of Public Administration*, 2nd ed. (New York: Macmillan, 1939).
3. Gordon, p. 7.
4. White, p. 7.
5. Cole Blease Graham, Jr. and Steven W. Hays, *Managing the Public Organization* (Washington, D.C.: CQ Press, 1986).
6. Ibid., p. vii.
7. Jong S. Jun, *Public Administration: Design and Problem Solving* (New York: Macmillan, 1986).
8. Ibid., p. 9.
9. E. S. Quade, *Analysis for Public Decisions*, 3d ed. (New York: North-Holland), 1989.
10. Ibid., p. 305.
11. Ibid.

12. Aaron Wildavsky, *The New Politics of the Budgetary Process* (Glenview, Illinois: Scott, Foresman, 1988).

13. Allen Schick, *Congress and Money: Budgeting, Spending, and Taxing* (Washington, D.C.: The Urban Institute, 1980).

14. Department of Political Science with the Institute of Government, Program Announcement for Master of Public Administration, Public Management and Public Policy Analysis (Chapel Hill, North Carolina: University of North Carolina, undated), p. 4.

15. Edwin O. Stene Graduate Program in Public Administration, Program Announcement (Lawrence: University of Kansas, 1988), p. 1.

16. Ibid.

17. Lyndon B. Johnson School of Public Affairs, 1988–90 Program Announcement (Austin: University of Texas, 1988), p. 5.

18. Ibid., p. 4.

19. School of Public Administration, Washington Public Affairs Center, Program Announcement for Graduate Studies in Public Administration, Course Offerings 1988–89 (Los Angeles, CA: University of Southern California, 1988), p. 5.

20. Ibid., p. 4.

21. 1986–87 Undergraduate Bulletin (Richmond: Virginia Commonwealth University, 1986–87), pp. 217–218.

22. Announcement for Administrative Science Programs (Monterey, California: Naval Postgraduate School, 1988), p. 32.

23. The past two decades have seen a mushrooming of specialized ASPA sections to eighteen that now include Budgeting and Financial Management, Conference of Minority Public Administrators, Criminal Justice Administration, Emergency Management, Environmental and Natural Resources Administration, Government and Business, Human Resources and Health, Intergovernmental Administration and Management, International and Comparative Administration, Management Science and Policy Analysis, National Security and Defense, National Young Professionals Forum, Personnel Administration and Labor Relations, Professional and Organizational Development, Public Administration Education, Public Administration Research, Science and Technology in Government, and Women in Public Administration. The same growth in specialized journals in public administration and public affairs is also evident. Fifty years ago (Spring 1940), the *Public Administration Review* began as the first generalist public administration journal in the United States; today, over 115 regular administrative publications are available, with more being added annually. Most are highly specialized and targeted to a specific group of administrative officials and readers, such as budget officials, police, or military personnel.

24. Standards for Professional Master's Degree Programs in Public Affairs and Administration, effective September 1, 1988 (Washington, D.C.: National Association of Schools of Public Affairs and Administration, undated).

25. Ibid., p. 3.
26. Ironically, the Kennedy School has been one of the trend setters in the field, having been one of the earliest schools to offer the MPA and the DPA, as well as various advanced public policy degrees. For an interesting current view of the Kennedy School, see J. Anthony Lukas, "Harvard's Kennedy School Is Complete," *New York Times Magazine* (March 12, 1988), pp. 24 ff. For the opposite view, see Derek Bok, "A Daring and Complicated Strategy," *Harvard Magazine* (May–June 1989), pp. 47–58.
27. John William Ellwood, "A Morphology of Graduate Education for Public Service in the United States," unpublished manuscript sponsored by NASPAA's Mellon Project, p. 1.

CHAPTER SEVEN

Modern Public Administration Theory as a Great State Debate: No State? Bold State? Pre-State? Pro-State?

In our days two contrary revolutions appear to be going on, the one continually weakening the supreme state, the other strengthening it; at no other period in our history has it appeared so weak or so strong.

ALEXIS DE TOCQUEVILLE ,
Democracy in America

At various points in this book the thesis has been advanced that America's public administration theory has followed state development. The absence of a nation-state in the first century of the U.S. Constitution made administrative thought unnecessary. The creation of the administrative state in the second century, however, made theorizing vital for both understanding and running America's new state system. Ideas about public administration were thus creatures of necessity: they were born from trial and error, not in the ivory tower. Yet, America's state itself was not static. Its early formation consisted largely of temporizing arrangements, and as these evolved so did America's administrative thought. As Chapter Five outlines, administrative doctrines elusively shifted from one, to two, into many forms. Each successively added new layers of complexity as well as difficulty for comprehending precisely "What is public administration?"

Much like the human mind, in which layers of experiences combine over time to define the identity of an individual, so, too, the identity of contemporary public administration thought is now composed of an immense complexity and diversity due to a rich heritage of layer upon layer of state-building experimentation and development. The present scene, as Chapter Six pictures, is defined by theoretical diversity, even extreme heterodoxy. How can modern administrative theory be best understood in light of this apparent unending variety of ideas, models, and perspectives? How can one make sense of this seemingly littered landscape of intellectual fragments that, taken together, today calls itself "public administration theory"? Do the consequences of such fragmented thought mark the decline or the evaporation of what we know as public administration theory? Do they mark the end of public administration?

Quite the contrary, as this chapter argues, its present-day diversity reflects its vitality, not as some suggest, its decline, or maybe its end. Much like in the late nineteenth century, the late twentieth-century literature in the field symbolizes a profound debate—implicitly and explicitly—over the fundamental values, purposes, and directions of America's modern state system. Public administration thought today can best be understood as a center-point in which critical normative issues collide and are being thrashed out: Who should rule? What is the meaning of the good life? What are the methods for realizing the good life? What are the appropriate criteria for action? What are the best organizational formats? What is the vision of the ideal state?

A century ago, such normative issues were debated among Sumnerites, Bellamyites, and Wilsonians, as Chapter Three discusses; today, they are wrestled with once again, now using different idioms and conceptual frameworks but with seminal importance to the future of American society and its government. Arguments over these and other unresolved value questions today turn public administration theory into something akin to a debating society or, more accurately, a great state debate, in which various analytical models, conceptual ideas, and normative values advocate various degrees of statism *or* statelessness. At either extreme today, clusters of proponents favor "no-state" or "bold-state" solutions; somewhere in the middle are those who favor "pre-state" (or "half-way") or "pro-state" (a professional technocracy) solutions. Imbedded within each vision of the good state, often drawn from past American state practices and thinking, are implicit or explicit views of what constitutes the good administration essential to turn that particular ideal state vision into reality. This dialectic among competing administrative approaches is thus rooted in broader, competing, alternative state models and designs, which may seem all very confusing and disjointed to many modern students of public administration. Yet it is not so complicated if viewed from the standpoint of a great state debate. This chapter attempts to summarize and sort out the characteristics of these competing contemporary state visions, the major schools of administrative thought they represent, and their key arguments, assumptions, central values, strengths, weaknesses, and implications for the field.

No-State (or Negative-State) Vision: Minimalist Public Administration

Monetarists and Public Choice Theorists

No-state or negative-state advocates achieved widespread popularity and support in many quarters of the United States during the past decade. They especially draw their ideas from monetarist and public choice economists. "Monetarists" heavily derive their visions of the good society from Adam Smith's eighteenth-century laissez-faire philosophy and the nineteenth-century Austrian School of economic thought, both of which view the state in any form with disdain and distrust. This rabidly anti-statist philosophy grew up essentially as a battering ram against state intervention in society by promoting a public policy of maximum industry and business action without government interference or direction. Quite literally, "laissez-faire" means "to let people do as they please." As a consequence, modern-day monetarists, such as Milton Friedman, George Stigler, Gary Becker, and others of the Chicago School who are heirs to this anti-state tradition, see it much like William Sumner did a century ago: ultimately the hero is the free market. For them, the market is an abstract mechanism for sorting out winners and losers in competition with one another, which is the only way real societal progress and human freedom can be attained. There is no "community" and little state as such in their writings, only calculating individuals in contest with each other, whose principal interconnections and attachments consist of monetary exchanges. Romantic love, loyalty to geographic place, religious devotion, family attachments, and national patriotism hold little value to them for achieving cooperative societal relationships; only money can be the true integrator and an effective force for societal actions. Here individual economic exchanges—not society, not sex, not politics, not religion, not nationalism, and not personal friendship—are the "basic units of analysis," at least in this world. Successful individual competitors in the free market can reap rich rewards by luck and skill; those who for various reasons are not successful fall behind, but overall efficiency and progress of society and "the good of the whole" results from the unfettered workings of free market mechanisms.

Their ideal, in short, is to allow natural adjustments in the marketplace to take place via natural competition and freedom from artificial state controls. At best, according to these authors, government therefore should keep stable monetary policies, promote slow economic growth in the money supply, and maintain open markets. Anything more is counterproductive. Woe to those who attempt to intervene, especially through any formalistic state intervention in free market transactions, for they will only make a mess of things. For "sound" monetarists, short-term government interventions to correct inequities in the markets will usually make matters worse economically, and politically will only advance the cause of authoritarianism and dictatorship. Thus, government should be kept as small as possible so as to promote the unseen, unplanned, and unpredictable workings of entrepreneurs in the marketplace. By-products of "the invisible hand" will in the end achieve economic and political benefits for everyone. A "natural community" of independent entrepreneurs working toward their own individualistic goals without state direction is ultimately the monetarists' ideal society.

Public choice theories, also highly popular in the 1980s, were, along with monetarism, highly influential in promoting limits on state development; however, unlike the monetarists, these theorists had no wish to dismiss state intervention entirely. Rather, writers such as James A. Buchanan, Gordon Tullock, William A. Niskanen, Vincent Ostrom, and others who have become associated with the public choice label see governments as nothing particularly special as human organizations go. They are neither better nor worse, but capable of making just as many mistakes and subject to as much special interest and self-centeredness as private organizations are. Hence, much of the focus of public choice theory is on the comparative study of public institutions in order to check the influence of special interests and self-centeredness on how agencies make decisions and influence public policy, as well as the mechanisms they use for the production of public goods and services. Government and society as a whole are seen not in political terms but, rather, as defined by economics in which transactions between individuals and government are measured in dollars and cents.

Like monetarists, public choice theorists view the world in largely economic terms, where people and groups pursue their own ends for self-interest. Their world is thus one of self-interested, atomistic individuals and organizations pursuing their own gain largely in economic terms.

Government in the public choice view is essentially an economic allocator of society's scarce resources, offering certain "benefits" to some at certain "costs" to others. Since government is viewed as a self-interested party like any other, the proponents of public choice ultimately seek the appropriate decision rules and decisional mechanisms that will keep government in check and ensure that the most efficient decision or policy is made—namely, one that will result in the most benefits for society at the least costs. Public choice writers thus look to the no-nonsense hard quantitative applications of cost-benefit analysis, i.e. weighing costs against benefits by mathematical formulas, and, much like monetarists, they prefer a range of free market solutions in order to promote the most economical allocation of scarce resources. As their name implies, they firmly believe human freedom and societal efficiency will result from expanding the range of public choice. But this point of view rests on an extreme economicization of human affairs, namely that in which every human transaction is calculated by self-interest in dollars and cents.

Throughout the 1980s, both monetarist and public choice doctrines had widespread impacts on public administration thought and practice. Their ideas in practical terms were adopted at the federal level in federal tax and spending policies. The drive to cut and index federal taxes, to deregulate business, to adopt a balanced budget amendment to the U.S. Constitution, and to promote "enterprise zones" and "tax limitations" initiatives at the grass-roots levels, as well as to cut government spending and revenues overall, reflect concrete applications of monetarist and public choice doctrines. In the 1980s, think tanks, staffed heavily with public choice and monetarist advocates, such as at the Hoover Institution at Stanford University, the American Enterprise Institute, and the Heritage Foundation in Washington, D.C., and journals such as the *Wall Street Journal*, *Public Choice*, and the *Public Interest* became especially important centers of advocacy for these ideas throughout the United States.

At the extreme, these writers take a sharply negative view of public administration. In the words of Stuart M. Butler's *The Privatization Option* (1985): "Public administration is negligent and wasteful, since public employees have no direct interest in the com-

mercial outcome. . . . bureaucrats will tend to adopt policies that
will ease their work load and make their jobs more pleasant. . . . As
a result, public enterprises' behavior will be less responsive to
demand and supply conditions, and will operate with higher costs
for any given output level, than private enterprises."[1] Bureaucrats
are frequently depicted as thwarting the natural markets by impos-
ing their own private interests and personal agendas, hence impair-
ing the "public good." Privatization of public functions is clearly
offered as "the answer." The major portion of Butler's book outlines a variety of privatization options for the public sector such as
volunteerism, fee-for-services, "load sharing," and "contracting
out" as successful remedies for avoiding bureaucratic interference
in the free market.

Similarly, in E. S. Savas, *Privatization: The Key to Better Government* (1987),[2] the free market is preferred for supplying goods
and services to the public. Government's role is largely viewed as a
producer of goods and services, and little more. As Savas defines
the subject: "Privatization is the act of reducing the role of government, or increasing the role of the private sector, in an activity or
in the ownership of assets."[3] Shifting to the private sector, in
Savas's thinking, leads to many advantages: more cost effective public services, less intrusive government, stimulation of the private
sector, and more choices for citizens in meeting their needs. Much
of the book details specifics of various "privatization options," with
such chapter titles as "How to Privatize" and "Applications." From
Savas's perspective, "Privatization means changing from an
arrangement with high government involvement to one with less.
The most important privatization arrangements from a policy perspective are the market, contract, voucher and voluntary arrangements."[4] For Savas these options are valued because they require
the minimal amount of state intervention: "Society is more than the
state," writes Savas; "it is made up of small, diverse communities. . . . Consequently, Americans are turning more to society's
other traditional institutions to satisfy local and individual needs,
through the family, neighborhood and church and through
ethnic and voluntary associations."[5] Here the "natural community" is preferred to "the artificial state" for fulfilling citizens'
needs.

Often the tone of these writings can turn into a heavy-handed
populist polemic that envisions *any* state intervention as thwarting
the popular will. One need only scan the chapter titles of another
recent book, Randall Fitzgerald's *When Government Goes Private:*

Successful Alternatives to Public Services (1988),[6] to glimpse the emphasis such writers place on "Giving Power Back to the People," "Making Government More Responsive," "Harnessing the Private Sector for the Public Good," "Unleashing Our Hoarded Assets," and so on. More democracy is achieved through less statism seems to be the clear, cogent message. Serious scholarly public choice writings, such as Vincent Ostrom's *The Political Theory of a Compound Republic: Designing the American Experiment* (2d ed., 1987),[7] show that limits on public action are connected directly to the U.S. constitutional framework. Through a careful exegesis of *The Federalist Papers*, Ostrom envisions the U.S. Constitution as layers of choice mechanisms reiterated to apply to many different units of the governmental system, where each is bounded by enforceable rules.

A "compound republic" is, in Ostrom's view, the by-product of these multiple, yet restricted autonomous decision structures within government and is maintained constitutionally by enforceable rules of law. The system would fail, according to Ostrom, if one decision structure or unit of government gains dominance over others. The stress is on finding the appropriate "choice mechanisms," "decision units," and "enforceable rules" to sustain personal freedom and individual liberty under a compound republican constitution. The Ostromist constitution is depicted therefore as a world of limits that sharply curtails public actions by promoting alternative private, nonprofit, or local options for collective action. It puts a premium on competition, pluralism, open choices, and constitutional alternative modes of collective action that maximize personal liberties. In short, it envisions a constrained, minimalist state within the republican constitution so as to expand individual discretion.

Administrative Consequences

The administrative consequences that follow from negative-state models are not merely advocacy of less public administration, one that only conducts the minimal essentials for society, but a field reduced to largely "technicalism" and mechanical applications. Public administrator roles, when they are discussed by monetarist or public choice writers, are visualized in terms of mainly low-level technical work, such as contract management, volunteer coordination, "load shedding," voucher administration, and rule enforcement. There is no large view for administrators' actions outlined here, no broad discretionary authority advocated, and no visionary administrative goal outlined. Administrative tasks are cramped and restricted.

Furthermore, career public service is little valued for fulfilling tasks, compared to a politically responsive and partisan one. Careerists are often seen in "the other camp" and opposed to limited administrative discretion. Indeed, there is in the writing general encouragement for a sharp split in the roles between "political appointees" and "careerists," with a tilt toward favoring the expansion of the political at the expense of careerist positions in order to achieve more responsiveness and loyalty to the elected chief executive's political agenda. "Government must be primarily political," writes former Office of Personnel Management Director Donald J. Devine, in *Steering the Elephant* (ed. Robert Rector and Michael Sanera, 1987).[8] Due to the need for political oversight and political loyalty to achieving political goals, Devine in particular argues for wider use of political appointees who possess "a clear vision of the President's agenda," are "politically loyal to the President," "have the courage to live with the inevitable negative reaction," and can "keep his [the political appointee's] agenda close" to his vest.[9] Toughness, loyalty to the boss, and commitment to partisan goals are prized, as opposed to promoting the values of nonpartisanship, expertise, and collegiality in the public service. It is, in other words, largely a top-down style of public administration, drawn from classic business management theory with a political appointee supremely in charge.

In the *President's Private Sector Survey on Cost Control in the Federal Government* (1984),[10] or the Grace Commission's report (named for the Commission's chair), a tightly controlled top-down business management model is specifically advanced as being most effective for the operation of the federal government:

> In the private sector corporate strategy is viewed as a means of reducing general corporate objectives to manageable proportions, thus enabling employees across the company to work in union toward the achievement of clearly defined goals and objectives. This unifying direction is critical for the successful coordination of management initiatives that cross departmental and functional boundaries, and for integrating disparate department projects. The same principles apply to the public sector.[11]

Administrative Practices

Many of these contemporary themes and ideas about good practices in public administration within the negative-state school are summed up in the Heritage Foundation's *Mandate for Leadership III* (1989).[12] This text ostensibly is not about public administration but is designed as a policy-action agenda for a newly elected administration. Nonetheless, the book implicitly contains a vision of the good administration. The book claims to draw from the experiences and writings of more than 400 scholars and practitioners, mainly those who had served the prior eight years in the federal government in key political appointee posts and who especially shared its conservative free-market values. It is, as its preface stresses, dedicated to a "public policy to reflect and strengthen the ideals of individual liberty, limited government, free enterprise, and strong national defense."[13] In order to carry out this agenda, the form of public administration generally called for by these authors collectively is one based on:

- Strong political leadership from the top down with strict adherence and loyalty to the President's agenda;
- Focus on "a handful of highly prized policy initiatives" with "consistency of purpose as the bedrock for all policy";[14]
- Strong top-down personnel, budgetary, and regulatory oversight considered critical in order to carry out policy objectives;
- Emphasis throughout on the widest use of the private sector and not-for-profit modes of service delivery such as contracting out, volunteerism, and wholesale privatization of entire government projects;
- Bottom-line results as what counts for effective policy implementation through use of business techniques and technologies, where possible, such as management by objectives (MBO) and pay-for-performance; also, heavy reliance placed on the use of economic methodology such as cost-benefit and other economic measures; use and application of these business techniques seen as fundamental to good management practices;
- A sharp split between careerists and political appointees assumed as necessary in order to promote and successfully implement the President's policy agenda; careerists are by

and large pictured as self-serving, unresponsive, and obstructionist and thus in order "to strengthen the ability of the President to control the executive branch, the new administration should increase the number of political appointees and strengthen their role in government";[15]

- At the root of all these administrative activities is the goal to decentralize and privatize government as much as is feasible in order "to promote more economic growth through less bureaucracy, fewer regulations, lower taxes and less government spending. . . . Washington performs poorly, inefficiently and often counter-productively."[16]

So let the invisible hand of free market mechanisms decide, say these authors, not the dead hand of bureaucracy.

Certainly not all followers of the limited state model of administration agree or subscribe to all its aforementioned points and the prescriptions found in *Mandate for Leadership III*, for there are many variations and differences in emphasis among the writers who favor the negative-state vision. Some, for example, favor a strong military buildup—more statism?—while others remain staunchly against large defense commitments. Some push privatization into virtually all aspects of governmental activities, while others see its limits and shortcomings to pursuing privatization options in many fields of public endeavor. Many varied shades of opinion and points of view are expressed in this camp about particular details of the ideal state and its administration. Negative-state writers are by no means of a unanimous opinion nor do they present a united front on such questions.

Strengths and Weaknesses of This Vision

Nonetheless, what can be concluded—pro and con—about this particular school of thought in regard to its overall prescribed administrative model? How can its central themes, ideas, and perspectives be evaluated on the whole in terms of contributions to modern public administration thought?

On the plus side, this school continuously reminds us—often loudly—of the limits and the down-sides of state action and that there are indeed alternatives to the formal routes to governmental administration. The best of this literature challenges, stimulates, and provokes thinking about the larger purposes and goals of public administration: What is administration's appropriate role in society? Can and should public administration be performed in different ways in order to improve economic efficiency and societal well-being? Answers to these and other questions have been a source of continued yeasty debate within the field, precisely because it reminds public administration that there are other options to achieving collective action.

"No-state" theorists have also brought about genuinely new innovations to the ways of doing the public's business in recent years. Their thinking sometimes has resulted in highly controversial ideas, such as enterprise zones or public-private partnerships. They often have asked public administrators to think carefully and more precisely about the costs and benefits of particular actions and programs they undertake in the name of "the public interest." What are the *real* costs and benefits? Are they carefully weighed? Are costs more considerable than benefits received? And to whom do the benefits actually go? For the public interest? or for personal gain? Who gains? Who loses? Such intensive questioning often sharpens thinking and critical understanding about the administrative enterprise and the purpose of its tasks. It further has renewed a necessary emphasis upon themes of efficiency and effectiveness in the public service. In fairness, it also should be noted that few of its advocates—not even the most hardline—propose to eradicate the state entirely. In reality, most advocate a limited state to decentralize and privatize but not to obliterate state institutions.

Yet, a con side is readily apparent in negative-state thinking. The emphasis on an enlarged, politically partisan cadre of loyalists to carry out the work of public administration can *and does* lead to wholesale corruption and ethical misconduct in office, not to mention poor and inefficient performance as well. It can and has opened up the government to opportunism and shady practices. Limited-state literature remains largely silent on these vital accountability issues. Their stress on expanding the values of political responsiveness in government and individual choice to such an extreme tends to neglect other equally significant ones, such as expertise, equity, and effectiveness in job performance. Furthermore, partisanship and broad-scale ideological attacks against government and public servants can undermine the basic legitimacy and popular confidence in government. It is even counterproductive to performance of tasks and responsibilities by impeding cooperation, informal collaboration, and sharing the vital information so necessary to carry out the work of modern government. Its approach can close off, rather than open up innovative solutions, practical achievement, and recruiting and nurturing qualified people into the ranks of government. In this sense, negative-state viewpoints ironically can fuel inefficiency and diseconomies of purpose, design, and implementation.

There is also a strange paradox contained in much of the current negative-state school's administrative paradigm: while it insists on the virtues of free enterprise, free markets, and natural cooperation as opposed to formalistic state intervention in the wider society context, it often prescribes the very reverse inside government—namely, an administrative approach that is strikingly authoritarian, top-down, and rigidly loyal to hierarchy, use of strict management controls, and task-oriented systems. The gap is great between what it envisions as the ideal for society compared to operating procedures within government. Anti-statism does not adhere to a democratic administrative model that invites broad-ranging participation from those within and outside government in order to make and implement public policies. Its thinking may be according to Adam Smith in regard to its societal vision, but according to Vladimir Lenin in terms of public administration prescriptions.

Finally, the stress on privatized and decentralized administrative solutions as being overall preferable, indeed superior, to actions by public administrators seems excessive and idealistic. Costs of private-sector contracts to perform public services can be just as significant: witness the repeated cost overruns in large weapons systems produced by private contractors. Business bureaucratic red tape can be just as prevalent as the government's: witness the problems of business responsiveness to environmental issues. Inequities, not to mention inefficiencies, can be rampant if programs are left entirely to private, state, and local options: witness the enforcement of civil rights throughout the United States until the federal government's intervention in the 1960s. Some problems will simply be ignored by industry unless firm government action is taken: witness the massive savings and loan scandal due to a weakness of government regulation. Blanket assertions in negative-state literature, in other words, about the virtues of private-sector over public-sector action tend to miss the mark or overvalue the capabilities of free enterprise in many instances. Especially in an era of fierce global competition, rapidly changing technologies, and advanced expertise, *public* action, planned and supported by government in cooperation with business and nonprofit agencies, is frequently necessary to cope with a vast array of complex issues confronting the nation. A privatized, decentralized public administration, both restricted in scope and staffed by amateur political loyalists, seems ill-equipped and ill-suited—even quaint—given the pervasive challenges confronting America. Thus the fundamental question: Can this negative-state model of public administration adapt well enough to the challenges ahead? Is it a realistic way to perform "the public's business"? Is it up to the tasks and responsibilities of the twenty-first century?

Bold-State (or Positive-State) Vision: Activist Public Administration

Public Institution-Building

If negative-state ideas fundamentally challenge the design, purposes, and ultimate legitimacy of public institutions and advance alternative methods and modes to formal bureaucratic action, bold-state writings reflect the mirror image. Bold-state activists are enthusiasts for the positive state and value its energetic role throughout society in order to promote and maintain the good life for citizens. They exhibit far less fear of government actions taken in the name of the public or the national interest compared to the weak-state writers. Indeed, they are cheerleaders for public institution-building that fosters strong, effective government organizations.

As Chapter Five outlines, this bold-state way of thinking grew up in the United States during the first half of the twentieth century and significantly shaped much of the founding doctrines of modern American public administration theory. It took root and evolved as a by-product of the explicit practical requirements for creating a stronger positive state in America to perform a variety of new national tasks and responsibilities imposed on the nation in the twentieth century. Within the public administration community, Leonard White, Louis Brownlow, and Luther Gulick were the founders of this strong management tradition.

Still today, these positive-state values dominate a considerable segment of the administrative literature, and these ideas continue to remain a vital, if not a fundamental, force in shaping contemporary public administration theory. By and large, such writings hold views that run directly counter to no-state thinking and in favor of:

- Expanded public roles and more activist institutions that can effectively respond to various societal challenges and individual needs;
- A national government that can take a positive lead in planning, coordinating, directing, managing, and implementing

public policies in various areas over states, localities, and the private sector;

- An emphasis on increasing overall institutional capacities so as to carry out public policies through government organizations;

- A focus on specific improvements in organizational effectiveness, such as staffing public agencies largely with career professionals who are well-trained and who are given adequate fiscal, planning, and managerial tools in order to carry out their assigned tasks;

- Encouragement for bold executive action in the name of the public, national, or community interest, as well as a clear preference for managers who are doers and movers;

- Limitations on political intrusions into public managerial roles and responsibilities in order to enhance public professionalism and expertise;

- Bottom-up accountability, rather than top-down direction, that is responsive to citizen, clientele, special interest, and legislative demands;

- Less emphasis on narrow economic theory and business values of economy and efficiency that constrain public action and more concern with the broader, elastic values of general management effectiveness as a basis to advance the community good and the public welfare.

This type of public administration model, as Chapter Five describes, had its clearest expression and widest appeal in the Brownlow Commission report (1937). Certainly it has not achieved the same fame or notoriety as the no-state school in the 1980s. Nonetheless, its influence remains strong among government insiders and professional public managers at all levels. Its expression is frequently found in government reports, professional association publications, and applied studies from government think tanks by individual students of public management. Often viewed as low-key and mundane, these publications nevertheless continue to be profoundly influential in the conduct of governmental practices.

Applied Administrative Studies

For example, the U.S. Government Accounting Office (GAO) series of recent reports on management practices in major federal departments reflects the creative application of classic good management principles according to Brownlow. One such GAO study reviewed the Environmental Protection Agency (EPA) and urges EPA's "management to identify ways the agency might improve its operational effectiveness and provide leadership essential to ensuring a clean and healthful environment."[17] Many of GAO's recommendations stress enhancing EPA's institutional capacity through "long-term planning to identify research needs," "developing a workforce embodying the skills needed to accomplish the tasks of today and the challenges in the years ahead," "more clearly communicate its goals and directives," "better integrate its planning and budgeting processes," "improve informational and financial systems," and "improve program implementation." Taken together, these prescriptions may not explicitly say POSDCORB; in fact such recommendations seek comprehensively to develop EPA's institutional capabilities through strengthening its overall managerial effectiveness. The words may have changed—that is, strategic planning and systems analysis—but this report remains squarely within the classic good management principles described by Brownlow.

At the grass-roots level, professional associations such as the International City Management Association (ICMA) and the American Society for Public Administration also continue to remain strong proponents for similar good professional management models. Typical of this perspective is the recent ICMA *Citizen Handbook: Retention of the Council-Manager Plan* (1988): "The Council-Manager Plan is a form of government developed in the United States to help communities overcome weaknesses in local government structure, and to cope with increasingly difficult and complicated local problems. . . ."[18] The report justifies adoption of these management practices embodied in council-manager government in order to enhance local problem solving, to assist elected officials in carrying out their assigned duties, and to improve ethical conduct and political responsiveness to the electorate. The normative assumption throughout is that expanding public institutional efficacy can be an invaluable asset for promoting responsible government in communities.

While "applied" administrative literature's norms continue to be fixed, as Brownlow's were, on finding ways for enhancing the public-sector's performance, much of the bold-state school today, unlike the Brownlow Commission's views, adopts a much more flexible approach toward principles of good management. They are less dogmatic about forcefully asserting the one best way, and their tone and emphasis are more qualified about asserting "the truth."

They exhibit considerably more selectivity and less certainty about overall schemes designed for "total" application. A good case in point is the major study by The National Commission on the Public Service (the Volcker report, named for its chair, Paul A. Volcker), *Leadership for America: Rebuilding the Public Service* (1989).[19] Rather than offering recommendations to reform all of government from the top down, as Brownlow sought, Volcker was more prudent and focused. Its blue ribbon panel composed of thirty-six men and women in prominent public, private, and nonprofit leadership positions produced one of the most significant public service reports since World War II that argued for a "renewed sense of commitment by all Americans to the highest traditions of the public service." The report prized strengthening governmental enterprises with a basic assumption that "the need for a strong public service is growing, not lessening" because Americans expect "our government to keep the peace," "pay the bills," "provide services with the highest levels of integrity and performance," and deal with a myriad of new issues such as international competition, the world economy, technological changes, and health issues like AIDS. Thus, argued this report, "we require a public service with professional skills and the ethical sensitivity America deserves."[20] In light of that aim, Volcker sought to target those federal institutional problems necessary to enhance professional skills within the federal service. Their key proposals included such pragmatic solutions as the following:

> "Cabinet officers and agency heads should be given greater flexibility to administer their organizations. . . ." (p. 6)
>
> "The growth in recent years in the number of presidential appointees [political appointees] . . . ought to be curtailed." (p. 7)
>
> "The President and Congress must ensure that federal managers receive the added training they will need to perform effectively." (p. 7)
>
> "The President and Congress should give higher priority to civil service pay. . . ." (p. 8)
>
> "It must be articulated early and often the necessary and honorable role that public servants play in the democratic process." (p. 13)
>
> "We should strengthen and expand the government's current programs for recruiting college graduates into public careers." (p. 26)
>
> "Federal productivity can and must improve. . . ." (p. 41)

In reviewing these "prescriptions," one senses a movement significantly away from the rigid POSDCORB doctrines of the 1930s; nonetheless, Volcker remains squarely in the Brownlowian camp of positive-state thinking. Their tactics and strategies—even their language—may differ, but their basic values remain much the same. As James Garnett recently observed, the orthodox doctrine of POSDCORB still permeates government administration in the United States today:

> Hierarchy, specialization, grouping by function, unity of command, and other orthodox precepts so shape organizational life despite their being debunked in academic circles that practitioners and scholars have difficulty thinking in different terms. Even when actions depart from orthodox theory, orthodoxy remains a frame of reference.[21]

Current Bold-State Scholarly Literature

The willingness to experiment and be less rigidly orthodox about good management, while enhancing public institutional roles and capabilities, is seen also in recent serious scholarly literature favoring a more activist state. Robert B. Denhardt and Edward T. Jennings, Jr. (eds.), *The Revitalization of the Public Service* (1987)[22] was a product of a conference sponsored by the Department of Public Administration at the University of Missouri at Columbia. The aim was "to bring together a diverse group of scholars and practitioners to assess the state of the profession and point the way to the future."[23] The authors were not so much interested in a defense of bureaucracy but, as the opening suggests, in "analysis of the current situation and a set of proposals that would support how the public service could be revitalized."[24] What is addressed in the dozen individual essays by the sixteen nationally prominent conferees are diverse ideas and prescriptions for strengthening America's public service. Some proposals reach back to old normative values, such as George H. Frederickson's call for "the recovery of civicism in public administration," while others seem genuinely new; such as Ann-Marie Rizzo's argument for "stake holder approaches to program design." Most provoke, stimulate, and challenge readers' thinking, but offer no "final cures." All authors, though, ultimately agree on the value of public services, its importance and worth in society, and stress the need for the improvement of its institutional capabilities and ultimate revitalization.

If the Denhardt and Jennings book calls for institutional

experimentations on a microlevel in order to enhance overall governmental effectiveness, Robert B. Reich's *The Next American Frontier* (1983) and *Tales of a New America* (1987),[25] in contrast, offer a macrolevel look at America in the modern political and economic world order and issue a stern warning that America's past political mythologies and present-day institutional practices are poorly designed and organized to meet the global and technological challenges in the years ahead. This prominent Kennedy School scholar calls for a new realism about the pervasive economic competition from abroad and about the rapid technological innovations that are transforming the world economy and American society. Reich's solutions are found in more subtle and experimental organizational designs that would strengthen government's capacities to respond to these dynamic international challenges. The answer is not "national planning," writes Reich, or "the blunt tools of historic preservation—broad gauge tariffs, desperate corporate bailouts, and prayerful microeconomics—but more subtle tools like restructuring agreements, training and employment vouchers, regional development funds and tax and financial codes that guide and accelerate market forces while discouraging paper entrepreneurialism."[26] Reich, in short, advocates bolder state action to foster the national interest by using more flexible, experimental organizational devices, initiated by government, yet carried out in cooperation with business and nonprofit organizations, in order to respond effectively to the changing global scene. He bluntly warns at the end that "either we will adapt to the new reality or following our historic predecessors, the American ascendency will needlessly come to a close."[27] For Reich, Americans ought to get their act together—politically, economically, and institutionally—for their own self-interest of survival in a new globally competitive era.

Positive-state authors, not only value institutional effectiveness—micro or macro—but often give special emphasis to individual managerial effectiveness as a principal means for improving productivity and performance of public administration as a whole. Steven Cohen's *The Effective Public Manager: Achieving Success in Government* (1988),[28] for example, takes the view that "the public sector can be effectively managed" and that it is through "an active and aggressive effort to overcome constraints and obstacles" by managers that great institutional effectiveness can be achieved. As he writes: "In large measure, effective public management is simply the product of a positive, can-do attitude."[29] Cohen believes that "effective public managers try to make things happen; they pursue programmatic goals and objectives by thinking and acting strategi-

cally. Effective managers attempt to understand why things are hap-
pening and how things can be changed."[30] Unlike no-state authors,
he sees them as doers, movers, innovators, and change agents, even
entrepreneurial risk takers who hope to ensure that government
programs succeed and that the public reaps the benefits of that success." Cohen even asserts that it is impossible to be an effective
public manager without being a risk taker. Furthering the public
good and community interest by their willingness to take on big
problems, to innovate, and to rethink programs from the bottom
up is their ultimate challenge—and their rewards. Much of Cohen's
book is oriented around specific practical advice to practitioners
for strengthening the public manager's role and operational effectiveness on the job as sample chapter titles illustrate: "How to Find
and Keep Good Staff," "Structuring the Organization for Optimum
Productivity," "Improving the Quality and Flow of Information,"
"Mastering the Budgetary Process and Controlling Resources," and
"Dealing with Superiors and Subordinates." Though it is all for a
good cause and worthy goal, as Cohen argues: "Modern American
society demands it all—plastic bags and a toxic-free environment,
fresh fruit and safe pesticides, material wealth and spiritual fulfillment. A free market alone will not produce the type of society in
which Americans wish to live."[31] An activist, energetic state
achieved through the talents of activist, energetic public managers
is Cohen's ultimate vision.

While many contemporary positive-state authors take such a
can-do, up-beat, and pragmatic "here's-how-do-it" point of view,
James A. Stever's *The End of Public Administration: Problems of the
Profession in the Post-Progressive Era* (1988)[32] provides a considerably more scholarly, deeper view of the problem today. Stever
seeks to examine the profound dilemmas of public administration
in what he calls "the post-Progressive era." He views the modern
era as fraught with a fundamental contradiction between fear or
dislike of public bureaucracy, on the one hand, and an "affinity for
programs and goals that generate increasing amounts of public
administration,"[33] on the other. This fundamental contradiction is
born from the problems of the post-Progressive era, as the subtitle
suggests, for it creates complications for legitimizing the role and
practice of public administration today.

According to the author, three alternatives for dealing with the
present situation exist: (1) let the contradiction continue, (2)
reduce dependency on government, or (3) "embark on the arduous
task of enhancing the status of public administration in American
culture." The first course is risky, suggests Stever, because "it is

increasingly unlikely that privately controlled administrative techniques in private hands will continue to complement the public or collective good. . . . A 'truly public administration' is here defined as one that seeks to apply the growing power of administration to the broad public interest as opposed to the ends of a few."[34] The second option is risky because it is both "infeasible and somewhat romantic," given that today "governments have become an integral part of a national service delivery network."[35] This leaves the third as the only real logical option, and the bulk of Stever's book is devoted to pursuing theoretically that goal: namely, finding a way to positively legitimate public administration in America. His challenging thesis is that public administration ought to develop as a profession, specifically what he terms "a polity profession," for through professionalism, "visible, legible authority is vital for the positive legitimation of public administration."[36] As Stever writes:

> Public administration must appear to both elected officials and the public as a critical function to the maintenance of society. Furthermore, the civil servant must acquire a certain mystique in the performance of these crucial functions.[37]

In the end he warns against the continued trend toward "pluralism by default" that leads to increasing institutional fragmentation, decay, and lack of a field's "locus or focus." It also dooms the field to illegitimacy or, as Stever writes:

> The pluralist bottom line is that public administration in America is destined to function without professional cohesion, without structural integrity, and without theoretical integrity. This is tantamount to claiming that public administration must be perpetually illegitimate.[38]

On the other hand, he sees that professionalization of public administration—an identity that combines theory, training, calling to service, an institutional network, and exercise of control—can allow it to have a positive impact on the public culture that will sustain and serve the needs of a liberal government and liberal society: "For the masses of people who constitute the greater portion of the citizenry, a public culture supported by a professional civil service would be a net improvement over what is occurring in the post-Progressive era."[39]

If Stever makes a strong case for "professionalization" in order to legitimatize the public administration role in America, Charles T. Goodsell's *The Case for Bureaucracy: A Public Adminis-*

tration Polemic (2d ed., 1985) simply outlines a full-scale frontal assault on the popular myths and wrongheaded characterizations of public administration that abound today in modern society. By marshaling a wealth of empirical data and qualitative evidence, plus reasoned interpretation, Goodsell attempts to clear away the fog of misperceptions and to make the case that public bureaucracy is one of the great, central institutions that sustain civilization and culture. It is a creative force for societal good, not ill, that emerges from this analysis. In the best sense, his book is a polemic attacking the stereotypes of bureaucrats that prevail in America. He concludes: "Even though the grand myth of bad bureaucracy probably can never be excised from American society, the grand assault on good bureaucracy can be countered and must be."[41] Goodsell ends with a plea for "the campaign of public action in behalf of this public asset to the entire country." For him, public education on a massive scale can be the only proper antidote for public administration's present-day misfortunes. By changing public attitudes, public administration may then find a supportive environment for undertaking its critical tasks and roles in American society and, thus, through citizen awareness, perhaps achieve, as Stever searches for, its fundamental legitimation and justified place within American culture.

An Assessment of the Bold-State Vision

On the whole, contemporary bold-state thinking in the late twentieth century appears in many forms and speaks with many voices. It is hard to classify easily, or as easily as no-state theorists. Neither its prescriptions nor its methods of analysis are monolithic. Some, like Goodsell, speak in an empirical and behavioral language, or, as Stever addresses it, in historical, normative theory; others, such as Reich, approach the subject in policy and economic terms; still others, like Volcker and Cohen, speak in highly pragmatic, applied managerial tones. Their approaches, like the reforms advocated, vary significantly from author to author. They present no united front in support of one idea or of several. Few if any, however, argue for creating a total state in which public administration does everything, as did Bellamy in the 1880s (see Chapter Three); nor do they accept the classic managerial orthodoxy of Brownlow (see Chapter Five). All these writers do prefer a bolder, more effective administrative system than what presently exists. Thus, their views place these writers squarely within the White, Brownlow, and Gulick tradition of American public administration thought that dominated the first half of the twentieth century. While no-state theorists have certainly held higher public visibility and national esteem in the 1980s, bold-state thinking has maintained a vital, consistent output and respectable influence throughout the last decade, especially among government insiders and professional scholars of public administration.

Above all, these writers remind us repeatedly of the operational realities and prerequisites for making American government operate successfully today and in the years ahead. Without effective institutional arrangements, professional expertise, and attention to the management details, effective government as we know it in a liberal society, they argue, will not long survive. The natural tendency in democratic nations is to overlook such essentials. These authors speak cogently to the continued necessities for wise planning, management, trained personnel, professionalism, and practical realism about doing "the public's business." Indeed, of all the schools, they have the keenest sense of promoting the public interest, the general welfare, the liberal society, the whole community, and the good society, and they are the most likely to worry about society's care and nurturing. Although they cannot quite tell precisely what the public interest is or how it can be defined, either in practice or in theory, these authors are stoutly sure "it" is there and worthy of a hard fight and their dedication and commitment.

Further, as mentioned before, writers today are far more open and less doctrinaire than were earlier management advocates of the one best way such as POSDCORB. They are less prone to want to take heaven by storm. Such new concepts as strategic planning reflect the remarkable appreciation by most of these authors today of the complexity and need for adjusting ideas to the pressures of societal change. Things in public administration in the late twentieth century are less simple; so are the ideas in relationship to describing, prescribing, analyzing, and advancing public administration.

In addition, these authors, compared to other schools, perhaps best collectively address the immediate needs and issues of insiders, those who operate as professionals on the firing line and who must make the system work on a day-to-day basis. It speaks their language and deals with their problems in a practical, timely, and direct manner. Good management, pragmatism, professionalism, and effectiveness are the terms they use and the criteria for action they espouse. This school of thought, unlike the negative-state school, generally recognizes that the unique qualities of public work make effective public management different from business management or other varieties of organizational endeavors, and therefore it must be studied and analyzed differently. Its angle of vision is, as a result, on much the same wavelength as those in government service and as such, stimulates, nourishes and speaks to the values and concerns of the practitioner audience.

On the other hand, positive-state writings today are not without their difficulties. Certainly there are some down sides. At times, these writings seem collectively to speak only to insiders and to take unflinchingly their view and stand only in their corner. At times, they appear to be cheerleaders for bureaucracy and the public service and, as a consequence, seem to turn a blind eye to its many flaws. They tend at times to prefer bureaucratic solutions and to ignore noninstitutional methods of achieving public goals, such as the nontraditional or economic alternatives proposed by negative-state theorists. It must be quickly added in their defense, however, that most bold-state authors are only attempting to bring some balance into a public debate in America that largely favors scapegoating bureaucrats. Americans are particularly prone to leap to hostile points of view about public officials and so, in this context, positive staters are simply, perhaps in fairness, trying to redress gross imbalances and injustices in popular thinking. Yet, just as the no-state view tends to get carried away with ideological attacks on formal public institution, so, too, do the bold staters lapse into easy, unsupported statements about the virtues of government action. And here and there they sound as if they are preaching to the choir, or talking to insiders, rather than to the general public. What justifies the bureaucratic action they tend to advocate over the alternatives? What are the virtues of this form of collective action over others?

Stever's book perhaps put the finger on the central problem that plagues positive-state thought today—namely, what legitimates creating a stronger, more effective role for state action within the context of American society? One is hard-pressed to find such support from a literal reading of the American Constitution. History seems to be on the side of the no-state theorists. The U.S. Constitution was designed *not* to be efficient, effective, or well-managed but quite the reverse: it created a system capable of smashing a strong administrative system in order to protect individual liberties and human freedoms. As a result, and as Chapter Three emphasizes, the American administrative state had to be chinked in between the cracks and was then, as well as now, seen as a temporary arrangement, not as a permanent constitutional fixture. An activist administrative model presupposes a positive-state design in the American Constitution, and thus some bold-state writings must resort to extraconstitutional devices in order to justify its place in America's constitutional system. As Chapter One emphasizes, the founders never conceived of a European-style positive state in creating the Great Charter of 1787. Specifically, therefore, how can Americans graft an activist administrative state onto a constitutional order that was designed to prevent its creation? Is professionalization, or what Stever terms "a polity profession," the answer? Are the felt necessities of a highly competitive international order, as Reich believes, ample justification for adopting a positive state? Most positive staters simply avoid the problem altogether and retreat into pragmatic solutions—i.e., what works is ok. Such practical arrangements can be put together—or put up with—for just so long before they become so complex, so piecemeal, and so unwieldy to operate that they finally can be seen for what they are: extraconstitutional, even slightly shady and illicit practices. Furthermore, what should be the end to the expansion of the positive state under these circumstances? Are there no limits? Positive-state writers certainly want a bolder state for various reasons, often quite good and justifiable reasons, but they fail, at least so far, to provide the appropriate means to legitimate state expansion within the existing American Constitution or to tell us where or how to limit state intervention once it is developed.

Bold-state thinking today needs a satisfactory conceptualization of the meanings of the good life, the public welfare, the public interest, and the liberal society. Positive-state writings use such concepts frequently as a basis for advancing positive-state prescriptions. Yet, from the context of these often idealistic slogans, it is hard to tell what precisely is meant by such terms. Descriptions tend to be sketchy at best and quickly passed over by these scholars as "givens." It is often assumed that everyone knows what these terms mean and agrees with their normative beliefs. What value or set of values ultimately justifies advancing the positive state and why? Today the challenges from no-state writings attach entirely different ideas to terms like the good life, the public welfare, the public interest, and the liberal society. Such words to no-state theorists take on new connotations, and they have not been shy in discussing their views on these subjects. Positive-state thinkers, on the other hand, have not often satisfactorily engaged in this level of discourse or countered their opposition in any profound or meaningful dialogue. Ultimate goals and ends are left more or less unarticulated, which leaves bold-state writings to appear on the whole as partial and incomplete.

Pre-State (or Halfway State) Vision: Temporizing Public Administration

Advocates of the Middle Ground

If negative-state and positive-state writings define the extremes on the spectrum of current dialogue about public administration, pre-state writers reflect a position somewhere in the middle. On the whole, these writers are more centralist in viewing the American state as well as its administrative system. They see the American state from a historical, philosophical, and evolutionary perspective and tend to understand "it" in light of its organic growth with all its many complexities and confused ways. Frequently, they do not even bother to try to define what a "state" or "public administration" is because its constitutional and institutional roots are so confused and complex. They do recognize public administration's central role and importance to society, but in their view defining public administration as a subject is a problematic exercise, given the immensely complicated history and jerry-built structures of the American state system. Their writings tend to be more descriptive and analytical rather than prescriptive or proscriptive. No major fundamental reforms to the existing system are found in these writings. These are more clear-eyed realists who accept things as they are, not ought to be. In many ways, they are our modern-day Edmund Burkes and Walter Bagehots who write from the point of view of evolutionary political realism, including public administration. Their thinking offers some of the most sophisticated and penetrating perspectives on the practice of public administration in the United States, but also it can be the most difficult to comprehend, pin down, and easily classify. Compared to the no-state and bold-state schools of thought, in addition, this school is less apt to propose clear-cut answers to problems confronting public administration and its authors are more tentative about their assumptions and cures for the creation of an ideal state and good administration. More "ifs," "maybes," and other qualifications dot their writings. They seem less certain about what is the best or how to reach it. Nonetheless, these writers from various disciplines individually and collectively articulate a vision that is intricately interconnected to the American constitutional framework.

Current Approaches of Pre-State Thinkers

Both John A. Rohr's *To Run a Constitution: The Legitimacy of the Administrative State* (1986)[42] and Don K. Price's *America's Unwritten Constitution: Science, Religion, and Political Responsibility* (1983)[43] are important recent contributions to this literature. Rohr's analysis attempts to legitimate existing public administration institutions in terms of constitutional principles. In Rohr's words, he seeks "to convince an interested public in the capability of the administrative state with constitutional principles." Rohr's argument is subtle and traces administrative legitimacy to U.S. constitutional origins. By no means does Rohr advocate a "bold administrative state" that emphasizes activist executive roles within the framework designed by the U.S. Constitution. Rather, he seeks to legitimate existing public administration with all its fragmented institutions and confusing complexities. From a close reading of the Constitution, Rohr sees the invention of public administration, as designed by the framers, to fill in the defects of the Constitution's separation of powers that "neither constitutes nor heads any branch of government, but is subordinate to all three."[44] Under the American constitutional system with its separation of powers, public administration, in Rohr's view, becomes something of "a balance wheel"—with "the grand end of maintaining the constitutional balance of power in support of individual rights."[45] Administrative duties are limited, circumscribed by constitutional values of checks and balances, always at the service of competing masters. And the competition never ends. Public administration is thus no monolithic giant or law unto itself, but is rooted in a competitive, pluralistic system, open to change, yet with concrete constitutional and legal boundaries. Rohr's constitutional ideal, while able to evolve, also clearly contains legalist limits for public administration within the confines of American society to fulfill the objective of "the oath of office to uphold the Constitution of the United States." As Rohr writes in this seminal treatise: "Administrators should use their discretionary power in order to maintain the constitutional balance of powers in support of individual rights."[46] Here is no bold-state Hamilton or negative-state Jefferson speaking, but Rohr, the good pluralistic Madisonian, is attempting to stake out a middle ground between extremes, as did Woodrow Wilson a century before.

Price also sees public administration as rooted in America's constitutional system, but he traces its roots further back than Rohr into the ideals of the Protestant Reformation and the later dissenting scientific attitudes that gave birth to America's confused legal and political authority in the United States. Authority was always being broken up and put under attack by the dissenting values inherent in America's Constitution. These uniquely American values directly led to decentralized American power in a public administration with "specialized practical concerns rather than general policy, legalistic controls rather than discretionary authority, and moralistic principles rather than political compromise." This peculiar system, says Price, works to keep "politics open to widespread popular participation, but at the cost of incoherence in policy and irresponsibility in legislation and administration."[47]

Price worries about the excesses of these tendencies but warns repeatedly in his important book against importing the British model of government or formally amending the U.S. Constitution "to fix problems." Such basic reforms, according to Price, would probably only make existing problems worse. Rather than grand redesign, he argues for adjustment "without amendment" by looking to "the unwritten constitution" that has grown up in the last century. These "unwritten" American administrative arrangements, he finds, hold the promise of providing tentative solutions to present national dilemmas. Through the "evolution of a richly varied unwritten constitution that can be adapted by political bargaining to new needs and circumstances,"[48] argues Price, the U.S. Constitution can evolve to meet modern challenges. Like Rohr, public administration stands for Price at the center of America's existing pluralistic, fragmented constitutional system today and is an important, even central, means for adapting constitutional values to modern realities. There are no visions put forward here for grafting a bold, positive-state system onto the U.S. Constitution. Indeed, Price opposes such basic reformulations as adopting the British Parliamentary design or other imports. Reforms are thus made on the edges and adjustments are added or subtracted in small increments, in accordance with existing American constitutional values, not at the center through wholesale reforms.

Contemporary agency histories in recent years written by prominent scholars of public administration also portray numerous examples of this pre-state view, or one partially developed with overlapping, decentralized authority and competing pluralistic institutional arrangements. Donald F. Kettl's *Leadership at the Fed* (1986)[49] is a good case in point, for it captures in vivid detail the development and evolution of the Federal Reserve System in a competitive and pluralistic context, which forces the Federal Reserve to constantly balance and adjust to presidential, congressional, and special interest demands. Emphasizing the political role of the Federal Reserve chairman as the man-in-the-middle, Kettl points out that the chair's critical leadership is vital to "building support, . . . developing credibility, or dealing with the complex and conflicting political environment in which the Fed finds itself."[50] How the chair "negotiates," "wheedles," "fine tunes," and "plays politics," according to Kettl, significantly affects the success or failure of the Fed's enterprise. Kettl sums up the seventy-plus years of powerful Federal Reserve administrative influence thusly: "For the Fed to survive, it must travel a politically acceptable course through irreconcilable demands."[51] These irreconcilable demands are imposed on the Fed, like other agencies, within the fragmented American administrative system, a system that radically decentralizes and breaks up political power.

No pat prescription, no answers, no cures, are advanced in much of pre-state literature on agency history, which is steeped in webs of U.S. history, politics, and constitutional values. Ample insights into the organic complexities and interconnections of modern public administration are contained in these studies that often show administrative activities as involving a continuous series of "no-win" trade-offs among competing values. Frederick C. Mosher's *A Tale of Two Agencies: A Comparative Analysis of the General Accounting Office* [GAO] *and Office of Management and Budget* [OMB] (1984)[52] is another good recent example of this perspective. Mosher provides a concise institutional history of GAO's and OMB's institutional development that creatively compares and contrasts the organic origins and development of both (both were created by the same legislation, The Budget and Accounting Act of 1921). As in Kettl's book, the central story is about two agencies caught throughout their histories in a tug of war between competing claims for "the maintenance of continuity, expertise, and credibility, on the one hand, and of political responsiveness on the other: in short, the relating within the same organization of professionalism and politics without damage to either."[53] How both agencies have coped with these intricate competing norms, according to Mosher, in large part depended on their leadership at the top and the distance or nearness to their political masters they served. OMB, being closer to power—the President—and serving only one party at a time, perhaps has had a tougher job "to provide a bridge between truth and power." In contrast, "GAO always must work for two different parties in two different houses and for many blocks and subdivisions."[54] As a result, says Mosher, intensive pluralism keeps GAO hugging the center ground of professional neutrality, whereas OMB's subservience to one political master, the President, has led it, at times willy-nilly, to being forced into political partisanship roles. Innovative leadership is demanded in both situations, but the situation itself largely defines the latitude for action and the possible variety of creative responsiveness that is allowable.

These and other administrative histories,[55] trace a particular organic development of America's administrative state and institutions of public administration. Administration is viewed essentially as a creative process of juggling competing claims of interests, professionalism, and political agendas within a vast landscape of the American setting. Here public administration is viewed as being interconnected and integrated fundamentally with politics, institutions, history, and constitutional values. Standing today at the center of the U.S. government, it serves essentially as a balance wheel, to use Rohr's apt phrase, profoundly rooted to America's pre-state constitutional design. America's administrative system is thus unique in contrast to other national administrative systems. So, too, is an administrator's role within this system.

The uniqueness theme is therefore another primary trademark of this literature, as Joseph L. Bower's *The Two Faces of Management: An American Approach to Leadership in Business and Politics* (1983)[56] underscores. The public sector is an enormously difficult arena in which to operate because of the various constitutional, political, and institutional constraints on public managerial roles in contrast to those of a business leader. Bower catalogues numerous comparisons with the private sector and emphasizes the political and institutional constraints imposed on government managers, such as "goals are diffuse or not operational"; "selectivity (of purposes) is not legitimate"; "budget control is tight due to line-item budgets"; "the public manager must operate in the open"; "few management information systems are available"; "organization is contingent on personality and current issues"; and "gossip and informal networks are keys to management success."[57] The constraints are so many, according to Bower, that often it is a wonder that *any* opportunity for successful management practices exist. Indeed his prescriptions for good management practiced in the public setting are few, if any.

For the public administrator, therefore, the message is clear: the need is to understand this unique context, to have the ability to work with trade-offs, to appreciate the different institutional realities and constraints, and to recognize the importance of chance, luck, and fate in being a successful public manager as much as technical proficiency. Thus, at best, if there is a prescription in pre-state writings today for practicing administrators, it is that they should recognize that they work within a highly unusual environment of a haphazard, fragmented administrative landscape, and that their work decidely involves creatively integrating, coordinating, knitting together, and innovating. Generally, unlike no-state or bold-state writers, pre-state authors avoid the mechanistic terms associated with efficiency, effectiveness, and economy as bottom lines for defining the "correct" administrative criteria for action. Rather, these writers envision a more creative, spontaneous, and humane role for public administrators, one in which outcomes are dictated by judgment, intuition, feelings, and the nonrational. They exhibit a keener sense of political dimensions, as opposed to strictly mechanical management practices in the work of administration, in which one has to work at the edges and interstices of problems in order to move things along.

Several recent authors speak forcefully to these themes of administrators as people-in-the-middle: Harlan Cleveland, in *The Knowledge Executive: Leadership in an Information Society* (1985)[58] pushes for "the-get-it-all-together-professional" role for today's public administrators. Cleveland argues that administrators must have a generalist's breadth of understanding of events and actions in order to see the big picture, yet they must be individuals who can grapple with specific details. It is integrative and demanding work, without exact formulas or clear road maps, but it is the most creative and rewarding process because of its potential for dealing with the future of society, indeed the world's fate. Cleveland uses phrases like "knitting together," "getting it together," "knowledge dynamic," and "generalist mindset" to explain executive roles.

Jameson W. Doig's and Erwin C. Hargrove's *Leadership and Innovation: A Biographical Perspective on Entrepreneurs in Government* (1987)[59] contains a dozen carefully culled and crafted biographies of prominent public administrators who were by and large credited with important achievements in their respective fields. A portrait emerges from these individual biographies—namely, that leaders do make a difference in the work they perform for government, but their innovations and influence on events very often come from a mysterious interplay among their leadership styles, their institutional roles, and the particular environments within which they operated. Timing, good luck, fate, accident, and simply being in the right place at the right time had a significant role in their success. Yet, individual administrative artistry and personal motivations of leadership, argue the authors, also made a mark on events. The sense of "artistry" in public administration is vividly underscored by these biographies.

In George W. Downs and Patrick D. Larkey's *The Search for Government Efficiency: From Hubris to Helplessness* (1986)[60], one can find a convincing case made for administrative "artistry" in advancing even a specific technical subject like efficiency in government. The authors argue that both efficiency and inefficiency basically have a political character. The tendency in the past has been either to oversell efficiency techniques such as planning, programming, budgeting systems (PPB) and management by objectives (MBO) (i.e., "hubris") or to undersell government's capability to do much to improve efficiency (i.e., "helplessness"). A more realistic middle ground is proposed by the authors: "In designing future reforms, it is important to view efficiency as one among many competing values in political processes. The problem in reforming governments to improve their efficiency is that of ensuring effective representation of the value of efficiency in the political process."[61] Working "not so much from overt, grandiose reform schemes as from a host of modest, tactical reform," say these authors, holds the key for improvements in government efficiency: in short, it is the middle way between extremes.

Pros and Cons of the Pre-State Vision

What emerges from current pre-state thinking, in the best sense, is a way of thinking, a normative philosophy if you will, that is politically realistic and humane for the practicing public administrator. It fits closest to the tradition of American public administrative experiences, rooted in the U.S. constitutional design, with a unique institutional history and complicated present-day reality. It is therefore concerned with organic connections between administration and constitutional values, between national history and institutional evolution—with all the perplexities and complexities involved. It is most mindful of constitutional legitimacy problems in the field and works to deal with them on a serious intellectual level. Indeed, this way of thinking fosters an appreciation of irony, ambiguity, and chance, even the irrational and nonrational in administrative affairs, and speaks more of limits, constraints, and cautions regarding any easy reforms or snap solutions to administrative dilemmas. There is no talk of sharp artificial separations between politics and administration here to enhance administrative efficiency; no pleas for big or small reform techniques. These writers are certain there are no quick fixes. In brief, they are excellent critics because they tend to describe, analyze, see the big picture, understand all sides, and weigh the trade-offs.

They call for insight, creativeness, wisdom, balance, and an appreciation of the context of the situation in any given situation in which public administration must operate. When they do recommend, it is most often on the margins favoring temporizing incremental changes that nudge improvements here and there, but they advocate reforms in no fundamental way. They tend to like to work in particular details of personalities, histories, and events. These are not revolutionary but, rather, evolutionary theorists of administration who feel uncomfortable with the excessive expectations, grand theories of reform, or major organizational changes in the administration system that are often prescribed by no-state and bold-state theorists.

These writings are not without flaws, however. For one, they are generally so sophisticated that they can see all sides of complexity and are so cautious about prescribing change that they can be accused at times of preferring the status quo over improving what exists. An inherent institutional conservatism characterizes this writing. Certainly, they lack the zeal for making bold moves, taking aggressive action, or questioning core assumptions about the American Way. There are no monetarists, Marxists, or Maoists in this lot of authors. It is a way of thinking with a special world view. In the language of economists, they prefer "satisficing" or "nonoptimizing" solutions, largely because their strong organic sense of historical and constitutional understanding tell them that this is the only realistic and prudent course of action to take. A high premium is placed on common sense or pragmatic "sensibility" by these authors; for them "what works" is the only suitable criterion for action for public administration. In a nation that prefers doers and movers to penetrating thinkers and critics, this more prudent school of thought basing action on wisdom and experience wins less popularity and influence today, even within the public administration community. It certainly attracts the fewest recruits to its banner, precisely because it avoids *raising* a banner. It is frequently too difficult to comprehend, follow, or get the point. So where's the message? In fairness to pre-staters, however, one must ask how it is possible to communicate "wisdom," which by its nature is complicated and only found through individual reflection and hard-won knowledge based on experience.

Intellectually from behavioral social science, also this vision is challenged for being mere description, for lacking rigor, and for missing a tight methodological design. Their thinking often focuses on the single case and thus tends to be hard to generalize from: Where is the "method"? the means for verification of their conclusions? the quantitative analysis to prove "the case"? the scientific approach? the clear categories? From the "hard" social scientific perspective, it is viewed as not worth reading since it deals with soft values, applied wisdom, mushy norms, and no techniques, and has little predictive power. "Why bother with such stuff?" say the rigorous social scientists.

Pro-State Vision (or a Professional Technocracy in the Global Society): Public Administration as Specialized "Analytics"

If pre-state writers draw on constitutionalism, institutional history, and political realism for their administrative framework, pro-state theorists today are creatures of the postwar American state system, in which globalism, professionalism, and technocracy define its administrative essence. As a result, a different set of normative values tends to prevail.

Aspects of this modern American state system, the global professional technocracy, have already been outlined in Chapter Four and need not be reviewed again here; briefly, the primary attributes defining its ideal public administration theory include the following:

1. Definition by little clusters of professional experts operating in a global context;
2. Hyperimpermanence and complexity of ideas and doctrines;
3. Blurring of the boundaries between public and private sectors, indeed among nations;
4. Fundamental commitment to the values of expertise, specialization, and merit;
5. Decisive shaping by driving technological imperatives;
6. Recognition of the central dilemma of our times: i.e., knitting together technical change with public purposes;

7. Higher education as the key legitimizer and theory-maker; and

8. An ultimate faith in the scientific paradigm and capacities for specialized professional-technical inventiveness.

Current Literature: The Perry Book as a Case in Point

While numerous books and articles today reflect aspects of these features, in part or as a whole, of this new American state framework for thinking about public administration, one of the most comprehensive noteworthy examples is James L. Perry's *Handbook of Public Administration* (1989).[62]

Perry's book, sponsored by the American Society for Public Administration, is an impressive major contribution to the field that attempts to summarize the vast scope of its present literature and complex current practices. As its book jacket suggests, the book attempts to be a "comprehensive volume that identifies and analyzes all major issues and problems facing today's public administration professionals. It provides guidance for contending with social and demographic trends, implementing and evaluating public programs, budgeting and accounting, establishing effective relationships with government officials, and more." It is a rich, authoritative, and varied collection by fifty-four nationally respected authors that seeks to synthesize the state-of-the-art of diverse aspects of public administration.

What emerges from the text, without going into specifics of the theses of the particular authors, is a general portrait of how we think about public administration in the modern era of the global professional technocracy, or way of thinking, a normative theory if you prefer, that defines public administration very much along the lines of the aforementioned eight features of pro-state thinking. The editor and authors did not explicitly set out to elaborate this or any specific view of public administration. Rather, the purpose for writing this text was to address all major issues and problems of public administration. In so doing, however, the authors collectively project a view of the field that features an implicit pro-state point of view.

First, the book is a team effort that draws on experts from a wide array of disciplines, from around the world, to analyze and describe important functions, roles, and elements of public administration. No longer the product of a lone scholar or single author,

like a Leonard White, this administrative text draws on top specialists from various fields and subfields of public administration—
budgeting, accounting, evaluation, and others—in order to identify, study, and comprehend the specific subfield's issues. In turn,
these recognized specialists largely summarize recent work of
many other experts within the narrow boundaries of a specialization. As a result, what constitutes today's public administration, its
ideas and mode of thinking, as a whole, defines its elements and
basic categories. Moreover, the central issues to address largely
emerge from discussions and research by and among experts.
Small clusters of specialists within the purview of tightly con-
stricted circles of expertise serve to define what are the problems,
how they are addressed, and which solutions, if any, have been discovered. Therefore, the field as a whole exhibits considerable complexity and depth but also projects a disjointed and disconnected
quality, as one might expect from any multiauthored writing with
numerous specialists expressing varied points of view, ideas, theses,
and outlooks. In short, it creates a segmented literature and perspectives on the field.

Second, and as a by-product, there is little in the way of concrete doctrines or unifying ideas advanced by these authors.
Knowledge is drawn for application to the field from many current
sources and interdisciplinary perspectives. The field seems open to
every new idea and perspective and thus there is a dynamic quality
to this text. The image of diversity and change without limits is
reflected throughout this book. But it is all *today's* theories, methodologies, and modes of thought. Most of the footnotes cite 1980s
literature with few references to previous historical books or documents. The past counts for little; only the present and future matter. In part, the editor of the handbook, as well as some of the
authors, attempts to pull things together and impose an orderly
theme of effectiveness in public administration as the central thesis, but, at best, what is prescribed are the various analytical techniques within various technicalities that are shaped and moving
with their own technical dynamics, apart from each other. There
are no correct doctrines beyond highly transitory and various specializations and devices for analysis. The authors speak of options
and trade-offs, not one best way. In these essays, the field reflects
an absence of a corporate purpose, without history, and so it can
be characterized as largely specialized analytics, without a clear
sense of wholeness beyond technical specialties and analysis. Specialization so defines the contours of public administration that,
ironically, none of the authors ventures to define what "it" (public

administration) is despite 660 pages supposedly devoted to that end.

Third, a global perspective is evident as well. Boundaries among nations and between public and private sectors are blurred in this handbook. The nation-state, as well as the discipline of public administration with a clearly defined scope and boundaries, seems to disappear. Much of the text's material is drawn from and about the United States, but much of it could pertain to any modern developed nation. The global overview of the contemporary public sector envisions its roles and scope interrelated and interconnected with private sectors as well as to other nations to the point that its distinctiveness as a "national identity" evaporates. Part I defines the new environment in which American public administration operates as no longer a closed nation-state but in the world context, as opening chapter titles indicate: "Coping with Global Interdependence," "The Explosion of Technology," and "Shifting Demographic and Social Realities." As one paper puts it, "The artful public administrator now becomes a 'weaver' who sees patterns and connections in the global environment and threads them into effective networks capable of local public action."[63] Here the traditional idea of "state" declines in relative importance. Neither the public sector nor its intellectual study is conceived as a traditional nation-state or government. American public administration has entered an entirely new era of the global professional technocracy in such writings.

Fourth, the trained administrator, expert, specialist, and "meritcrat" are pictured as critical for guiding, deciding, and directing administrative systems. The assumption throughout most of these essays is that competent individuals are essential—indeed central—to the effective operation of this new global professional technocracy and these specialists need to be afforded discretion, latitude, and respect for their public roles. No longer is public administration simply confined to carrying out, implementing, or doing the public's business, efficiently and economically; now it entails a whole range of public activities, some decidedly political functions as certain chapter titles indicate: "Empowering and Involving Citizens" and "The Public Administrator's Role in Setting the Policy Agenda." The Perry handbook envisions public administrators' tasks and responsibilities today to cover a wide range of actions and roles formerly reserved for politicians. Indeed, the political role seems to shrink significantly as the administrator's expands within this handbook's perspectives. It concludes with a plea for public administration to be seen as a profession with competence, expertise, and merit as keys for the field's future development. "Joining competence to commitment," argues Perry in his concluding chapter, "is a necessary formula for meeting the challenges that confront today's public administrator . . . which stem from the American system of public administration and the technical, social, and international development that currently surround it."[64] The book takes as axiomatic that expert knowledge, not the generalist dilettante, will be essential for the vast range of tasks of running a modern global professional technocracy.

Fifth, hard and soft technologies are the driving forces of this world of public administration thought. Clearly hardware and software including computers, telecommunications, information systems, and cybernetics are seen in the handbook as critical for guidance, control, direction, and management of public administration. Discussions in individual chapters also feature significant soft technologies that have been invented in recent decades for study, analysis, and implementation of public agendas: i.e., policy analysis, program evaluation, accounting, audits, performance appraisals, coordination structures, procurement processes, and intelligence devices. Here is fundamentally a technique-driven world, an artificial world as opposed to a natural world. Critical instrumentalist technologies and soft technologies that have been invented largely by social scientists in recent decades and that guide and direct public-sector actions toward more rational and well-defined ends are given the most prominent attention and elaboration in these writings. Frederick Taylor's one-best-way is thus the grandfather of this handbook. The image of machine technology emerges and dominates this book's thinking. Much of public administration as an idea and process therefore is pictured here, not as a generalist, get-it-all-together profession but as a bag of tools, technologies, analytical techniques, and applied instruments that decisively create and influence the direction of the global professional technocracy. Discontinuities and disconnections between and among these technologies are apparent so as to make it overall a less than perfect, well-ordered, rational machine model. Nonetheless, the machine image is strikingly apparent in this handbook.

Sixth, individually and collectively, these writers view oversight and accountability of these hard and soft technologies of public administration as a significant problem. Concluding chapters in the handbook emphasize these themes: "Balancing Competing Values," "The Liability of Public Administrators," and "A Guide to Ethics for Public Servants." Accountability themes are raised in the discussion of new forms of public delivery systems—third-party and "coproduction" arrangements—that involve central questions of control and oversight. Ethical questions pervade the various technical problems of administrative duties. How can both hard and soft administrative technologies, as well as administrators themselves, serve public ends rather than the goals of the technocrats and technologies? Who will integrate and direct them? Who *is* the public and how best can it be served? How can the public control the controllers and for what ends? What should the values of administrators be? These intellectual issues nag at readers throughout the Perry handbook. There is much to ponder and worry about—with few definitive answers offered up—by authors of this handbook.

Finally, legitimacy for the field is ultimately a by-product of social science knowledge generated from advanced education and research. All fifty-four authors of articles in this book are members of university faculties, consulting firms, or think tanks. None is currently a practitioner of public administration or simply a generalist lay citizen. By implication, the foundation for public administration as both ideas and practice rests on acquiring professional expertise and advanced training from a wide range of fields in higher education, which affords status, recognition, and authority. It allows an individual, in other words, to speak as an expert. As indicated before, this text provides understanding the field largely in terms of specialized analytics and draws heavily on positivist social science thinking, particularly from policy analysis, management science, and organization theory, all of which are largely generated by higher education research and all of which stress rational analysis, science, and theory as the most appropriate modes of thinking and reasoning. It places considerable optimist faith in seeing and reasoning, based on rational, empirical ways of thinking that dominate modern social science. Ultimately, it is built on a positivist eighteenth-century faith that happiness and justice will result from rational, applied research for the general public and social progress for all.

This bright belief in social progress through technical application and scientific inventiveness is profoundly shared by these writers. Nonrational, intuitive judgment, wisdom, and personal insight are given little, if any, treatment. Unlike pre-state writers, pro-state writers give short shrift to application of historical, political, literary, poetic, and philosophical knowledge.

From these and other writings, the diversity, complexities, values, and realities of modern global professional technocracy are apparent. Above all, the strength of this writing is its overview of the contemporary American state in the world setting as governed by clusters of experts, techniques, and technologies. The authors collectively provide stimulating understanding—a vision?—of the changing nature of the public sector and its roles and responsibilities in the world context by emphasizing the driving forces of globalism, professionalism, and technologies. The focus is interdisciplinary, drawing on a wide range of skills and knowledge, offering up-to-date macrolevel and microlevel perspectives. Although the authors prefer to describe, analyze, and evaluate, not propose doctrines or normative solutions, in fact, they collectively capture the truth or much of the truth about the modern administrative enterprise, perhaps more so than they realize.

An Assessment of the Pro-State Vision

Much can be learned from this handbook about the modern state and how we think today about its administration. But there are also limits or problems of this writing, including the following. First there is the tendency to see the field of public administration in mechanistic and positivist terms, as simply a series of tools or analytics that experts need to grasp in order to perform their work. The technical vision of the state is as a political belief system with its own values and norms different from other state systems. It is a unique political philosophy. A technical view of public administration, which frequently (though certainly not entirely) is evidenced in this handbook, can fail, if taken to the extreme, to deal adequately with normative considerations such as serving the public good as well as attaining the good life. What are the appropriate goals and means for achieving these ends and the collective integration of various methodologies? How can integration of specialties in public administration be achieved for the common good? How can national values and ideological preferences of individuals and groups values be included in decisions? How can appreciation of historical backgrounds of public agencies and the particular constitutional context be understood? What purpose and larger ends should these technologies and experts in public administration serve? How can limits and checks be imposed on these techniques?

Second, is the fact that such an approach, which tends to take an empirical, analytic, and technological point of view, also tends to be blind toward the creative, intuitive dimensions of dealing with politics, institutions, and "people problems" involving administration. The expert in the technical view can easily take over the whole of the enterprise of public administration; its language and belief systems can easily encompass everything without most people ever realizing it. But at a price—opportunities for creative leadership, nonrational solutions to people problems in human organizations, and actions based on practical intuitive insight, judgment, and applied moral wisdom can be lost or underemphasized. A technique-driven state can impose rigidity, centralization, mechanistic solutions, and a homogeneity on governmental processes. In brief, it can easily dehumanize government and squeeze out vision and idealism for the men and women who work in it *and* its clientele.

Third are the assumptions, often hidden in these writings, that knowledgeable experts, or those with knowledge of such techniques and analytical tools, are the chosen ones who can and will influence in better ways than the nonexpert and generalist the direction of the public sector for the public good. There is a certain antidemocratic elitism thus found at the root of many of these writings, that value an educated meritocrat for directing and controlling public issues. Some, in other words, are "better" for government service than others. If they do not so explicitly state it, at least many of these authors tend to favor the technocratic and administrative norms with the technocrat and administrator in charge over the free market, natural cooperation, and informal arrangements. There is little room left for the amateur or unitiated in arcane techniques and administrative jargon.

Finally, an instrumentalist thinking can be fostered in arguments for using technical policy analysis, implementation, statistics, and evaluation research. Those devices are hardly neutral, as some of their proponents claim. They represent a way of explaining the world and apprehending human action—but only *one way*. In this world vision, facts, analysis, data, and manipulation techniques can become individually and collectively ends in themselves. Technical and quantitative analysis applied to human situations incur value judgments, though this reality is often lost because of the non-dialectic, formalistic, and linear formulations imbedded in technocratic thought. A tool of administration never is entirely free of value choices, and the public administrator who comes somehow to believe it can be so runs the risk of being dangerously optimistic, even naive, about the potential for the application of administrative technology. Technical approaches taken by themselves or in bits and pieces as in Perry's handbook, in other words, can promote unrealistic and unwarranted expectations about their effects. Thus, the key unanswered question is: Where and how can limits be placed on the technique-driven vision of administration so that we will not ultimately be captured by the triumph of technique or the technical faith?

Other State Visions, Other Administrative Models

The foregoing state visions and their concomitant ideal administrative models may well be the dominant visions and models in public administration today, but they by no means exhaust the possibilities in contemporary literature. Numerous minor critical voices are heard as well, proposing still other ideas about state design with an implicit or explicit administrative apparatus inherent in its operational design. There are arguments advancing Marxist visions; others advance a developmental state or a contractual state; still others advance an associational state design. Frequently, these criticize the status quo and offer strikingly different alternatives. Voices of the 1960s from the new public administration movement are still heard from today—though in far more muted tones—advocating a state devoted to enhancing human equity in which administrators consciously pursue the goals of promoting fairness and justice for the less fortunate in society. These writers press for a public administration arranged and organized toward pursuing those normative ends, possibly a new kind of "equity state."[65] Other writers, from the phenomenological or critical social theory vantage points, conceive of a state that enhances human interaction, personal growth, and individual freedom through reason and intuitive understanding. Here public administration is generally viewed in-the-small where enhancing face-to-face interaction and personal development becomes a chief aim. In the words of one proponent of this line of thinking, public administration should be a "catalyst for community or client participation in decision making" that "facilitates consensus" and is motivated by "love and mutual fulfillment."[66] Here the state almost evaporates from view, and so does public administration in this world of naturalism and personal interaction. Is this a return to the natural community without a state?

Still another prominent scholar, Theodore J. Lowi, in *The End of Liberalism: The Second Republic of the United States* (2d ed., 1979),[67] makes a strong case for "a judicial democracy." According to Lowi, responsiveness in American government has declined due to the vast expansion of government activities, which have been pushed by special interest needs. This rapid expansion has led to

Table 7.1 *Contemporary Visions of the American State and Their Inherent Models of Public Administration*

	No State	Bold State	Pre-State	Pro-State
Ideal Role for PA in Society	Sharply limited	Broadly expanded	"A balance-wheel"	Global, all-encompassing
Constitutional Legitimacy	Strictly constrained by constitutional rules, etc. (Ostrom)	Uncertain relationship to U.S. Constitution	"Fills in the cracks" (Rohr); "unwritten constitution" (Price)	Technique-driven and unrelated to U.S. Constitution
Federal Role	Decentralized; sharply restricted	Feds and public service take lead roles	Mixed according to needs and tasks	Professional expertise at all levels in charge
Reliance on Free Market	High	Low	"It all depends"	No such thing; planning by experts
Source of Policy Direction	Top down with politicals in command	Bottom up with citizens, interests, and officials involved widely	Influenced "from all sides"	Responsive to globalism, technology, and professional expertise
Key Staff Elite	Political appointees	Career bureaucrats	All three branches and administrators	Specialized experts
Political/Administrative Relations	Sharp split between politics and administration	Cooperative relationships between politics and administration	Complex and indefinable relationships	A nonrelationship; technocracy takes command
Criteria for Action	Economy and efficiency	Managerial effectiveness	Pragmatic, muddling-thru norms	Technical rationality and specialization
Ideal Model of Administrator	Temporary political appointee	Careerist; a doer, leader, and innovator	A fixer, negotiator, or bargainer	Specialist or professional expert
Historic Founding Father	Adam Smith	Louis Brownlow	Woodrow Wilson	Frederick Taylor

numerous new programs assuming vast powers to carry out their activities. Too much discretionary power, asserts Lowi, has been taken up by the various administrative agencies with the result of undermining democratic oversight and responsiveness. Instead of the status quo, Lowi presses for "a judicial democracy" in which the courts through legal principles and judicial action would restore and expand the rule of law by limiting the administrative state's power of coercion. He advocates clear rules, procedures, and laws to guide government actions: "The judicial principle puts the burden upon the law itself; and the law, when clear, would displace vague public expectations as the criterion by which the performance of governments and government officials would be judged."[68] In Lowi's world, the state would ideally be governed by lawyers, judges, and rules of law. In many ways, administration here becomes a total triumph of technique, the legal technique.

And what sense can be made out of all these competing state visions?

As Barry D. Karl once observed, history may not repeat itself, but often it seems to rhyme. Much like the late nineteenth century when various alternative visions of a new social order were debated with intensity—Sumnerism, Bellamyism, Wilsonianism—now, a century later, various alternatives for the American state are being vigorously advocated. Whether or not permanent changes will occur and what directions they may take remain problematical. However, as Table 7.1 attempts to sum up, the four dominant visions of an American state ultimately shaped the scope and boundaries of the current debate over public administration theory in America. As the United States enters the twenty-first century, the question is whether the parameters and the content of this dialogue will change as new and unforeseen types of state visions appear.

Notes

1. Stuart M. Butler, *The Privatization Option: A Strategy to Shrink the Size of Government* (Washington, D.C.: Heritage Foundation, 1985), p. 7. For an even more explicit discussion of this strategy, see Stuart M. Butler, *Privatizing Federal Spending* (New York: Universe Books, 1985).
2. E. S. Savas, *Privatization: The Key to Better Government* (Chatham, New Jersey: Chatham House, 1987).
3. Ibid., p. 3.
4. Ibid., p. 90.
5. Ibid., p. 291.

6. Randall Fitzgerald, *When Government Goes Private: Successful Alternatives to Public Services* (New York: Universe Books, 1988).
7. Vincent Ostrom, *The Political Theory of a Compound Republic: Designing the American Experiment*, 2d ed. (Lincoln: University of Nebraska Press, 1987).
8. Donald J. Devine, "Public Administration: The Right Way," in Robert Rector and Michael Sanera, eds., *Steering the Elephant: How Washington Really Works* (New York: Universe Books, 1987), p. 130.
9. Ibid.
10. *President's Private Sector Survey on Cost Control: A Report to the President* (Washington, D.C.: Privately Printed, January 15, 1984), vol. 2.
11. Ibid., p. 19.
12. Charles L. Heatherly and Burton Yale Pines, *Mandate for Leadership III: Policy Strategies for the 1990s* (Washington, D.C.: Heritage Foundation, 1989).
13. Ibid., p. xi.
14. Ibid., p. 19.
15. Ibid., p. 361.
16. Ibid., p. xi.
17. United States General Accounting Office, *Environmental Protection Agency: Protecting Human Health and the Environment through Improved Management* (Washington, D.C.: GAO, 1988), p. 8.
18. ICMA Endowment, *Citizens' Handbook: Retention of the Council-Manager Plan* (Washington, DC: ICMA, 1988), p. 3.
19. The Report of the National Commission on the Public Service, *Leadership for America: Rebuilding the Public Service* (Washington, D.C.: privately printed, 1989).
20. Ibid., p. 2.
21. James L. Garnett, "Operationalizing the Constitution via Administrative Reorganization: Oilcans, Trends, and Proverbs," *Public Administration Quarterly*, vol. 47, no. 1 (January/February 1987), p. 41.
22. Robert B. Denhardt and Edward T. Jennings, Jr., eds., *The Revitalization of the Public Service* (Columbia: Extension Publications, University of Missouri-Columbia, 1987).
23. Ibid., p. 10.
24. Ibid.
25. Robert B. Reich, *The Next American Frontier* (New York: Times Books, 1983) and *Tales of a New America* (New York: Random House, 1987).
26. Reich, *The Next American Frontier*, 278.
27. Ibid., p. 282.
28. Steven Cohen, *The Effective Public Manager: Achieving Success in Government* (San Francisco: Jossey-Bass, 1988).
29. Ibid., p. 13.
30. Ibid.
31. Ibid., p. 18.
32. James A. Stever, *The End of Public Administration: Problems of the Profession in the Post-Progressive Era* (Dobbs Ferry, New York: Transnational Publishers, 1988).

33. Ibid., p. 4.
34. Ibid., p. 6.
35. Ibid., p. 6.
36. Ibid., p. 20.
37. Ibid., p. 171.
38. Ibid., p. 180.
39. Ibid., pp. 183–184.
40. Charles T. Goodsell, *The Case for Bureaucracy: A Public Administration Polemic*, 2d ed. (Chatham, New Jersey: Chatham House, 1985).
41. Ibid., p. 177.
42. John A. Rohr, *To Run a Constitution: The Legitimacy of the Administrative State* (Lawrence: University Press of Kansas, 1986).
43. Don K. Price, *America's Unwritten Constitution: Science, Religion, and Political Responsibility* (Baton Rouge: Louisiana State University Press, 1983).
44. Rohr, p. 182.
45. Ibid.
46. Ibid., p. 181.
47. Price, p. 13.
48. Ibid., p. 180.
49. Donald F. Kettl, *Leadership at the Fed* (New Haven, Connecticut: Yale University Press, 1986).
50. Ibid., p. 193.
51. Ibid., p. 197.
52. Frederick C. Mosher, *A Tale of Two Agencies: A Comparative Analysis of the General Accounting Office and the Office of Management and Budget* (Baton Rouge: Louisiana State University Press, 1984).
53. Ibid., p. xix.
54. Ibid., p. 181.
55. A useful recent effort to collect and summarize historical cases for use in decision making is found in Richard E. Neustadt and Ernest R. May, *Thinking in Time: The Uses of History for Decision-Makers* (New York: Free Press, 1986).
56. Joseph L. Bower, *The Two Faces of Management: An American Approach to Leadership in Business and Politics.* (Boston: Houghton-Mifflin, 1983).
57. Ibid., pp. 42–43.
58. Harlan Cleveland, *The Knowledge Executive: Leadership in an Information Society* (New York: Dutton, 1985).
59. Jameson W. Doig and Erwin C. Hargrove, *Leadership and Innovation: A Biographical Perspective on Entrepreneurs in Government* (Baltimore: Johns Hopkins University Press, 1987).
60. George W. Downs and Patrick D. Larkey, *The Search for Government Efficiency: From Hubris to Helplessness* (New York: Random House, 1986).
61. Ibid., p. 256.
62. James L. Perry, ed., *Handbook of Public Administration* (San Francisco: Jossey-Bass, 1989). Other worthy books that might have also been cited

include Christopher C. Hood, *The Tools of Government* (Chatham, New Jersey: Chatham House, 1983); Lester M. Salamon, ed., *Beyond Privatization: The Tools of Government Action* (Washington, D.C.: The Urban Institute, 1989); and Franz-Xavier Kaufman, Giandomenico Majone, and Vincent Ostrom with the assistance of Wolfgang Wirth, eds., *Guidance, Control, and Evaluation in the Public Sector: The Bielefeld Interdisciplinary Project* (Berlin: Walter de Gruyter, 1986).

63. Jeffrey S. Luke and Gerald E. Caiden, "Coping with Global Interdependence," in Perry, p. 90.
64. James L. Perry, "The Effective Public Administrator," in Perry, p. 625.
65. For the most recent expression of several of these writers, see the entire issue, "Minnowbrook II: Changing Epochs of Public Administration," *Public Administration Review*, vol. 49, no. 2 (March/April 1989). Also, see H. George Frederickson, "Public Administration and Social Equity," *Public Administration Review*, vol. 50, no. 2 (March/April 1990), pp. 228–237.
66. Michael M. Harmon, *Action Theory for Public Administration* (New York: Longman, 1981), p. 163.
67. Theodore J. Lowi, *The End of Liberalism: The Second Republic of the United States*, 2d ed. (New York: Norton, 1979).
68. Ibid., p. 299.

CHAPTER EIGHT

The Future of American Public Administration Theory: A Dialectic among Competing State Visions?

The principle of equality, which makes men independent of each other, gives them a habit and taste for following in their own private actions no other guide than their own will. This complete independence, which they constantly enjoy in regard to their equals and in the intercourse of private life, tends to make them look upon all authority with a jealous eye and speedily suggests to them the notion and the love of political freedom. Men living in such times have a natural bias towards free institutions. Take any one of them . . . he will soonest conceive and most highly value that government whose head he himself elected and whose administration he may control.

ALEXIS DE TOCQUEVILLE
Democracy in America

As this text argues, public administration theory in America lives within a peculiar cocoon of American state development. The values that surround and influence public administration in the United States remain unique compared to the rest of the world. Whereas the rise of nation-state systems in Europe created centralized concepts, rationalized doctrines, even authoritarian prescriptions, and clear-cut academic training for educating state administrators by the eighteenth century, America's missing state at birth gave a completely different cast and color to its ideas about public administration. The U.S. Constitution that inaugurated a *novus ordo seclorum*, a new order of the ages, was a product of a unique historical confluence of ideas, institutions, events, and mythos that framed a new order without a state in the fashion of the European state. At the time, as Dwight Waldo underscored, "we did not *want* a European-style state, we did not need a European-style state, and we did not develop a European-style state."[1] And so partly by chance and partly by choice, the founders designed a Constitution that effectively pulverized stable state institutions. To this day, Americans retain this rock-hard, populist prejudice against state authority, or, in the words of Barry D. Karl, fulfilling the hope for the opportunity of the American dream "was to be there without significant interference by the state; it was to be created by individual efforts at self improvement. This was the key to the American meaning of individualism. Individual achievers would thus be beholden only to themselves, not to the government."[2] Grafting in effective state institutions or even recognizing their value thus continues to be a peculiarly challenging dilemma for Americans.

For a century the United States was able to ignore the problem and get along reasonably well without a nation-state. At the dawn of the twentieth century, however, the forces of urbanization, technological change, international involvement, industrialization, and other stresses and strains imposed severe system overload on existing constitutional arrangements. By then, the nation's back was against the wall and it had no choice but to opt for some limited forms of state mechanisms. What Americans settled for—or, rather, were forced to settle for—were temporizing administrative arrangements that chinked in just enough of a state system that was necessary to cope, but no more than necessary. Here, of course, was the genius of American public administration that made it different from the rest of the world's—namely, formulating pliable administrative arrangements that could cope, adapt, *and get by*, but that were limited, fragmented, and largely invisible to the general public. More important, they did not threaten, at least in any fundamental way, Americans' ingrained love of political freedom. Americans not only created "the first new nation"[3] but truly designed a most original one.

The contemporary global professional technocracy, America's modern state system, is a special by-product of this continuing contradiction between, on the one hand, the necessity to chink in a system that will get by and cope without, on the other hand, creating a formalized state that would challenge the ingrained American love of individualism, freedom, and equality. Americans who have continued to temporize administrative patterns have concocted not only chaotic institutional arrangements but also a chaotic intellectual landscape in terms of modern public administration thought. The Wilsonian middle way that balanced competing values and created, in turn, a crazy quilt pattern of administrative arrangements was what the United States had opted for during its Constitution's second century. As a result, theories of public administration have not taken on one doctrine, or only two, but many, as Chapter Five outlines. Yet, would an increasingly complex and specialized heterodoxy of doctrines be an adequate response for the problems facing America in the third century of its Constitution? Would simply getting along by "muddling" through or by balancing off competing values suffice for the future? Or is something new required? Perhaps American exceptionalism will end with the rise of the global professional technocracy and so, possibly, will an entirely new world order appear, and with different values.

The nation-state system, as has been repeatedly underscored, is a comparatively recent historical invention, and it is by no means certain that it will continue in its present form. Throughout recorded human history, numerous alternative, less rational, less centralized, and less ordered arrangements have predominated for organizing human affairs: families, tribes, city-states, religious orders, confederations, and feudal empires, to name a few. Each of these historic social institutions requires administration, to a greater or lesser degree, but nowhere near the scope or intensity of that found within modern, secular, bureaucratic societies. Administration plays a part in many types of human organizations, but it is not the whole ball of wax: Families are sustained by the knowledge of household management; tribes, by rudimentary organization for agriculture and warfare; city-states, by implementation of popular mandates; religious orders, through the performance of rituals; and empires and confederations, through the basics of decentralized administration. In contrast in the modern nation-state, public administration permeates everywhere throughout society and is, in the words of Carl J. Friedrich, the core of its government.[4] Hence, the ideas, concepts, and theories about public administration that were largely forged from recent nation-state experiences have an all-encompassing, all-inclusive quality, which Americans have repeatedly rejected in practice—at least in the past.

Whether the United States moves toward the traditional centralized nation-state model or other looser forms of human cooperative arrangements—or an entirely new international order—remains an open question today, though, as this book has argued,

America's "stateless" origins make such adaptation possible, but its directions not easily predictable. The Wilsonian middle way is a good historic example of institutional innovation in response to change. In whatever directions America's state system moves in the future, however, will ultimately determine the shape and destiny of America's future public administration theory. Just as the 1880s saw the emergence of new Wilsonian temporizing arrangements, so, too, as the last chapter stresses, we are witnessing in the 1980s and 1990s "a great state debate" in which alternative state forms with different implicit or explicit administrative models are being put forward, argued over, postulated, tested, and analyzed. It is an era of debate and dialogue without any settled principles, methods, or doctrines of public administration. Contemporary public administration thought, in other words, is an argument, a dialectic among competing models, ideas, and concepts that ultimately turns on the questions: What is the ideal state? the good society? the purpose of community? Big questions, big subjects that are unlikely to be settled in the near future for they involve the most profound, important, and difficult questions any society can address.

Public administration theory will undoubtedly remain confused, complex, and unresolved for some time to come until such big questions are resolved. The challenge for students of the field and practitioners who operate within the present context of vast, administrative systems in the United States is to recognize that realistically there exists no overarching theory, no one best way, at least for now, and that they must thread their way among competing theories, confused models, and contradictory approaches. Realism is required, but so too is optimism, for the opportunities and possibilities exist for learning from each of these fragments of ideas and approaches. There is the possibility of taking bits and pieces from the various approaches and by creative synthesizing and reconceptualizing find new names entirely to advance the art and science of public administration. Perhaps at first such innovations will be only on the margins, working toward someday achieving a new synthesis for the field. This task requires insight and sensitivity as to the strengths and limitations of competing administrative designs, what they can offer, as well as what they fail to provide for the field as a whole and for its individual practitioners. In short, it requires the best critical capacity from scholars, practitioners, and students in the field to pick and choose but not to swallow any one idea whole. Therein lies the challenge and excitement today in public administration—as well as its frustration—for there are no neat formulas or pat answers available on its present highly fragmented, diverse, intellectual landscape. Instead, what is needed is understanding, insight, and wisdom about public administration, its historic evolution, central role, current options being debated, relationship to state visions, and how the future public administration theory that evolves will ultimately be shaped by the directions for their future state design. It is a vital and exciting era in which opportunities abound to develop an imaginative capacity for judging, evaluating, and learning from all of the major alternative models now on the horizon: no state, bold state, pre-state, and pro-state. To recap, the sorts of issues, challenges, and possibilities that can be gleaned from each approach include the following.

The negative-state model assumes a backward evolution of the nation-state where much of the public tasks now in the hands of government officials revert back to for-profit, nonprofit, family, or neighborhood organizations. Administration in this world view increasingly becomes more privatized, decentralized, and "less public." Thus, in the best sense, this school of thought challenges the field to think about the role of government in society: What is its purpose and boundaries? What are the relationships to individuals and third parties? Where can it head in decentralized and privatized directions? Where *ought* it to be heading? In practical terms, it asks public administration to define with more precision the meaning of "public" and think about new, nontraditional, and innovative methods of servicing the public such as "enterprise zones" and "coproduction" techniques. No-state writings also ask the field to assume new roles and responsibilities for administrators, such as contract administrators, and work in public-private partnerships. These new tasks can stimulate and reinvigorate administrative thinking. It already has. The negative-state school, nonetheless, needs to confront, or be confronted with, the feasibility problem inherent in its thinking—namely, how is it possible to adapt its administrative prescriptions to the realities of a twentieth-century environment of government by a global professional technocracy? Can state mechanisms based on free market or public choice decision making operate effectively or at all within the context of a world driven by globalism, professionalism, and technocracy? Will the outcomes be fair and equitable? in the name of the national interest? Or are the tasks and responsibilities so large and complicated today to be beyond privatization, beyond the family and neighborhood, and beyond business's capacities to deal with them adequately? Will privatization of public power ensure its responsible use for public purposes? How is it possible for a politicized cadre of officials to inspire accountability and achieve responsibility to the general public? In short, how can proponents of this model reasonably ensure that this state design can work? The jury is still out on whether or not this school of thought can meet the acid test of workability in America, given contemporary world affairs.

Current bold-state writings advance arguments, ideas, and pragmatic solutions for strengthening institutional actions. They are our modern-day institution-builders. Quite the opposite from no-state writers, their language and concepts very often focus on issues that confront the men and women who must grapple with the daily operational problems of administration. Therefore, this positive-state model is the most easily understood and in many ways the most attractive to practitioners. Its direct application and sympathies are in tune with the many critical problems facing administrators. For those on the firing line, often under extreme pressure to perform, or just survive, there is much to recommend in these writings. But pragmatism, as a world view or operational philosophy, is also not without flaws. Bold-state writings, precisely because they most often come in bits and pieces that apply to this or that administrative situation, lack integration and a sense of the whole. No longer do the arguments for the overarching classical orthodox models of Leonard White or Louis Brownlow seem plausible or acceptable; yet the assumptions of these orthodox models are found in the fragments that are advanced here and there throughout positive-state writings. Fragments therefore persist without an overarching intellectual framework to legitimatize their application. So here, for positive state thinking, is the central challenge and opportunity—namely, how to justify and integrate activist conceptions of an administrative state within America's constitutional framework that was created to negate just such an energetic state system? The Brownlow report, as well as many of the writers of the 1930s, argued for pragmatism as the basis for framing bold state action (recall that Brownlow began, "The President Needs Help"). Modern writers like James Stever argue for adoption of a consciously professional paradigm, a "polity profession." Scholars during the past half century unfortunately have been unable to discover a respectable integrated framework to legitimate the positive administrative state. Historical and constitutional factors, as this text has observed, mitigate powerfully against finding one. So, again, more questions than answers are inherent within this school of thought: What, short of fundamental constitutional redesign, can legitimate a bold state within the American constitutional framework? How can positive state arrangements be grafted into a system organized to prevent its appearance? What justifies bold state action as a theory: promotion of the good society? liberal society? self-protection? the national interest? What is meant by those terms, and is the attainment of these goals worth the trade-offs and costs required? Can there reasonably be any agreement on these ends? Where and how can limits be imposed on a positive-state design? If extraconstitutional means are used to graft in a positive-state system in America, what will ensure its checks and balances?

Pre-state thinking, as the last chapter stresses, is by contrast highly sensitive to normative, historical, and constitutional questions. The writers willingly and readily see administration wrapped within the complexities of an unusual tradition of political values. They recognize that public administration thought and practice do not operate outside history but within the unique context and constraints of the American scene. On the whole, these writings most closely describe the realities and traditions of American public administration. They remain the true heirs of Wilson's middle way, for they understand most profoundly public administration's limits, its temporary qualities, and the requirements for balancing, negotiating, bargaining, and making incremental fixes in the margins in order to make it work. There is much to learn from these writings, for they can yield the richest insights and profound understandings about the organic qualities of American administrative operations within its unique contextual setting. Pre-state writers, however, also tend to be highly particularistic and ideographic. Their observations, are often confined to a single agency and program, with limited generalizations made beyond the immediate problems under discussion. These writers tend to be quite sophisticated when they analyze, describe, define, and criticize the particular, but they can be timid about developing their prescriptions beyond the narrow confines of what they know as the status quo. Thus the challenge for these pre-state writers is how to be more responsive to the present by means of advocating broader generalizations for changes and innovations. What do their writings mean for developing tomorrow's agendas, challenges, and opportunities? Are past norms and values a suitable guide to the future? How to inspire? lead? innovate? move ahead? envision tomorrow's challenges and serve up new solutions as answers? Being too uninspiring, backward-looking, bound, and limited to the past traditions of the American state—conservative?—*may* be the Achilles' heel of these writings.

Pro-staters are bustling about on many specialized fronts—budgeting, policy analysis, evaluation, and much, much more.

These writers advance narrow, technocratic subfields of public administration. There is found here much depth and high degrees of specialization. Much can be learned in the various specialties and technicalities contained in this literature for advancing the multitude of particulars of modern administration. Yet, therein lies the rub, for specialized analytics do not necessarily add up to meaningful and purposeful administrative action. Keeping the trains running on time may be a worthy enterprise, but it can also miss the larger issue: Are the trains going in the right directions? Should they even be moving in the first place? Without worrying about the worth of the central purpose or fundamental goals, Big Questions and Big Issues can be overlooked or missed entirely. Reliance on a technique or a cluster of techniques to give meaning and purpose to public administration can even allow means to become ends in themselves. When there is only the refinement of the status quo at the margins by technical tinkerings the vision of the whole goes unaddressed: What is the objective(s) of expertise? its role and place in society? the relationship between experts and the application of their techniques? the source of ultimate legitimacy? Do they individually and collectively advance the public interest? What are the more general purposes or public interest(s) for which these techniques are aimed or targeted? How can pro-staters be encouraged to see the Big Picture in order for their techniques to be integrated into the broader American constitutional framework? How can they weave together their rich, varied techniques and sources of knowledge to broaden and enrich the public purpose and advance constitutional goals? How can specialized analytics organically be connected together and related into the wider purposes of the human and constitutional enterprise in America? What are the means and methods by which we can prevent ourselves ultimately from becoming prisoners of the very techniques and expertise we invented to run the modern global professional technocracy? To ensure, according to the aphorism of Paul Appleby, that experts remain "on tap, not on top"?

These four schools of thought about the future of the American state—no state, bold state, pre-state, and pro-state—do not exhaust the possible options. Others exist. Today, however, these four are the most prominent and speak to and advance very different roles and purposes of public administration. Ultimately, other state models may well define the scope and purposes of public administration, in turn raising new problems and possibilities for the field. Heretofore unrealized, unarticulated state visions, or combinations of present ones, may well offer a new synthesis for public administration. Whatever the future patterns of human society may be devised—except, of course, the absence of any future—one thing can be said for sure: there will be public administration inherent in any future social system and it will play a critical role in defining its purposes and shaping its future. For public administration involves the central problems and issues in coping with complexities and changes in every society, especially our own. However, within the American context, its ideas and ideals have been fashioned very differently, so differently, in fact, from the rest of the world's, that it is at times possible to overlook its special angle of vision as well as the peculiar challenges and potentialities found in its ideas, ideals, and practices. Developing a sensitivity to its special nuances, a critical capacity for evaluating alternative schools of thought, and a creativity to remain open and inventive in our administrative thought may well be the central challenge today and in the years ahead for students and practitioners of public administration.

Notes

1. Dwight Waldo, *The Enterprise of Public Administration* (Novato, California: Chandler & Sharp, 1980), p. 189.
2. Barry D. Karl, *The Uneasy State: The United States from 1915 to 1945* (Chicago: Chicago University Press, 1983), p. 233.
3. From the title of the book by Seymour Martin Lipset, *The First New Nation* (New York: Basic Books, 1963).
4. Carl J. Friedrich, *Constitutional Government and Democracy: Theory and Practice in Europe and America*, 4th ed. (Boston: Ginn, Blaisdell, 1968), p. 38.

A Brief Bibliography

Within the past decade or so there has been a surprising outpouring of literature on "the state" in the social sciences and history. Indeed, the revival of interest in "the state" as a focus of intensive research and discussion has perhaps been the most important intellectual event to occur in recent years in these fields. For an excellent dialogue—pro and con—by prominent political scientists on this topic, see: Gabriel Almond, Eric A. Nordlinger, Theodore Lowi, and Sergio Fabbrini, "The Return to the State: Critique," *American Political Science Review*, vol. 82, no. 3 (September 1988), pp. 867–901 (the last two pages contain a good bibliography of recent writings on the state). While the quality of writing is uneven, some of the best recent literature examining this issue within each of the major fields include: from sociology, Gianfranco Poggi, *The Development of the Modern State: A Sociological Introduction* (Stanford, California: Stanford University Press, 1978) and Charles Tilly, ed., *The Formation of Nation States in Western Europe* (Princeton, New Jersey: Princeton University Press, 1975); from political science, Eric Nordlinger, *On the Autonomy of the Democratic State* (Cambridge, Massachusetts: Harvard University Press, 1981) and Stephen Skowronek, *Building a New American State: The Expansion of National Administrative Capacities, 1877–1920* (Cambridge, Massachusetts: Cambridge University Press, 1982); from political sociology, Peter Evans, Dietrich Rueschemeyer, and Theda Skocpol, *Bring the State Back In* (Cambridge, Massachusetts: Cambridge University Press, 1985) and Roger King, *The State in Modern Society* (Chatham, New Jersey: Chatham House, 1986); from history, Ellis W. Hawley, *The Great War and the Search for a Modern Order: A History of the American People and Their Institutions, 1917–1933* (New York: St. Martin's, 1979) and Barry D. Karl, *The Uneasy State: The United States from 1915 to 1945* (Chicago: University of Chicago Press, 1983); from comparative and international perspectives, William D. Perdue, *Terrorism and the State: A Critique of Domination Through Fear* (New York: Praeger, 1989); James A Caporaso, ed., *The Elusive State: International and Comparative Perspectives* (Newberry Park, California: Sage, 1989); and Chambers Johnson, *MITI and the Japanese Miracle: The Growth of Industrial Policy, 1925–1975* (Stanford, California: Stanford University Press, 1981); and from the economic development literature, Nora Hamilton, *The Limits of State Autonomy: Post-Revolutionary Mexico* (Princeton, New Jersey: Princeton University Press, 1982) and Steven Langdon, *Multinational Corporations in the Political Economy of Kenya* (London: Macmillan, 1981). Much of this renewed emphasis in the social sciences on "the state" comes from neo-Marxist writings, and for an excellent overview of this literature, read Martin Carnoy, *The State and Political Theory* (Princeton, New Jersey: Princeton University Press, 1984).

Seminal scholarly essays within individual disciplines have also been key sources for renewed interest in institutional factors influencing the way a discipline thinks about intellectual issues, for example in political science see James G. March and Johan P. Olsen, "The New Institutionalism: Organizational Factors in Political Life," *American Political Science Review*, vol. 78 (1984), pp. 734–749 and their book, *The Organizational Basis of Politics* (New York: Free Press, 1989); in geography, Roy E. H. Mellor, *Nation, State, and Territory: A Political Geography* (New York: Routledge, 1989); in economic history, Douglas C. North, "A Framework for Analyzing the State in Economic History," *Explorations in Economic History*, vol. 16 (1979), pp. 249–259 and later his book, *Structure and Change in Economic History* (New York: Norton, 1981); or in political sociology, Theda Skocpol, "Bringing the State Back In: False Leads and Promising Starts in Current Theories and

Research," a paper originally prepared for a Social Science Research Conference on States and Social Structures: Research Implications of Current Theories, at Steven Springs Center, Mt. Kisco, New York, February 25–27, 1982, and later published as "Bringing the State Back In: Strategies of Analysis in Current Research," in the previously cited book by Peter Evans, Dietrich Rueschemeyer, and Theda Skocpol, *Bringing the State Back In*, pp. 3–18. Also the entire issue of *Daedalus* (Fall 1979) is devoted to exploring "The state," and contains several interesting essays.

Within public administration literature there has been an equally rich outpouring of scholarly literature, but, remarkably, with little or no conscious reference to "the state" or the theorizing about the subject that has occurred and is occurring in other fields. For a good sampling of the recent literature in public administration, read Fred Lane, ed., *Current Issues in Public Administration*, 4th ed. (St. Martin's, 1990) or for the earlier writings, see Frederick C. Mosher, ed., *Basic Literature of American Public Administration, 1787–1950* (New York: Holmes & Meier, 1981). For the best bibliographical guide through the complex and vast maze of writings on this subject, read Daniel W. Martin, *The Guide to the Foundations of Public Administration* (New York: Marcel Dekker, 1989); and for some useful sketches of many of its key intellectual contributors to the administrative state-building enterprise, read Brian R. Fry, *Mastering Public Administration: From Max Weber to Dwight Waldo* (Chatham, New Jersey: Chatham House, 1989). Perhaps of all the current writers today in public administration, those in comparative administration have the keenest appreciation of the role of "the state" and the best book summarizing comparativist thinking in the field is Ferrel Heady, *Public Administration: A Comparative Perspective*, 3d ed. (New York: Marcel Dekker, 1984). In addition, excellent current overviews of major administrative state systems in developed nations can be found in Donald C. Rowat, ed., *Public Administration in Developed Democracies: A Comparative Study* (New York: Marcel Dekker, 1988).

Older scholars, trained prior to World War II in comparative, constitutional, and historical studies, frequently exhibited a strong appreciation of the development of the state and the rise of the theory and practice of public administration. Several of these works that are well worth reading today include Thomas F. Tout, *Chapters in the Administrative History of Medieval England*, 6 vols. (Manchester, England: University Press, 1920–1933); Ernest Barker, *The Development of Public Services in Western Europe, 1660–1930* (London: Oxford University Press, 1944); Dwight Waldo, *The*

Administrative State: A Study of the Political Theory of American Public Administration (New York: Ronald Press, 1948); Dwight Waldo, *The Enterprise of Public Administration* (Novato, California: Chandler & Sharp, 1980); Carl J. Friedrich and Taylor Cole, *Responsible Bureaucracy: A Study of the Swiss Civil Service* (Cambridge, Massachusetts: Harvard University Press, 1932); Frederick C. Mosher, *Democracy and the Public Service* (New York: Oxford University Press, 1968), as well as Leonard D. White's four-volume history of the institutional development of American public administration, all published by Macmillan: *The Federalists* (1948); *The Jeffersonians* (1951); *The Jacksonians* (1954), and *The Republican Era* (1958).

As Chapters 6 and 7 of this text argue, the current scene in public administration literature is vast, confusing, and often lacking in any conscious connection with "the state." Nonetheless, implicitly contemporary books, essays, and monographs reflect normative orientations toward no-state, bold-state, pre-state, or pro-state points of view. It is therefore recommended that one can profitably selectively read recent prominent examples from each, such as: for the no-state perspective, Vincent Ostrom, *The Political Theory of a Compound Republic: Designing the American Experiment*, rev. ed. (Lincoln: University of Nebraska Press, 1987); for the bold-state view, Robert B. Reich, *The Next American Frontier* (New York: Times Books, 1983); for the pre-state ideas, John A. Rohr, *To Run a Constitution: The Legitimacy of the Administrative State* (Lawrence: University of Kansas Press, 1986); and for the pro-state vision, James Perry, ed., *Handbook of Public Administration* (San Francisco: Jossey-Bass, 1989). Any of the writings discussed or cited in Chapters 5 and 6 could also usefully be studied and compared.

Since the literature in public administration has been so diverse and rich in recent years, one should not neglect looking through current issues of the major scholarly research journals in the field, such as the *Public Administration Review, Administration and Society, American Review of Public Administration, Annals of Public Administration, Journal of Public Administration Research and Theory, The Bureaucrat, Journal of Policy Analysis and Management, International Review of Administrative Sciences, Public Administration Quarterly*, and *Administrative Science Quarterly*. In reviewing these journal articles, one should note how few explicit references there are in the serious literature to "the state." A noteworthy exception is Paul P. Van Riper, "The American Administrative State: Wilson and the Founders—An Unorthodox View," *Public Administration Review*, vol. 43 (November/December 1983), pp.

477–490 or the entire bicentennial issue of the *Public Administration Review* (January/February 1987) devoted to exploring the theme, "The American Constitution and the Administrative State," edited by Richard J. Stillman II. One is also encouraged to compare any of the several current basic texts in the field today with older pre–World War II classics such as Luther Gulick and Lyndall Urwick, *Papers on the Science of Administration* (New York: Institute of Public Administration, 1937) and Leonard D. White, *Introduction to the Study of Public Administration* 1st, 2d, 3rd, or 4th editions (New York: Macmillan 1926, 1939, 1948, and 1955).

In contrast to such "classics," some recent general reconsiderations of the entire field by various current scholars are also worth sampling for comparisons and include: Naomi B. Lynn and Aaron Wildavsky, eds., *Public Administration: The State of the Discipline* (Chatham, New Jersey: Chatham House, 1990); Gary L. Wamsley, Charles T. Goodsell, John A. Rohr, Philip Kronenberg, Orion F. White, James Wolf, Camilla M. Stivers, and Robert M. Bacher, *Refounding Public Administration* (Newberry Park, California: Sage, 1990) and Henry D. Kass and Bayard L. Catron, eds., *Images and Identities in Public Administration* (Newberry Park, California: Sage, 1990).

Index